Wildflowers of the Eastern United States

Wildflowers of the Eastern United States

John Eastman

STACKPOLE
BOOKS

Published by
STACKPOLE BOOKS
5067 Ritter Road
Mechanicsburg, PA 17055
www.stackpolebooks.com

Printed in the United States

10 9 8 7 6 5 4 3 2 1

First edition

The text in this book is adapted from material first published in *The Book of Forest and Thicket* (1992), *The Book of Swamp and Bog* (1995), and *The Book of Field and Roadside* (2003), all copyright by John Eastman and published by Stackpole Books.

Cover design by Tessa J. Sweigert
Cover photo by Buslick/Shutterstock.com

Library of Congress Cataloging-in-Publication Data

Eastman, John (John Andrew)
Wildflowers of the eastern United States / John Eastman. — 1st ed.
p. cm.
ISBN 978-0-8117-1367-2
1. Wild flowers—East (U.S.) I. Title.
QK115.E286 2014
582.13—dc23
2013043594

Contents

Fields and Clearings

WENDY MEDER/SHUTTERSTOCK.COM

Alfalfa
(*Medicago sativa*)

KRIS LIGHT

Pea Family. Short spikes of blue flowers, three-part cloverlike leaves, and spiral seedpods identify this alien perennial forage plant. The terminal leaflet, turned upward, is longer than the two side leaflets, and leaflets are toothed only at their tips. Other names: lucerne, medick.

About eighty *Medicago* species exist, mostly in Eurasia. Several alfalfa subspecies, forms, and hybrid varieties exist, but in eastern North America the plant typically consists of several stems and a taproot that may extend ten to fifteen feet down, occasionally farther. Like most legumes, alfalfa grows nitrogen-fixing nodules on its roots. *Rhizobium* bacteria in the nodules convert atmospheric nitrogen into substances that the plant uses in forming amino acids, also enriching the surrounding soil with nitrogen.

Another characteristic that alfalfa shares with many legumes is the trip mechanism of its flower, flinging pollen on the bodies of insect pollen or nectar collectors. Both male and female sex organs, held under tension by the basal keel petal of the flower, "trip" when an alighting insect dislodges the keel petal. "The organs hit the bees on the lower portion of the head," as biologist Bernd Heinrich wrote, depositing pollen from the stamens, "while the female organ of the flower becomes dusted with pollen the bee has picked up at a previous flower." Tripping can also occur, however, when petal tissues become weakened by high or low temperatures, an event that usually results in self-pollination. Untripped flowers do not set seed. Fertilization—that is, when pollen tubes penetrate to the ovary—occurs about twenty-four hours after pollination. Seedpods, spiral in shape with four or five coils, contain several yellowish seeds.

Bushy, often half prostrate, alfalfa has flowered along with human agriculture and civilization from ancient times. Today it frequently overlaps its cropland borders, appearing in open areas everywhere. Alfalfa requires well-drained, limy soils.

Although many insects seek nectar and pollen from alfalfa flowers, relatively few are effective pollinators—that is, can trip the stamens, retrieve and carry the pollen, and cross-fertilize the plants with consistent regularity. These few are mainly bees of various genera—honeybees, bumblebees, and alfalfa leafcutting bees. A pollen-collecting bee may visit twenty to forty alfalfa flowers in a single trip from the hive, tripping most of the flowers it visits. Honeybees, however, favor pollens from other plants and visit alfalfa mainly for nectar.

Probably alfalfa's foremost mammal feeder (excluding livestock) is the cottontail, though almost all vegetarian grazers also consume it. Alfalfa fields provide prime nesting habitat for pheasants, but first mowing of the year may destroy many nests.

Many farmers rank alfalfa first among crop legumes. It is said to furnish more green forage, more pasture, and more dry hay per acre than any other hay or grass. The quantity of atmospheric nitrogen fixed by *Rhizobium* bacteria in any given stand of alfalfa, though difficult to measure, is probably about a hundred pounds per acre. Alfalfa may yield from three to twelve tons of hay per acre. This plant grows poorly, however, in soils not already rich in nitrogen. A successful alfalfa crop requires soil priming or preparation with manure or nitrogen fertilizers. Such inoculation enables nodule bacteria to produce all the nitrogen required by the plants, thus further priming the soil for the potential benefit of other crops. Yet, since an alfalfa stand may last three to ten years or longer, many farmers do not rotate it with other crops, allowing it to regenerate each year until it loses vigor and declines. Somewhat offsetting its soil fertility value for other crops is deep-rooted alfalfa's tendency to lower the water table, especially in arid regions where it is grown, causing hardship for more shallowly rooted crops sown afterward.

Herbalists set great store by this plant, claiming it as the source of eight essential amino acids along with useful laxative, diuretic, and other medicinal properties. According to homeopathic lore, almost any ailment one might think of having can benefit from a swig of bland alfalfa tea steeped from leaves and flowerheads. Alfalfa provides a source of commercial chlorophyll and carotene as nutrition supplements, is rich in vitamins A, D, and K, also the antioxidant tricin. Alfalfa sprouts are widely marketed as salad items, and most honeys sold as clover or clover blend actually come from alfalfa. On the negative side, reports indicate that canavanine, found in alfalfa sprouts and seeds, may adversely affect lupus conditions. Alfalfa's main commercial use is cattle feed; overfeeding alfalfa, however, may cause a condition called bloat in livestock.

Alfalfa is said to be a native of Asia, but nobody really knows for sure—its place of origin is lost in time. Earliest mention may have been in Babylonian texts around 700 B.C.E. Alfalfa became the main forage for the horse cavalries of ancient Persia and Greece as well as Rome. Probably Roman farmers first planted it about 200 B.C.E. The Arabs, to whom we owe the plant's English name, called alfalfa the "father of all foods" for its hay forage value. Spaniards brought alfalfa to the New World in the fifteenth and sixteenth centuries, and it arrived in the southwestern United States about 1750. In 1793, Thomas Jefferson raised a field of it in Virginia. A cold-hardy strain developed in 1858 by a Minnesota farmer enabled northern hay growers to raise alfalfa. Today alfalfa remains widely cultivated (and widely escaped) throughout the country. After centuries of cultivation, horticultural tinkering, and deliberate hybridization with other *Medicago* species, it has also become a genetic mixture of characters far removed from those of earlier cultivated strains in both ancient and recent times—even farther from those of the original plant.

The word *alfalfa* is the Spanish modification of an Arabic word for the plant. *Medicago,* from the Greek word *medike,* probably refers to the region of Media in Persia, an early source of the plant.

Amaranths
(*Amaranthus* species)

Amaranth family. Most amaranths have large leaves and green flowers, the flowers occurring in dense, bristly spikes. Two of the most common species are *A. retroflexus*, called redroot, and *A. hybridus*, smooth pigweed. Both annuals are native to tropical America. Seedling leaves often show bright red undersides. Other names: green amaranth, careless weed.

About twenty *Amaranthus* species reside in eastern North America. These include tumbleweed (*A. albus*), love-lies-bleeding (*A. caudatus*), and prince's feather (*A. hypochondriacus*). The two familiar "weed amaranths," abundant in gardens and along roadsides, reproduce solely by seed each year. Redroot flowers are distinctively surrounded by three to five spiny bracts; the plant's shallow taproot is pinkish or red. Smooth pigweed looks less coarse, is darker green, and has slender, bending flower spikes. Both plants stand from one to six feet tall. Seeds mature from late summer through fall in one-seeded pods that uncap to release the seed. Reputedly a single plant may produce more than a hundred

KRIS LIGHT

thousand seeds, and amaranth seed may remain viable for at least forty years. The bisexual flowers appear throughout summer, are pollinated by wind, and also commonly self-pollinate.

Most green plants transform raw materials into plant tissue by a process of photosynthesis known as the C3 carbon-fixation pathway. Amaranths, however, use a C4 carbon-fixation process. The chemistry is complex, but essentially the C4 process more efficiently absorbs atmospheric carbon dioxide; it also requires less water and adapts the plant for higher temperatures, brighter sunlight, and drier conditions. Since grain amaranths probably evolved in the Andes, benefits of the C4 adaptation for mountain habitats are obvious.

Redroot typically appears in bare ground soon after fire, rototilling, or other disturbance, but it thins out quickly as grasses and old-field herbs become established. Also chemically inhibited by the growth of curly dock, it is sometimes root-parasitized by branching broom-rape. It may, however, become a major pest in corn and other field crops. Smooth pigweed also grows as a cosmopolitan weed of roadsides, vacant lots, and gardens.

Before the Spanish conquest of South America in 1519, an amaranth species was planted and harvested by both Aztecs and Incas as a grain crop; they cooked the seeds for cereal and ground them for flour. This crop may have provided the main agricultural base for the Aztec economy. The Spanish conquerors, aided by their priests, banned its growth and usage, apparently in the nervous belief that the food provided too much energy for a defeated people; also, its use in native rites and rituals made it anathema to the missionaries. Thus widespread amaranth cultivation disappeared from the New World for many centuries, though remote pockets in Andean and Mexican locales preserved the grain amaranth species from extinction. During the 1960s, the Rodale Research Center in Pennsylvania led in the reintroduction of grain amaranth as an agricultural crop.

The tiny seeds yield a protein content of sixteen percent, higher than wheat, corn, and rice. Large amounts of vitamins A and C plus calcium, iron, and potassium also make these plants nutritionally exceptional, as does the unusually high lysine content in the plant's amino acid balance.

The leaves, especially of young plants, make edible cooked greens. These leaves concentrate nitrates, however—they are known to poison cattle and pigs that forage on the plants—so boiling to eliminate the toxic materials is essential. An astringent tea made from the leaves has served as a homeopathic treatment for external and internal bleeding, diarrhea, dysentery, and ulcers.

The word *amaranth* originates from a Greek word meaning "everlasting."

Asters
(*Aster* species)

VALERIE POTAPOVA/SHUTTERSTOCK.COM

Aster family. Aster flowerheads consist of aggregate flowers; another name for the plant's family, descriptive of its flowerheads, is composites. Field and prairie asters, most standing 2 to 5 feet tall, include both white-flowered and blue-flowered species. Common white-flowered ones include calico aster *(A. lateriflorus)* and heath aster *(A. ericoides)*. Blue asters include arrow-leaved aster *(A. sagittifolius)* and New England aster *(A. novae-angliae)*. All asters are perennials.

Some 66 native Aster species reside in eastern North America; more than 200 species exist worldwide. The aster family, second largest in the plant kingdom, consists of more than 1,000 genera and some 20,000 species.

For the professional botanist, aster taxonomy poses tough quandaries; for the rest of us, the field manuals often (except for a few well-marked species) force highly tentative identification decisions. The genus *Aster* remains difficult to sort out or even define. Many taxonomists believe that the traditional aster classification scheme is incorrect and must be replaced by another arrangement based on chromosome number or DNA relationships. In broad terms of their structure and form, however, all asters look enough alike to be lumped as loosely, if not closely, related.

The flowerhead disk florets, often yellowish or reddish, center the fifteen to one hundred strap-shaped ray florets, depending on species—which appear white, pale lilac, or deeper blue (color in asters is not always a reliable identifier to species). The flowerheads, though bisexual as in all aster family species, are dominantly female in *Aster* species since the ray flowers bear only female pistillate flower parts (in many plant genera—as among organisms generally—the male sex is far more expendable than the female). The disk flowers bear both male pistils and stamens. Many asters exhibit so-called sleep movements, with the ray flowers closing around the disk at night.

Asters usually require pollination from other aster plants to produce seed. Some *Aster* species grow colonially and can clone from underground stems, called rhizomes; others produce new shoots from the bases of old stems in spring. Most cloning asters survive for only three or four years.

From summer to fall, aster plants produce several rosette shoots—flat, leafy circles of growth at the plant base—from rhizomes or at the base of flowering stems. Rosettes remain green and dormant on the ground over winter, often beneath snow. In the spring, they produce erect shoots that become flowering stems.

Most wild asters flower after goldenrods in summer and fall. Individual flowerheads mature from the outside in—that is, the ray florets become pollen receptive before the disk florets open. As the asters in any given area are in multiple stages of development at any given time, opened disk flowers of some plants may be producing pollen before the disk flowers in other plants have opened. Also, asters begin flowering at their branch tips, the flowerheads nearest the stems blooming last. Depending on aster species and local weather conditions, insect-pollinated flowers remain pollen receptive for five to ten days.

Aster fruits consist of one-seeded achenes, which mature a month or more after flowering ceases. Bristles on the dry achene end curl and spread, catching air currents that disperse the seeds. Cold stratification, a period of freezing necessary to the germination of some plant seeds, though unnecessary for aster germination, nevertheless increases germination rate.

Most meadow asters favor open, sunny areas, including roadside, garden, and pasture habitats. At least one wild aster species *(A. pilosus)* appears consistently associated with farm habitats. It invades abandoned fields, usually in the second year after field cultivation ceases; quickly becomes a dominant plant; and typically remains so for about two years in old-field plant succession.

Pollinators include a variety of insects. Anglewing butterflies frequently visit aster flowers, as do yellows, sulphurs, checkered whites, common buckeyes, plus painted ladies, several skippers, and south-migrating monarch butterflies. Adult butterflies and moths generally favor the blue and purple asters, whereas white asters are mainly pollinated by honeybees, bumblebees, and flies. Asters do not provide favored or frequent wildlife food resources. New spring shoots of heath aster may provide livestock forage, but the mature plants are rarely eaten.

The word aster comes from a Greek word meaning "star," as in asterisk. The flower was considered a sacred emblem in the pantheon of Greek divinities. The "star-flower" or its images were sacred to various gods and adorned altars of every size. In one myth, asters are the goddess Astraea's grieving tears fallen and sprouted on earth. An early English name for the flower was "starwort," and various species were named Michaelmas daisies because they flowered around St. Michaelmas day, September 29.

New England aster roots provided a tea for native tribal treatments of fevers and diarrhea, and various other asters were smudged, smoked, or steamed as tranquilizing inhalations. Aster roots, according to one anonymous source, "were crushed and fed to bees in poor health" (a statement that is worth a double take).

Beardtongues
(*Penstemon* species)

RON ROWAN PHOTOGRAPHY/SHUTTERSTOCK.COM

Figwort family. Recognize these native perennials by their tubular, stalked, unevenly lobed flowers—white, pink, lavender, or violet—surmounting the stem. Flower clusters rise from paired stalks; leaves are also paired but stalkless and toothed. Probably the commonest species in the Northeast are the foxglove beardtongue *(P. digitalis)*, with white or pink-tinged flowers; hairy beardtongue *(P. hirsutus)*, with woolly stem and magenta-tinged white flowers; and eastern beardtongue *(P. laevigatus)*, with pale violet flowers. Most *Penstemon* plants stand two or three feet tall. About 275 species of Penstemon exist, all endemic to North America. Only eleven of these reside in the Northeast.

The tonguelike, "bearded" sterile stamen rising amidst the four fertile, pollen-loaded ones gave these flowers their name. Beard-tongue's flower is technically bisexual but—as with many flowers—is actually sequentially unisexual. The flowers first become staminate, developing pollen on their male anthers; when the stamens decline, the small female pistil matures, its sticky tip curving down from the roof of the flower tube. Individual plants or flowers exhibit different phases of sexual sequencing at once, so that some are pollinating and others receiving pollen. A flower in the staminate phase drops pollen on a bee's hairy body as the insect jostles the anthers in seeking the nectaries at the base of the tube. A female-phase flower, on the other hand, partially blocks the insect's visit with its pistil, to which adhere grains of pollen snagged from the insect as it brushes past. Beardtongue's sequential sex change, called protandry, helps ensure cross-pollination (as opposed to self-pollination, an added option for many flowers).

Most beardtongues flower from May to July, some later. Many white-flowered beardtongues show violet or purple lines radiating from the flower's center; these nectar guides may help lead pollinating insects to the nectaries. Many *Penstemon* plants also have dense root masses and maintain a winter basal rosette of leaves, from which rises the new stem in spring. Fruit capsules, ripening in late summer or early fall, contain the seeds.

Look for beardtongues in old fields, sandy outwashes, and open woods. The many species vary considerably in their shade and moisture tolerances; some prefer fairly dry, sunny conditions, whereas others require more mesic soils, thriving as well in partial shade.

Few genera show such wide diversity as *Penstemon* in flower form and adaptation for various pollinators. Some fifteen western species are pollinated mainly by hummingbirds. In the East, a 1966 study discovered that two beardtongues—the eastern and slender—are pollinated extensively if not exclusively by a single genus of mason bees *(Osmia)*, which depend upon the plants for pollen and nectar. Since these bees also frequently pollinate clovers, research suggests that planting of *Osmia*-associated beardtongues in clover fields might increase clover seed production.

Penstemon, like the common name beardtongue, refers to the plant's vestigial stamen; the original Greek words mean "almost a stamen." Naturalist Thomas Nuttall, during western trips in 1810–11, collected and first described several *Penstemon* species. This complex genus, it is said, contains the most species of any flowering plant group restricted to North America. Various *Penstemon* species hybridize readily, and this propensity has led to the development of many ornamentals—notably, the common beardtongue *(P. barbatus)* and garden beardtongue *(P. hartwegii)*—of which many colors and cultivars exist.

Beggarticks
(*Bidens* species)

MARTIN FOWLER/SHUTTERSTOCK.COM

Aster family. Mostly yellow-flowered herbs standing one to three feet tall, the many species of beggarticks show much variation. The two common *Bidens* considered here are beggarticks *(B. frondosa)* and Spanish needles *(B. bipinnata)*. Both are native annuals, and both have yellowish flowerheads that somewhat resemble sunflowers with their ray flowers missing. Other names: sticktights, tickseeds, tickseed-sunflowers, bur-marigolds, pitchforks, devil's pitchfork, old ladies' clothespins, beggar-lice, stickseed, devil's bootjack.

The genus *Bidens* consists of some 280 species, most of them native to Africa and the New World. Plant guides often identify *B. frondosa* and *B. bipinnata* as rayless. Close inspection, however, reveals that yellowish ray flowers, though rudimentary and inconspicuous, are indeed present. Flowerheads in both species grow at the ends of long, sparsely leaved branches. Both plants reproduce entirely from seed. A single *Bidens* plant can easily produce more than a thousand seeds.

Flowering from late summer into fall, beggarticks become most conspicuous to hikers after the flowers are gone. Bidens are pants pests; the barbed seed packages hook onto one's clothing, hitchhiking there until removed by hand, brush, or comb. With trouser legs crusted and solidly armored by the achenes in October, "it is as if you had unconsciously made your way through the ranks of some countless but invisible Lilliputian army," wrote Thoreau, "which in their anger had discharged all their arrows and darts at you, though none of them reached higher than your legs." *B. frondosa* has two-pronged flat achenes, allowing for wind distribution, whereas the black, long, and narrow Spanish needles have four short adherent barbs. Both kinds appear in central clusters protruding from the former flowerhead. *B. frondosa* has a shallow, much-branched taproot; *B. bipinnata's* taproot is thicker and plunges deeper, with numerous side branches.

Although these two *Bidens* annuals can rapidly colonize disturbed areas, they seldom compete for very long with perennial plants as old-field plant succession advances. These sun-loving plants help stabilize the soil after digging, erosion, or other disturbance.

Bidens seeds, though not a significant food for larger wildlife, are consumed by several waterfowl, gamebirds, and finches. *Bidens* seeds can be dispersed by almost any mammal or bird that comes into contact with the plant. Sheep wool, especially, often becomes matted with the achenes—these animals stand at just the right height to snag *Bidens* barbs in passing.

Drab and scrubby *Bidens* conveys some interesting items besides its sticktights. Since most (though not all) *Bidens* species are native plants, they provide refreshing exceptions to the idea that all our weeds are alien intruders. Also, the adaptation of barbs and hooks on seeds as a way of dispersal represents a complex level of evolution—that is, they are apparently adaptive to self-propelled life forms. Without the later appearance on earth of fur and feathers, no impetus for the evolution of barbed or sticky seeds would have occurred. "How surely the *Bidens* . . . prophesy the coming of the traveller, brute or human," wrote Thoreau.

Native tribes and homeopathic practitioners found several medicinal uses for *B. bipinnata*. The Cherokee drank a tea of the leaves to expel worms, also chewed the leaves for sore throat. European doctors prescribed infusions of *Bidens* as astringents and cathartics and to induce sweating, menstruation, and urination. A strong infusion of *B. frondosa* was said to have effectively remedied croup in children. *Bidens,* like many herbal brews, serviced its patients by giving them the feeling they had been genuinely treated, if not cured. The generic name, meaning "two teeth" (Latin *bis* and *dens*), refers to the prongs on the achene.

Bird's-Foot-Trefoil
(*Lotus corniculatus*)

MARTIN FOWLER/SHUTTERSTOCK.COM

Pea family. This low, alien perennial legume exhibits yellow, pealike flowers and three cloverlike leaflets (actually five, with two opposite leaflets at the base of the "trefoil," or triple leaflets; despite its name, this trefoil is the only legume with five leaflets). The plants often sprawl, though sometimes stand erect up to two feet tall. Other names: broadleaf trefoil, poor man's alfalfa.

More than two hundred *Lotus* species exist worldwide. Some forty western species are known as deer vetches. Two other northeastern species, likewise aliens, are narrowleaf trefoil *(L. tenuis)* and Spanish clover *(L. purshianus)*.

Planted both as a nourishing forage for livestock and for erosion control—its extensive root system branching from a strong taproot binds loose soil effectively—bird's-foot-trefoil has received, like dandelions, an "OK status" from most of our plant guardians, though unquestionably it competes with native prairie vegetation. Like most legumes, it produces root nodules; *Rhizobium lupine* bacteria in the nodules convert atmospheric nitrogen to ammonia, enriching the soil and providing a usable form of nitrogen to plants. This self-supply eliminates the need for nitrogen fertilizer.

Numerous branched stems rise from a basal clump, or crown. Four to eight bright yellow, sweetpealike florets, sometimes tinged with orange or reddish striping, cluster at the ends of the flower stems. Each floret is bisexual and can self-pollinate, though the plant has a self-incompatibility mechanism that limits self-seeding, and most seeding results from cross-pollination between plants by insects. Pollen in this flower actually matures before the flower opens. Filaments push the loose pollen forward into the closed tip of the united lower petals, and pollination occurs when an insect's weight on the keel forces a ribbonlike mass of pollen from the keel opening, some of it adhering to the insect's underside. Further pressure as the insect seeks the nectaries causes the female stigma to slide onto the same contact area, where its stickiness may pick up pollen on the insect from another trefoil plant. Flowers unvisited by pollinators remain open eight to ten days, but frequently visited flowers usually last less than four days as fertilization occurs. Inch-long seedpods, each containing ten to fifteen dark, tiny seeds, ripen about a month after pollination. The five or six pods attached at right angles to the peduncle somewhat resemble a splayed "bird's foot," accounting for the plant's name. They split and twist open spirally, scattering the seed, in a process called shattering. "On a hot, still day," wrote one observer, "anyone standing in a field of trefoil will be conscious of a rustling sound, often almost a steady undertone, as the ripe pods snap and the seeds patter on the foliage."

This is a so-called "long-day plant," requiring some sixteen hours of daylight to flower. At night, the leaflets fold along the leaf stems, probably conserving moisture. The plant also reproduces vegetatively; although this species does not extend subsurface stems, its roots can and do develop clonal shoots.

Fields, expressway medians, and roadside areas throughout North America display this bright yellow ground cover from late spring through summer. Bird's-foot-trefoil favors well-drained, acid-neutral soils, but it also tolerates acid, infertile soils, and periods of flooding and drought.

Hay farmers like to graze livestock on bird's-foot-trefoil and raise it for hay because, unlike alfalfa and some other hays, it does not cause bloat and is more palatable. It also tolerates poor soil conditions and resists numerous legume-foraging insects. The wise farmer leaves this crop unharvested during late summer and fall, a procedure known as stockpiling; this allows the plant's root reserves to accumulate, improving its winter survival and spring growth. The plant can still be grazed as pasture forage in late fall since it holds its leaves after frosts.

A native of Eurasia and still cultivated there as a forage legume, bird's-foot-trefoil probably came to North America along with European livestock about 1900. It was first discovered growing wild in 1934 in New York. Bird's-foot-trefoil honey is the only human food derived from this plant.

Blazing Stars
(*Liatris* species)

VLADIMIRA/SHUTTERSTOCK.COM

Aster family. These native perennials, most of them two or three feet tall, show magenta or purple (rarely white) flowerheads crowded on dense, wandlike spikes; the feathery, thistlelike flower rises from a scaly-bracted base. Leaves are narrow, grasslike, alternate, and show resin dots. Most commonly seen are the large blazing star *(L. scariosa)*; rough blazing star *(L. aspera)*; and dense blazing star *(L. spicata)*. Other names: gayfeather, liatris, colic-root, rattlesnake master, button snakeroot, devil's bit, prairie pine, throatwort.

About thirty *Liatris* species exist, all in temperate North America. Some thirteen species inhabit the East. "It has a general resemblance to thistles and knapweed," Thoreau noted, "but is a handsomer plant than any of them." *L. spicata* is probably our most commonly seen species. Some *Liatris* species readily hybridize with others, creating plants with intermediate characters. *Liatris* flowering may occur irregularly from year to year. Some plants may produce flower stalks as early as the second year, many (notably *L. aspera*) not until their eighth or ninth year.

Unlike many other plants with tall flower spikes, such as purple loosestrife or vervains, blazing stars begin flowering from the top of the spike, progressing downward as the summer season advances; look for developing seedheads above the flowering portion of the spike, unopened flower buds below it. Each flowerhead is an aggregate, consisting of many separate bisexual florets, as in all aster family plants (the composites). The number of florets on each flowerhead varies with the species. Florets are insect-pollinated and are obligate outbreeders, which mean that they cannot self-pollinate.

Liatris flowers produce one-seeded achenes with barbed or feathery bristles (depending on species) that aid seed dispersal. In winter, Thoreau observed, "the now bare or empty heads of the *liatris* look somewhat like dusky daisies surmounted by a little button instead of a disk." This "base on which its flowerets stood is pierced by many little round holes just like the end of a thimble. . . . it readily scales off and you can look through it."

Most *Liatris* species rise from a winter basal rosette of leaves atop a thick, rounded rootstock called a corm. *Liatris* corms may be aged by their cross-sectional rings, annually formed like tree rings. Typical corms may live eleven to seventeen years; an extreme of thirty-four years has been recorded. The corms may be fire adaptive, for most *Liatris* species grow in frequent fire habitats, and corm food storage enables survival of the plant following ground burns.

Liatris species range across the continent. Frequent fires probably turned many presettlement prairies into summer vistas of blazing stars, visible as far as the eye could see. Today we see them more often as solitary stalks or small stands in a field or along a fencerow. Most *Liatris* species favor open, dry, sandy ground or roadsides; a few prefer wet meadows and sandy shores. Although *L. spicata* often becomes a dominant forb in tall-grass prairie, on rangeland *Liatris* species are generally considered decreasers, transitory plant dwellers being replaced by less desirable rangeland species, resulting either from grazing pressure or plant succession. *L. spicata* also pioneers plant succession in strip-mined spoils and in old fields. Ordinarily, *Liatris* is easily outcompeted by grasses and other grassland herbs.

Neither seeds nor foliage of *Liatris* rank as an important wildlife food. *L. scariosa* and *L. punctata* are palatable, nutritious livestock pasture forages, especially in early growth stages; the latter is especially relished by sheep. Some sources state that the hairy stems of some *Liatris* species make them unpalatable to white-tailed deer, thus maintaining the plants in heavily foraged deer areas.

Native Americans found *Liatris* useful for several medicinal purposes. The Chippewa called *L. scariosa* "elk tail," probably because of its tall flower spike. They drank the root tea for treatment of dysentery. Other tribes, as well as white settlers, used the infusion as a diuretic, a gargle for sore throat, and in poultices for snakebite. Plains tribes apparently ate the bulblike corms of *L. punctata,* said to have a carrot flavor, in early spring.

Almost all *Liatris* species have been cultivated and hybridized as popular native garden flowers. They dry and preserve well as winter bouquets.

Blue-eyed Grass
(*Sisyrinchium* species)

JOHN L RICHBOURG/SHUTTERSTOCK.COM

Iris family. Not grasses but so called because of their stiff, grasslike leaves and flat, wiry stems, these native perennials typically stand four inches to a foot tall. They exhibit six-petaled, mostly blue-violet flowers with white, six-pointed centers accented with golden yellow. Each blunt petal is tipped with a bristlelike point, an infallible identity mark. Flowers open solitarily at the end of branched or unbranched stems. *S. angustifolium* is probably the most common species. Other names: eye-bright, blue star.

About seventy-five blue-eyed grass species exist; most are New World natives, and few are distinguished by separate English names. Some eight species, separated on the basis of technical characters, grow in the Northeast.

The apparent petals of iris family flowers are actually tepals, a term for both sepals and petals when they look alike and occur together in the flowerhead. In the blue-eyed grasses, three sepals alternate with three petals in each flower, but all of these "tepals" resemble petals in color and form. Dark lines on the tepals serve as possible nectar guides, leading insect pollinators to the yellow center. Usually about three flower buds occur at the end of a stem, but buds open separately—often a day or so apart—and stay open for only a day or less; they never remain open at night. Time windows for cross-pollination are thus very brief; but what an individual bisexual flower lacks in exposure time may be compensated for by the more or less constant flowering of the plant from May through midsummer or later. Blue-eyed grasses also reproduce vegetatively, rising from masses of fibrous rhizomes, subsurface stems that also store food. Seed capsules are round and three celled.

Blue-eyed grasses occupy both moist and dry open habitats, depending on species—meadows, sandy flats, gravel banks, grassy pastures. Thoreau noted that flowering blue-eyed grass marked dry footing through wet fields: "You can cross the meadows dry-shod by following the winding lead of the blue-eyed grass, which grows only on the firmer, more elevated, and drier parts."

Pollinators are mainly bees. Prairie-chickens and wild turkeys are known to consume the seed capsules. Probably other ground-feeding birds and mammals do likewise.

Sisyrinchium lore is not large. The rhizomes provided a tea that native Americans drank for treating both diarrhea and constipation, say the sources. The leaves made a tea for stomach ailments.

Bluestems
(*Andropogon* species)

KRIS LIGHT

Grass family. Bluestems, native perennials, are usually identified by technical characters of the flower clusters. The three most common species, however, show distinctive features that can be easily recognized without a hand lens. Bluestems flower in summer and fall. They remain standing when dry, turning conspicuously straw yellow or other tan or reddish shades.

Big bluestem *(A. gerardii)* stands six or more feet tall. It has long flower stalks that branch radially from the tip of the plant stalk. The bristles that project from the flowers are sharply bent, and the bases of lower leaf blades and sheaths are often silky haired. Little bluestem *(A. scoparius)* usually stands two or three feet tall. It branches along the stem, with fuzzy flowers and wiry branches that extend beyond the leaves, which tend to fold; the flower clusters each bear a long, projecting bristle. Clumps of dried stems in fall and winter show a distinctive orange color. Broom-sedge *(A. virginicus)*, the most common bluestem, resembles little bluestem but is leafier, its flowers more fuzzy and feathery and tucked inside the leafy bracts. From a distance, the downy clusters, which grow on the upper stem portion, may appear silvery. Its color in fall and winter is bright straw yellow. Other names: beardgrasses, bunchgrasses, forked beardgrass, turkeyfoot, broom beardgrass, prairie beardgrass, broom, wiregrass, purple wood grass, broom-sage.

Some one hundred Andropogon species grow in warm temperate climates worldwide. Of the thirty or so species native to North America, about six inhabit eastern fields and prairies.

Like most grasses, bluestems are bisexual and wind-pollinated. *Andropogon*, however, is distinctive in the fact that its flower spikelets occur in pairs, one stalked and one unstalked. Also, *Andropogon* stems are solid or pithy, not hollow as in most grasses.

Impressive indeed is big bluestem; vast seas of this tall, splay-flowered prairie grass greeted American pioneers, revealed good soil, and told them where to settle and plow. Fire-maintained big bluestem often stood taller than a man, and its sod, built through millennia of prairie growth, provided—and still provides—the rich loam soils that underlie America's heartland agriculture.

Big bluestem has short, scaly rhizomes and fibrous roots that may plunge twelve feet. This grass grows in large clumps, new stems cloning from the rhizomes; its lower leaves curl up when dry. Little bluestem likewise propagates by short rhizomes, seed, and tillers or sprouts. Length of little bluestem's dense roots usually exceeds the plant's height, reaching up to eight feet down. Broom-sedge roots are much shallower, densely fibrous. All three species exhibit a bushy growth form, but the dense sods created by big and little bluestems produced prairie grassland that only John Deere's steel plowshares could break. Broom-sedge clumps, poor sod formers, tend to grow in isolated, single-plant patches.

Big and little bluestems produce seed irregularly and often do not develop abundant seed every year; indeed, some stands produce only once every five to ten years. Requirements of these two species are surprisingly exacting. They apparently demand a combination of optimal conditions, including abundant moisture and moderate temperatures at flowering time, in order to produce seed. Most of their reproduction, in fact, occurs vegetatively by means of their rhizomes.

Much research has focused on the relationship of fire and bluestems. A 1968 study, which indicated that a maximum interval of three years between burnings maintained the most vigorous stands of big bluestem, is fairly representative of recent work. The rejuvenative effects of prairie fire on bluestem growth have long been noted, but exactly how the process operates remains largely speculative. What makes the plants fire adaptive consists mainly in their dense, subsurface root systems that can rapidly "green up" a grassland burn with new sprouts. The present consensus is that fire benefits, and causes a growth surge in, bluestem mainly by removal of dead grass litter, thus exposing the new sprouts to more sunlight and warmth—rather than by fire release of plant nutrients that fertilize the soil, as has also been theorized.

Big bluestem's main habitats are the moist, highly fertile loams of the central states and eastern Great Plains. Little bluestem tolerates drier, more gravelly soils, and it extends farther west than big bluestem. Big and little bluestems have broadly overlapping ranges, however, and often associate. Broom-sedge is the "poor relation"; an indicator of low-fertility soils, it grows throughout the eastern half of the continent, often invading sandy fields.

Big and little bluestems make nutritious livestock forage, especially in their earlier growth stages. Farmers plant them in some areas for pasture forage and hay. Broom-sedge is coarser, not favored as forage; in pastures, it is usually regarded as a weed.

Several American tribes found *Andropogon* roots and rhizomes beneficial for various ailments. The Chippewa used a decoction of big bluestem for digestive problems; the Catawba boiled broom-sedge as a treatment for backaches. The Cherokee drank a leaf tea of broom-sedge for diarrhea (apparently a common ailment among Indians, to judge from the number of herbal remedies they used for it); and they and other tribes also used *Andropogon* leaf teas as a skin wash for sores, rashes, and other irritations.

Andropogon means "man's beard" in Greek, indicating the characteristic long, feathery awns—certainly a more descriptive term than "bluestem."

Bouncing-Bet
(*Saponaria officinalis*)

KRIS LIGHT

Pink family. This common alien perennial spreads five scallop-tipped, slightly notched, white or pinkish petals, bent slightly backward, from a quarter-inch-long floral tube (the calyx, consisting of the fused sepals). Flowering from July into fall, the plant stands one to two feet tall, often in large colonies. Other names: soapwort, hedge pink, bruisewort, fuller's herb, scourwort.

About thirty *Saponaria* species exist, all natives of temperate Eurasian regions. The spicy-scented flowers occur in tight clusters on short stems at and near the top of the plant. Both double flowers and double petals may commonly be seen, indicating that this species is probably in a current state of evolutionary flux. Each insect-pollinated flower projects from its center of ten stamens in two sequential sets and one pistil divided into two stalks. Indeed, the reflexed petals surrounding the sexual organs give the impression of flagrant thrust. The entire plant appears somewhat coarse in form and feature, ranking low in the consensus qualities of beauty and grace.

Bouncing-bet's flower, about an inch across, is sequentially unisexual—the male parts develop and decline before female parts mature. Its pistil remains hidden until the flower's abundant pollen is gone, then opens up, exposing itself and exhaling fragrance, luring insects from younger, still-pollinating flowers, and thus averting self-pollination. The flower's fragrance tends to increase at sundown, attracting night-flying moths. The sexual stages sometimes overlap, however, and individual bouncing-bet flowers can and do self-pollinate. Seeds develop and spill numerously from oval capsules. This plant also reproduces vegetatively, cloning itself into colonies by sprouting from short, branched, almost woody rhizomes.

Some of the first American colonists brought bouncing-bet from Europe as a medicinal and useful household herb. The plant rapidly escaped colonial kitchen gardens and yards and now ranges throughout most temperate regions of North America, and the globe. It favors disturbed, desolate spots—vacant lots, roadsides, railroads, ditch banks, sometimes fields and pastures. Although it thrives best in moist, sandy soil, it is also drought-tolerant, thus widely adaptive to many habitats. In most areas, the plant seems quite thoroughly naturalized (that is, not extremely competitive with native vegetation).

Romans of two thousand years ago called this plant *herba lanaria,* "wool herb," for its usage in washing and shrinking wool. Though long used by many peoples and cultures as an important, gentle substitute for soap, this plant does not contain or produce real soap, though it duplicates lather in its foamy suds and grease-cutting effects. The soapy substance is a glycoside called saponin, brought forth by crushing the stems, leaves, and roots in water. Native to Eurasia, bouncing-bet arrived in England during the Middle Ages. The plant decorated most European cottage gardens, was especially used for washing delicate linens, silks, woolens, and fragile fabrics such as old curtains and tapestries. Even today, a bouncing-bet solution can clean and polish glass and china as well as or better than most commercial formulas.

Probably bouncing-bet's rapid spread in North America owes to "the aid of thrifty settlers fond of clean laundry," as one observer wrote. Along with its sink-and-basin utility, however, the plant has a roster of remedies for everything from leprosy to liver ailments, with coughs and kidney stones between. Saponin, anti-inflammatory, encourages bile flow and is not only laxative but purgative. Herbalists have widely recommended it as a poultice for boils and skin rashes, including poison ivy. Saponins are also mildly toxic; all parts of the plant, especially the seeds, may cause gastric distress to people and livestock. Drying and storage do not dispel the toxin. Thus soapwort has no food value, even in direst emergency. Saponins exist in hundreds of plants, but the proportion in bouncing-bet measures more than in most.

The plant's generic name *Saponaria* derives from the Latin *sapo,* "soap." *Officina,* the species name, means "workshop," denoting a plant for practical uses. Its common name is said to stem from an old term for a vigorous washwoman, "bouncing Betty." "The inflated calyx and scalloped petals of the flower," according to one folklorist, "suggested the rear view of a laundress, her numerous petticoats pinned up."

Buckwheat
(*Fagopyrum esculentum*)

MHOLKA/SHUTTERSTOCK.COM

Smartweed family. Recognize buckwheat by its arrowhead-shaped leaves attached in swollen joints to the reddish stem. Other names: brank, crap, cornheath, duck-wheat, goose buckwheat, Indian-wheat, Saracen's-corn, Saracen's-wheat.

Some fifteen Eurasian *Fagopyrum* species exist. India wheat *(F. tataricum)*, along with buckwheat, is widely cultivated. Buckwheat is unrelated to wheat *(Triticum aestivum)*, a grass.

A crop plant that has widely escaped, buckwheat has a long flowering season, from June into September, so plants in almost every stage of development may be seen throughout summer. Sprouting anew from seed each year, buckwheat forms a low ground canopy where sown as a crop, effectively shading out competing weed growth.

F. esculentum displays a floral form called heterostyly, consisting of flowers differing in length of their styles (the stalklike parts of the female pistils). Two types of flowers exist, both lacking petals: pin-type flowers, with long pistils and short stamens; and thrum-type flowers, with short pistils and long stamens. Such dimorphism in flowers induces self-incompatibility, increasing the likelihood of cross-pollination from other buckwheats. Buckwheat begins flowering five to six weeks after it germinates, and the insect-pollinated flowers can produce mature seed in about two weeks. The triangular, beechnutlike, one-seeded fruits protrude from the sepals, readily dropping when mature. Buckwheat's taproot, along with fibrous lateral roots, may extend up to two feet deep.

Buckwheat tends to transpire so rapidly that it may wilt in the midday sun, recovering at night. Yet its water requirements are not large, and it tolerates a wide range of soil moisture and acidity. The plant may also lean over or break in the wind and heavy rains. It is extremely sensitive to cold, so its entire life cycle occurs between the last spring frost and the first one of autumn.

Buckwheat thrives along roadsides, fencerows, and railroads. It favors cool, moist climates for optimal growth. Numerous insects forage on the plant, as do deer and rabbits. For many waterfowl, gamebirds, and songbirds, buckwheat seed is a choice food.

Human usage of buckwheat consists mainly of flour ground from the seed, often an ingredient of pancake mixes and pastas. Most buckwheat grown in North America is exported to Japan, where it forms the chief ingredient of soba noodles, a diet staple. The inner parts of the dehulled seed are used in cereals or, roasted, as kasha in traditional Jewish and Polish dishes.

The plant produces high amounts of rutin, a flavenoid glycoside that reduces cholesterol and blood pressure in humans; of vitamins B1 and B2; and of lysine and iron. Some people, however, become allergic to buckwheat protein. A continuous diet of buckwheat cakes may produce skin rashes, and occupational asthma occurs among workers in Japanese soba shops. The other main food produced from buckwheat is honey; dark and distinctively flavored, it is prized by gourmets. One beehive per acre of buckwheat may produce up to 150 pounds of honey per year.

Other uses of buckwheat include livestock feed and green manure. Buckwheat hulls have been collected for mulches, pillow and mattress stuffing, and packing material. One of the plant's most important agricultural uses is as a smother crop for controlling weeds such as quack-grass, thistles, leafy spurge, and Russian knapweed. Decomposing buckwheat roots seem to chemically inhibit the germination of weed competitors. Buckwheat plants also acquire phosphorus from the soil by means of root exudates and transform it to a usable form for other plants.

Once a much more common crop and food than today, buckwheat was apparently one of the first plants cultivated by American colonists, who brought it to the New World. Its origins are obscure; perhaps a native of China, it was introduced into Europe about 1400. Foremost world producers today are Belarus, the Ukraine, and China.

Scots, it is said, coined the word *buckwheat* from the Anglo-Saxon *boc* ("beech") and *whoet* ("wheat"), apparently because of the achenes' resemblance to beechnuts.

Bush-Clovers
(*Lespedeza* species)

Pea family. All bush-clovers have untoothed trifoliate leaves and terminal, often bristly spikes. Otherwise, bush-clover species appear variable in size, lifestyle, and form. Some of these legumes are annuals and some are woody shrubs, though native lespedezas are all perennial herbs. Some trail and sprawl, though most stand erect one to three feet tall. Flowers vary from white and yellowish to purple and pink, depending on species. Bush-clovers also hybridize widely, so species identification is not always simple. Native perennial bush-clovers include round-head bush-clover *(L. capitata)*, with cream-white bristly, knoblike flower clusters; slender bush-clover *(L. virginica)*, with short purple flower clusters; violet bush-clover *(L. violacea)*, with solitary purple flowers in loose terminal heads; and trailing bush-clover *(L. procumbens)*, with a reclining or trailing stem, downy stems and leaves, and purplish flowers. The names bush-clover and lespedeza are interchangeable for most species.

T. TRAVIS BROWN

Bush-clovers produce two kinds of bisexual flowers: showy, five-petaled, cross-pollinated blossoms conspicuously displayed on terminal branches; and much smaller, budlike, inconspicuous, unpetaled, self-pollinated flowers. The latter flowers usually appear later than the former, though individual plants occasionally produce only a single kind in a given year. Both kinds produce viable seeds, but the self-pollinated flowers apparently produce most. The insect-pollinated chasmogamous flowers can also self-pollinate, however, and visiting insects may facilitate this process. As lespedeza researcher Andre F. Clewell wrote, "The possibility of selfing is enhanced in that bees usually visit several flowers on one plant before visiting another plant"; also, unlike many flowers, bush-clovers have floral mechanisms that hardly hinder self-pollination. Clewell concluded that more lespedeza flowers are self-pollinated than cross-pollinated. This tendency reduces the likelihood of hybridization in many populations while maintaining species identity, even as it reduces the adaptive benefits of outcrossing. Asexual, or vegetative, reproduction—by the extension and fragmentation of woody, horizontal rhizomes—also occurs. Researchers believe that connecting rhizomes may sometimes rot away, separating individual clonal plants.

Lespedeza seeds, with their thick, impervious seed coats, may remain viable for a half century or longer. "The scarcity of seedlings in natural populations," wrote Clewell, "suggests that few seeds germinate the year after their formation and that seeds may remain dormant for many years pending . . . natural scarification." Such aids to germination include frost-cracking of the seed and fire. Controlled-burn programs have demonstrated that many native lespedezas are fire-adapted species, often sprouting vigorously after fire passage. Game managers and agricultural technicians alike have used burn programs to encourage lespedeza growth for wildlife food patches and livestock forage growth.

Lespedezas, beloved of livestock farmers for forage and game managers for wildlife food plantings, also commonly appear in prairies and old fields and along roadsides. Most bush-clovers favor open land, sandy soil, and disturbed habitats, though trailing and violet bush-clovers can tolerate the light shade of open woods.

Like most legumes, bush-clovers have root nodules with nitrogen-fixing bacteria, which convert atmospheric nitrogen into ammonia for protein production. Thus lespedezas increase soil fertility wherever they grow.

This genus could have been labeled *Cespedes.* The name *Lespedeza* is apparently a misnomer. A French botanist in America, André Michaux, intended to pay tribute to the Spanish governor of East Florida, one Manuel de Cespedes, by naming bush-clover after him. But somehow the name, probably through a copying error, came out as *Lespedeza,* thus saving the world from another memorial to a politician.

Lespedezas, which thrive in open and disturbed sites, probably occur much more abundantly now than in presettlement times. Clewell believed that the probable original centers of distribution were the deciduous forest-prairie and coastal savanna borders of the East and Midwest.

Moxa, a variation on acupuncture practiced by Plains tribes, used small pieces of bush-clover's dried stems. Moistened and stuck to the skin, they were ignited on the other end and allowed to burn down to the skin, supposedly relieving (replacing?) pains of neuralgia and rheumatism. Other tribes boiled the leaves to make a tea for unknown benefits. Researchers are finding that lespedezas are apparently loaded with biologically active compounds, most of which await further investigation. Extracts of the plant demonstrate considerable activity against certain types of cancerous tumors and also apparently lower blood cholesterol and blood nitrogen levels.

Butter-and-Eggs
(*Linaria vulgaris*)

Figwort family. Recognize this one- to three-foot-tall alien perennial by its terminal spikes of fifteen to twenty bright yellow, lobed and spurred flowers appearing in summer and fall. Petals are five but united; the pouch-shaped lower lip protrudes with three lobes plus an orange spot or palate and a drooping conical spur. Leaves are narrow, often densely crowded, appearing opposite because of crowding but actually mostly alternate. Other names: yellow toadflax, eggs-and-bacon, flaxweed, brideweed, wild snapdragon, common linaria.

About one hundred *Linaria* species exist, mostly Eurasian (as is *L. vulgaris*) and South American. Annual toadflax *(L. canadensis)* is a native American species.

The yolk-colored palate, serving as a nectar guide in this insect-pollinated flower, covers the throat of the petals. Weight of a landing insect depresses the lower lip, admitting the insect over the palate and through a restricted opening into the long, narrow spur, wherein pools the sucrose-rich nectar. In pushing through this tight slot, the insect brushes against the pollen-loaded stamens projecting overhead, receiving a load of dust on its back.

MARTIN FOWLER/SHUTTERSTOCK.COM

Between the two stamens—a short and a long one—projects the stigma. The visitation sequence for a bumblebee bumbling its way into the flower would be, first, an overhead caress by the sticky stigma, relieving the bumblebee fur of a few pollen grains deposited on it elsewhere; then a liberal pollen dusting from the long stamens; then, as the bee backs out of the plant, a second dusting from the fur-snagged short stamens. A single bumblebee can thus pollinate most flowers of a spike in a single visit to each, easily invading some ten flowers per minute.

Most reproduction in this plant occurs vegetatively; a single plant can rapidly produce a thriving colony of clones, often circular in form, by means of budding from both taproots and laterals and from root fragments. "The importance of the root system for persistence and local spread," wrote a 1995 Canadian research team, "is illustrated by subarctic populations that are unable to produce seeds but that increased in abundance from 'scarce' to 'frequent' between 1959 and 1989." Individual taproots, which may extend three feet down, may survive at least four years, probably longer. The combination of poor seed dispersal/germination and quick duplication once colonies are established often results in dense, thriving local populations. Stems die back to the roots in the fall, but the small, blue-green shoots at the base of old stems remain visible through winter.

Butter-and-eggs occurs in a wide range of open habitats, mostly disturbed areas, throughout the continent. Most frequently it appears in gravelly and sandy soil, along roadsides, on railroad embankments, and in vacant lots, dry fields, and waste ground. As a garden escapee, it thrives, like lilacs, around old homestead sites. Because it does not require a long growing season or high seed production in order to survive and reproduce, it adapts well to hostile environments, survives fire, grazing, and herbicides with aplomb. Today the plant has a virtually global distribution.

Pollinators of butter-and-eggs are mainly the larger, long-tongued bees that can reach into the long-spurred nectar reservoir of the flower. These include several species of bumblebees and halictid bees.

Native to the steppes of Eurasia, butter-and-eggs probably arrived in North America with New England colonists, brought as a garden ornamental sometime before 1672. Additional introductions, probably in crop seeds and baled hay, hastened its spread across the continent. Botanist John Bartram, writing in 1758, called "the stinking yellow *Linaria* the most hurtful plant to our pastures that can grow in our northern climate." "It is a troublesome weed," wrote Thoreau, parenthesizing that "flowers must not be too profuse nor obtrusive; else they acquire the reputation of weeds." Not until the 1930s did butter-and-eggs become well established in western rangeland, where by 1950 it had become a seriously invasive grain and pasture weed. Since about 1960, it has somewhat declined in abundance and distribution, probably because of insect biocontrol species.

American natives had no acquaintance with this plant, but pioneer homeopaths widely prescribed it as an astringent, laxative, and diuretic. Infusions treated dropsy and liver ailments, while external poultices and ointments made from the plant soothed hemorrhoids and skin sores. Other historical uses have included insecticide—boiled in milk, the flowers are said to produce an excellent fly poison. They also produce a yellow dye.

Butterfly-weed
(*Asclepias tuberosa*)

MARK HERREID/SHUTTERSTOCK.COM

Milkweed family. Its bright orange flowers, hairy stems, and alternate, lance-shaped leaves (unlike the opposite leaf arrangement of most milkweeds) help identify butterfly-weed. A native perennial, it stands one to two feet tall. Other names: pleurisy-root, orange-root, orange milkweed, chigger flower, Canadaroot, Indian-nosy, coralweed.

Our only "milkless milkweed" has watery sap, not the milky juice characteristic of most *Asclepias* species. It is also the showiest milkweed, its orange glow impossible to miss in a field where it grows. That color, however, varies somewhat depending on geography. In some locales, the flowers are clear yellow rather than orange; in others, they are bicolored. Leaf shape also varies; a study often cited by students of evolution detected a geographic progression of gradual changes in leaf shape for this plant in eastern North America. These manifest changes are believed to be subtle adaptations for drought conditions.

Floral and reproductive biology of this plant closely resembles that of common milkweed, though it lacks the cloying fragrance of its relative. Looking closely, one can see that petals of the small florets are sharply bent back; the erect, petal-like hoods are actually appendages of the stamens and secrete nectar. The four- to five-inch-long, hairy, spindle-shaped seedpods ripen to maturity by late September. This plant reproduces both by seed and by root sprouts.

Butterfly-weed has a long, fibrous taproot, giving the plant drought resistance. Several clonal stems rising from the root crown often form a small patch or colony, flowering from May into July, sometimes later. Butterfly-weed may not flower for its first few years, however, and it may take four years to reach full size. Once established, though, individual plants may survive as long as adjacent plants do not shade them out.

Butterfly-weed favors dry, sandy soil and full sunlight; it can also tolerate light shade. A plant adapted to dry conditions, it will not survive where soil is too moist. The plant resides throughout most of the continent in temperate areas.

Pollination in this plant, as in other milkweeds, involves an insect's ensnarement by yoked pairs of pollen masses, or pollinia, in a floret, then pulling them loose and depositing them in the floret of another plant. The floret's device is a kind of slot adaptation into which long legs—specifically, the legs of butterflies, many species of which are attracted to the colorful blooms and ample nectar, thus aptly naming this milkweed—become snagged. Butterfly pollinators include several large swallowtails, monarch butterflies, checkered whites and European cabbage butterflies, little sulphurs, painted ladies, and many others. Bees—digger bees, honeybees, bumblebees, halictids, and leafcutting bees—also pollinate the plant. Often trailing the pollinators come nectar thieves. "Lacking the quantity of sticky milky juice which protects [common milkweeds] from crawling pilferers," wrote botanist Neltje Blanchan, "the butterfly-weed suffers outrageous robberies from black ants."

Like all milkweeds, butterfly-weed is loaded with cardiac glycosides, making it extremely toxic to mammals as well as to many insects. Whereas boiling water renders other milkweeds harmless and edible, butterfly-weed is best left alone even by the hungriest devotee of cooked greens.

Yet many native tribes as well as pioneer doctors found the taproot medicinally useful. Teas and infusions treated pulmonary conditions such as pleurisy, bronchitis, and asthma. Externally, the pulverized root formed poultices for all sorts of skin and arthritic ailments, plus cuts and bruises.

The generic name *Asclepias* derives from Aesculapius, a Greek physician, later deified as the god of healing.

Canadian Thistle
(*Cirsium arvense*)

SARI O'NEAL/SHUTTERSTOCK.COM

Aster family. This colonial alien perennial, common almost everywhere, has small, pale lilac to rose-purple or pinkish, brushlike flowerheads. Extremely fragrant, they occur in branching, somewhat flat-topped clusters atop the plant. The crinkled, lobed, and very prickly leaves are gray-green. Degrees of leaf lobing and spininess differ among individuals and varieties of this plant. Unlike many thistles, this species has smooth, unspined stems. It stands up to five feet tall. Other names: field, cursed, creeping, corn, hard, prickly, or way thistle.

Some two hundred *Cirsium* species exist worldwide, some of them native to North America. Canadian thistle, the most abundant thistle on our continent, is also the only dioecious North American thistle (that is, with male and female flowers occurring on separate plants). "Occasionally," as botanist Arnold Appleby noted, "a male flower will produce a seed, so separation is not absolute." Indeed, some studies indicate that up to a quarter of all "male" plants can self-pollinate and produce seed. Actually, all the flowers are bisexual, but female pistils are vestigial or abort in some flowers and male stamens do likewise in others, producing functionally unisexual flowers. The functionally male flowerheads appear rounder in shape and somewhat smaller than the female flowerheads, which look more flask-shaped.

This "long-day" plant requires fifteen hours of day length in order to begin flowering, usually in middle June or early July, lasting into September. Thistle flowerheads consist exclusively of tubular disk flowers; no ray flowers are present. The shaving brush–like purple heads, massive in some thistle species, appear modest in size, less than an inch across, but emit a very sweet-smelling aroma in Canadian thistle. The flowerheads typically contain about a hundred florets. Healthy plants may produce thirty to sixty flowerheads in clusters of one to five per branch atop the plant.

The insect-pollinated flowers produce one-seeded achenes. An average plant may develop as many as 70 achenes per flowerhead some ten days or so after flowering; a single plant typically produces about 1,500. Seeding success depends upon the extent of pollination, hence nearness of a male thistle clone. Studies have shown that female clones separated by only 50 to 100 feet from a male clone produce much larger amounts of seed than clonal colonies sited 500 feet or farther apart. The feathery plume (the thistledown) attached to the achene, existing in many aster family plants, aids in wind dispersal up to a mile or more. Many observers have noted the tendency of thistle plumes to float free, however, leaving their achenes back in the seedhead; those little wisps of fluff so often seen riding the breezes in late summer and fall are parachutes gone astray. Thistle seeds can germinate immediately, sprouting best at temperatures of 70 degrees F and above. Seedlings form leafy rosettes in the fall, and flowering stems emerge the following spring. Unsprouted seeds, dormant in the soil until spring or later, may remain viable for twenty years.

But Canadian thistle reproduces most successfully not by seed, but by vegetative means. The plant lacks rhizomes, despite assertions otherwise in various plant manuals, but it buds extensively from creeping roots. New plants can develop from root fragments as small as a quarter inch in size. A single plant may extend foot-diameter clonal thicket in three seasons, eventually spanning more than one hundred feet. The subsurface root connections last only about two years before decaying, eventually isolating clones or clonal groups from the parent, but each individual also proceeds to send out its own budding roots. Seed production depends upon the proximity of both male and female plants in an area. Thistle's aerial stems die back to the roots in the fall.

Canadian thistle—not a native of Canada, where it ranges widely, but of southeastern Europe and the eastern Mediterranean region—has long gone worldwide, today occupying almost every continent. Adaptable to numerous soils and habitats, Canadian thistle thrives best in open, sunny, fairly moist locales where soil has been disturbed—roadsides, old fields, overgrazed pastures, fencerows, campgrounds, recent burns, often in marshy ground or ditches (these last may provide invasion corridors). It favors clay soil or silt loams but can grow on almost any soil except peat and in waterlogged sites. Although it often invades cropland and native vegetation, Canadian thistle rapidly declines in shade.

The best-known bird feeders on thistle are American goldfinches. The birds, which are summer nesters, raid the seedheads for fluffy nesting materials as well as food; a ring of thistledown seen on the ground beneath the plant usually means that goldfinches have been pillaging. The white thistledown nests of goldfinches, easily visible in shrubs after leaves drop in the fall, remain compact, so tightly woven that they hold rainwater, yet so flexible that they expand as nestlings grow.

Cattle and horses avoid thistle foliage (which is more highly nutritious than alfalfa) because of its spines and prickles. In some national parks, Canadian thistle has invaded along horse trails, apparently as a result of horses consuming unprocessed hay containing thistle seeds. Sheep and goats, however, relish the tender rosette leaves in spring. Canadian thistle probably arrived in New France sometime in the early 1600s as a contaminant in crop seed or ship's ballast. It is said to have entered the American colonies via the hay for British general Burgoyne's horses during the Revolution

Thistles produce a fine honey, and beekeepers are never sorry to see them (unless they begin taking over clover fields). The plants, mainly the peeled young stems, are not only edible but highly nourishing, making a fine survival food, cooked or raw. Young leaves with spines removed can be served as salad or cooked greens. Removing thistle spines is not a simple job, however; it requires thick-gloved hands.

Thistle's astringent properties were well known to herbalists from ancient times. Leaf teas, prescribed as tonics, also treated dysentery and diarrhea; externally, thistle brews poulticed skin sores and rashes. American tribal healers quickly adopted the alien plant, especially its root, for treating mouth sores and upset innards.

The word *thistle* derives from various similar names meaning "something sharp" in old European languages. *Cirsium* apparently stems from *kirsos,* Greek word for a swollen vein, which a thistle poultice may have remedied; *arvense* refers to "cultivated fields," where this weed seems most at home.

Catnip
(*Nepeta cataria*)

BRUCE WORKS/SHUTTERSTOCK.COM

Mint family. Recognize this alien perennial herb by its softly furry, gray-green aspect and its opposite, toothed, arrowhead-shaped leaves with whitish undersides; its crowded terminal spike of white or pale violet flowers with pink or purple spots; and the strong aroma of its crushed flowers and leaves. The plant stands six inches to two feet tall. Other names: catmint, catnep, catrup.

Some 150 *Nepeta* species exist, all of them Eurasian, as is catnip itself. Most mints have square-sided stems, and all have opposite leaves. Otherwise they appear in two flowering forms: with flowers growing in the angles of leaves or side branches, or with flowers in terminal spikes. Catnip exemplifies the latter group. The plant's odor and taste resemble that of no other mint—neither unpleasant nor often relished as a taste treat but strong and thoroughly distinctive. Aromatic oils, plus nepetalactone, account for this odor and taste.

New leaves in early spring may show purple-tinged undersides. The bisexual, insect-pollinated flower is tubular with a three-lobed lower lip. Flowers occur from July through October, even into early winter if mild. Fruits are nutlets, four to a pod. The summer's growth dies back to the fibrous taproot in late fall.

A common resident of weed patches and vacant lots throughout North America, catnip also appears along roadsides and railroads and in old fields and thickets. It favors lime-rich soils.

This plant's name derives from its well-known effect on cat behaviors (called "the catnip response"), which nobody yet fully understands. Many researchers believe, however, that nepetalactone mimics feline sexual scents. This aphrodisiac odor affects about eighty percent of all house cats and other felines, including lions, tigers, leopards, and lynxes. Many cats exhibit loopy behaviors in reaction to it, nuzzling, chewing, rolling in it, losing all semblance of cat dignity, apparently becoming virtually intoxicated if not hallucinating. The catnip response seldom exceeds a period of fifteen minutes or so, after which a cat seems to get sleepy. Research suggests that cats with a friendly disposition react most overtly to the plant; young kittens, however, are not affected.

Catnip tea, brewed from the leaves, is a traditional folk remedy for colds, fevers, diarrhea, and a variety of ailments. It induces sleep (nepetalactone is a mild sedative) and promotes sweating. The plant also exhibits herbicidal and insect-repellent properties. To Thoreau, the aroma of catnip leaves in early spring "advances me ever to the autumn and beyond it. How full of reminiscence is any fragrance!"

Catnip is raised commercially in a few places, mainly for herbal teas and cat toys.

Chicory
(*Cichorium intybus*)

FOKIN OLEG/SHUTTERSTOCK.COM

Aster family. Blue, stalkless flowers with squared-off, fringed rays along a rigid, almost leafless stem characterize this summer alien perennial. Basal leaves appear dandelionlike. Chicory typically grows two or three feet tall. Other names: succory, blue or ragged sailor, bunk, blue daisy, coffee-weed, wild endive, forage chicory.

Some nine *Cichorium* species exist, all European and Mediterranean region natives—among them, endive *(C. endiva)*, a popular salad green.

Chicory's blue, radiating flowerheads on straggly stems are familiar sights along summer roadsides. The flowerheads, an inch or more across, occur in loose clusters on the upper stem, but only a single flowerhead in a cluster blooms at a time. Some guidebooks state that chicory flowerheads typically open in early morning and close by noon, but I have seen chicory flowering at all hours of the day; it seems more accurate to say that they probably flower most vigorously early in the day and gradually close and "lose face" as the afternoon advances. Occasional plants may bear white or pink flowerheads.

Unlike many of its aster relatives, which display both disk and ray flowers, chicory has only flat ray florets on each flowerhead, usually some twelve to twenty of them. Each straplike, insect-pollinated floret is bisexual, bearing five stamens and an ovary at its base (the florets can, in the absence of insects, self-fertilize). The single-seeded fruits are angular, fringed achenes. Reproduction occurs solely by seed. Chicory blooms from July to the first frost.

Chicory produces long, thick, and fleshy taproots, typically extending six inches down or more. These plants have a milky, bitter sap, similar to dandelions (the substance taraxacine is common to both). After frost, the stems die back to a basal rosette of leaves much resembling those of dandelions. The rosette may overwinter, lowly and unnoticed, above the crown of its root or may itself die back to the crown, which sprouts new rosette leaves in the spring.

Chicory favors open, disturbed-soil habitats—roadsides, old fields, vacant lots—but seldom thrives in cultivated fields (except where it exists as a crop itself). It also favors limestone over acid soils. Chicory plants often emerge from cracks in pavement and asphalt. A 1992 study found that chicory germinated much more successfully on dry, rocky roadsides than in adjacent ditches with deep, fertile soil; the microhabitat of crevices formed by rock-soil interfaces sheltered the seedlings and supplied moisture for germinating chicory, whereas the plant litter on smoother, more fertile surfaces prevented such lodgment.

Chicory has a long history of human usages. Ancient Egyptians and Romans knew the plant well, and Europeans have cultivated it for at least a millenium. It continues to be grown as a vegetable and salad crop, especially in France, Belgium, and the Netherlands. The white subsurface leaflets are the tastiest parts of the plant.

Four groups of agricultural chicory exist: loose-leaf chicories, used for salad greens; heading chicories, forced varieties also used in salads; root chicories, cultivated for food and chemicals; and forage chicories, raised as livestock feed. Salad chicories are known in Europe as "Italian dandelion" potherbs, and French or Belgian endive is force-grown for its root as a salad delicacy. In North America, recent interest has focused on growing chicory as a root crop. In addition to its uses as a noncaffeine coffee additive or substitute, chicory root contains large amounts of a fructose carbohydrate called inulin, used as a sweetener. Not fully digestible itself, inulin reduces caloric content of foods while increasing bulk and is medically beneficial as a prebiotic in the colon. Chicory root extracts may prove useful in treating heart irregularities as well. The ground-up root is also used in the food industry as a seasoning and flavor enhancer, and some commercial dog foods contain chicory.

Chicory, along with several other plants, has evoked recent interest as a possible agent in phytomining—that is, the retrieval by plants of metallic substances or pollutants from soil. Gold, changed to soluble form by use of sodium thiocyanate, can be root-absorbed by chicory, though whether in sufficient quantity for economic benefit remains questionable. Recently chicory has also been used in fructan research; fructan polymers, containing fructose sugars, form carbohydrate reserves in plants and play important roles in plant metabolism.

Native to the eastern Mediterranean region of Europe, chicory was first introduced to America in 1785 by Massachusetts governor James Bowdoin, who liked it in his salads. It remained an import, however, both before and after the 1890s, when a few American farmers began cultivating it for salad greens and coffee.

The word *chicory* may have originated in the Arabic name for the plant—*chicourey*—reflecting the influence of Arabian physicians in medieval Europe. "With only minor modifications," as weed botanist Pamela Jones wrote, "the word *chicory* has traveled through the millennia and been absorbed into virtually every European language."

Cinquefoils
(*Potentilla* species)

MOTOROLKA/SHUTTERSTOCK.COM

Rose family. Some of our most familiar summer yellow wildflowers, cinquefoils suggest Virginia strawberry in the disk shape of their five-petaled flowers. Most cinquefoil species also show distinctive five-parted leaves splayed like fingers. The most common *Potentilla* species include common cinquefoil *(P. simplex)*, a low, sprawling, native perennial with arching stems and a single flower to a stalk; sulphur cinquefoil *(P. recta)*, an alien perennial standing one or two feet erect with hairy stems and foliage and large (up to an inch across), notched, pale yellow flowers in flat terminal clusters; and rough cinquefoil *(P. norvegica)*, sometimes an annual, sometimes a biennial or short-lived perennial, native to both Old and New Worlds, standing one to three feet tall, and exhibiting three instead of five leaflets. Other names: five-finger, five-leaf, old-field, creeping, and sulfur cinquefoil; sulphur five-finger, strawberry-weed.

Some two-hundred *Potentilla* species reside in the Northern Hemisphere worldwide, almost twenty-five in eastern North America. Several alien cinquefoils have become common weeds of lawns and roadsides.

The broad petals and disk flower form seen in most cinquefoils also appear in unrelated plants such as marsh-marigold and other buttercups, frostweeds, and others, as well as in closely related plants like strawberry. The shallow bowl prototype of these plants has evolved independently as an efficient host of nonspecialized insect pollinators. Cinquefoil can, however, also self-fertilize in the absence of insects. Some sources say this happens at night when the flowers close and the anthers touch the stigma.

One botanist described the cinquefoil pollination procedure thus: "The flowers secrete honey [nectar] on a ringlike ridge surrounding the base of the [male] stamens. Insects alighting on the petals dust themselves with the pollen but do not touch the stigmas, as the honey ring extends beyond. If they alight in the middle of the next flower, they dust the pollen against the stigma and cross-pollinate it." Individual flowers last for a day, strewing their petals on the ground in the afternoon, with new flower buds opening the next morning. The seeds, encased in achenes, develop loose inside the dried, goblet-shaped urn of the former flowerhead.

Common cinquefoil rises from a short subsurface rhizome, producing trailing stolons or runners up to four feet long that may also root at widely spaced nodes or joints. This plant also reproduces by "leapfrogging"—that is, by producing a terminal tuber and new plant where the bowed stem arches to the ground. Like the other perennial cinquefoils, *P. simplex* produces a basal rosette of leaves in the fall; it remains green beneath the snow, and from it rises a new flowering stem in spring.

Sulphur cinquefoil usually exhibits five leaflets, occasionally seven. It has a woody taproot with short, branching roots, but no rhizomes. This species displays a characteristic mode of regeneration from the root crown: New shoots encircle the root crown as the latter gradually rots away (over a period of six to eight years); the eventual result is a circular stand of erect clones surrounding a central gap, in which grasses and other plants usually sprout. Otherwise this cinquefoil reproduces only by seed, which average some 60 per flower; a single plant may produce some 1,600 seeds. Many remain viable for four years or more in the soil. Cinquefoil plants as old as twenty years are not uncommon, the aging based on total diameter of a clonal colony. These plants often produce a continuous cover over large areas of roadside and in old-field patches. Common cinquefoil favors open sun and typically inhabits dry, sandy ground—fields, roadsides, and open woods. Sulphur cinquefoil favors dry or wasteland sites from southern Canada throughout North America. Rough cinquefoil adapts to both moist and dry soils and has a more northern distribution.

Bright yellow flowers such as cinquefoils do not look yellow to the compound eyes of pollinating insects but reflect ultraviolet "bee purple," invisible to human eyes (whereas the flowers we perceive as purple often look greenish to them). The scientific lesson here is that there is no absolute yellow—or any other color. The way one perceives the plants of field and roadside—indeed, one might say the visible world generally—depends greatly upon the kinds of radiant energy one's eyes have evolved to detect. Cinquefoil seeds bear oily appendages called elaiosomes that are attractive to ants, which collect and store the seeds, aiding the plant's dispersal.

Cinquefoil is Middle English for "five-leaf"; *Potentilla* means "little powerful one," presumably referring to the plants' abundant tannins, making them potently astringent. Common cinquefoil found frequent usage among native tribes; the pounded rhizomes made medicinal tea, which was used to treat diarrhea, poultice sores and stop bleeding, and as a skin wash. Use it "as a gargle for loose teeth and spungy gums," recommended aging botanist Manasseh Cutler in 1785. Certain modern antiwrinkle cosmetic preparations contain *Potentilla,* as did love potions and witches' brews and banes in medieval Europe. Roots or rhizomes of Eurasian cinquefoils "have been employed medicinally since the time of Hippocrates and Dioscorides," according to one source. Young shoots and leaves of cinquefoil are edible as salad greens.

that, however, it may produce its large-leaved basal rosette for several years in succession.

The key trigger for burdock flowering is size rather than age of the plant. The rosettes of basal leaves (each one "not infrequently long and wide enough to hold a baby," wrote weed lorist Pamela Jones) must reach a critical size before flowering can occur. (This size index can be figured by multiplying the total number of leaves by the centimeter length of the longest leaf blade; a product number in the range of 150 indicates imminent flowering.) Rosette size does not accurately indicate the plant's age, however, since competition and crowding from surrounding plants may slow rosette development considerably.

Unlike many flowers of the aster family, burdock has only tubular disk florets, no radiating ray florets as in daisies and sunflowers. Flowers appear from July into October. Burdock's tubular florets are bisexual and insect-pollinated. The half-inch disk becomes the hitchhiking bur.

Burdock produces heaps of biomass. One study indicated that amounts of above- and below-ground biomass were about equal. The plant's large, fleshy taproot may descend three feet or so, and each rosette or lower leaf may extend more than a foot long and broad. The photosynthate energy stored in the taproot ultimately produces the flowering stems, a process called bolting.

Burdock cannot be labeled a truly invasive weed, for it rarely intrudes into cultivated fields. Tilling usually controls and eradicates burdock populations. Its favored havens are the disturbed soils of roadsides, railroads, fencerows, vacant lots, and around sheds and old buildings. It tends to favor partially shaded sites over those in full sun. Especially in the rosette stage, when leaves are large and sprawl low to the ground, burdock shades out competing plant growth. In later erect growth, the arrangement of leaves on the stem, with each level angled by its petioles and the upper leaves smaller than lower ones, results in a vaguely pyramidal form that allows maximum light exposure on each level.

The name *burdock* derives from the Latin *burra,* or lock of wool, presumably owing to the intimacy of sheep with the burry seedheads. Common burdock apparently arrived in North America with early English and French colonists. The burs are dangerous only when they lodge in skin, eyes, or ears of grazing mammals or pets or when ingested with other vegetation—if swallowed, the bur may form the core of a "hairball" mass in the digestive tract. Occasionally a small bird such as a hummingbird or kinglet becomes ensnared by a bur cluster, fatally exhausting itself in trying to pull loose.

Burdock's food, medicinal, and camp uses have long been known. The peeled, raw or boiled stem provides a nourishing, asparagus-like food; roots and young leaves also become edible after boiling to remove their bitterness. Root and leaf teas, both taken internally and applied externally, treat a variety of ailments. The leaves make effective poultices for skin sores or rashes. Some sources say that native Americans used the plant extensively for medicinal purposes, but this seems unlikely, given its immigrant history.

The strongly adherent burs find practical use as substitute buttons or temporary patchwork devices for cloth or clothing. Indeed, it is claimed that the fabric fastener Velcro, invented by Swiss engineer Georges de Mestral in 1948, originated from his microscopic examination of burdock's spiny seedheads when he removed burs from his dog's coat.

Common Buttercup
(*Ranunculus acris*)

BASPHOTO/SHUTTERSTOCK.COM

Buttercup family. Buttercups display yellow, wet-shiny, five- to seven-parted flowers and deeply cut palmate leaves resembling those of celery. This alien perennial species, the most common, stands two or three feet tall, with overlapping wedge-shaped petals, hairy stems, and an erect, branching form. Other names: tall buttercup, meadow buttercup, blister-plant, tall crowfoot, kingcups, goldcups, butter-flower.

About 250 *Ranunculus* species reside worldwide. More than 30 species, both native and alien, occupy wetland, woodland, and meadow habitats in eastern North America.

Relatively few yellow wildflowers appear in April or May—most yellows are summer flowers—but common buttercups are conspicuous exceptions. This species continues flowering into September, then dies back to a basal rosette of leaves, which remains green over winter and from which the flower stalk rises in spring. Buttercup stems rise from thick, fibrous roots.

For the novice botanist, buttercups are among the easiest flowers for identifying male and female parts, since the flower demonstrates the prototypical dish-shaped form, with sexual organs plainly evident. The stamens surround the domed, central pistils, a simple arrangement that becomes variable and complex in more highly evolved plants. Buttercup flowers are protogynous—the green pistils mature first, thus reducing chances of self-pollination; later, the stamens bearing the anthers expand in a fringed circle around the declining pistil. At the inner base of each shiny petal exists a tiny flap, the nectary, holding the flower's liquid invitation and reward to pollinating insects. Each flower lasts for about a week, opening only in daytime—or not at all, if the weather is overcast or rainy.

Notice the small, hooked seedcases, called achenes; some observers have thought they resemble tiny frogs in shape (*Ranunculus,* the Latin genus name, means "a little frog"). Seeds may germinate in either spring or fall. The plant reproduces mainly by erecting stems from short, budding rhizomes that rarely produce clonal colonies.

Common buttercups have adapted to many habitats in North America: pastures, hayfields, streambanks, roadsides, among others. The plant favors moist meadows and usually does not persist among cultivated crops. In England, its abundance in pastures and meadows is taken as an indicator of the ecological health of the field; its frequency increases with overgrazing (since cattle generally avoid it) and hay cropping.

At least sixty species of insects are known to frequent buttercup flowers—mainly bees, syrphid flies, wasps, and beetles. Many of these pollinate the flower as they collect pollen or nectar. The flower also attracts numerous butterfly feeders. Buttercups are not important wildlife food plants. A variety of birds and mammals consume the foliage and seeds, but in relatively small amounts. Ruffed grouse chicks, however, may feed extensively on the leaves soon after hatching. Cattle usually avoid the plant—its acrid juices can blister their mouths—though they can also develop something like an addiction to it, consuming it until it kills them. Wild animal grazers apparently do not suffer similar effects. Once the plant is dry (as in hay forage), the toxins vanish and it becomes harmless.

In a childhood game, the reflected glow of buttercup petals under a chin supposedly identified a lover of butter—or today we might say a person with a future cholesterol problem. From chin to mouth, however, is not a wise move. Similar warnings apply to most plants in the buttercup family. The acrid toxin is ranunculin, a volatile yellow glycoside that causes acute oral irritation and gastrointestinal distress if eaten. On skin contact in allergic individuals, the substance can cause rashes and blisters.

Buttercups represent one of the most ancient flowering plant groups that survive from the early Cenozoic era. Although this species originated in northern Eurasia and remains one of England's most common wildflowers, its presence in North America probably dates from the earliest colonial settlements. It may have been first brought and planted as a medicinal herb, a caustic "deep-heat rub" once widely applied for treatment of arthritis and rheumatism. American natives, though probably not familiar with *R. acris,* used native buttercups for similar ailments. Illinois tribes pulverized the roots and used them in a solution to treat cuts and wounds, and the Montagnais inhaled the odor of crushed leaves for headache. According to an old herbal, a decoction of buttercup splashed on the ground will make earthworms rise for a fisherman's plucking.

Common Chickweed
(*Stellaria media*)

GRESEI/SHUTTERSTOCK.COM

Pink family. Its five tiny, white petals, so deeply cleft that they appear as ten atop the threadlike trailing stem or branching from leaf axils, and its paired oval leaves identify this low, inconspicuous, alien annual. Stems and lower leaf petioles show a fringe of hairs on one side. Chickweeds tend to spread out in extensive succulent mats. Other names: starweed, starwort, star chickweed, chicken-weed, white birdseye, winterweed, stitchwort, chickwhirtles, skirt buttons.

More than one hundred *Stellaria* species exist, most in north temperate and arctic regions of the globe. Some twelve species reside in eastern North America; the narrow-leaved species are called stitchworts. Mouse-ear chickweeds *(Cerastium)* have shallower-notched petals, and some have hairy "mouse fur" leaves.

Chickweed may bloom and be seen from earliest spring to latest fall and even later. Yet the tiny flowers are not easily seen except during the plant's two main growth flushes: before tree leaves emerge in early spring, and after they fall in late autumn. Thus chickweed inversely reflects the deciduous seasonality of the year in its early and late ignitions on the ground.

Starlike bisexual chickweed flowers open anew each day, survive for only a day or so.

They attract insects with copious, sometimes visible drops of nectar. The pollen-shedding anthers typically mature at the same time as the female stigmas, a timing confluence called homogamy. Chickweed does not depend exclusively on insects for pollination, however; during the colder seasons, when few insects are abroad, the flowers can and do self-pollinate. Cleistogamy, self-fertilization in unopened flowers, also occurs. The wind-dispersed seeds spill from cylindrical capsules (usually nine or ten seeds per capsule) that fracture at maturity. A typical plant produces more than two hundred capsules, and seeds can remain viable in the soil for forty years or longer, requiring sunlight to germinate. In milder climates, chickweeds often germinate in the fall and remain dormant over winter—though a warm spell in winter may bring on rapid flowering. Thoreau once found frost-bitten chickweed blossoms in early February, concluding that "apparently it never rests." Lifespan of a spring or summer chickweed is about five to seven weeks. The plant also reproduces by rooting at the nodes of the creeping stems. Chickweed roots are shallow and fibrous.

This plant's lengthy flowering season, ability to self-pollinate, extensive seed viability, and concurrent vegetative reproduction enable it to survive as one of the world's most successful weeds. Chickweed is also one of the world's most common plants, its green carpets appearing wherever humans settle in the Northern Hemisphere. It favors lawns, cultivated fields and gardens, disturbed soil of today, yesterday, or the day before. Preferring cool temperatures and moist ground, it can tolerate cold but not drought.

Many if not most seed-eating birds relish chickweed seeds—birds are probably this plant's foremost dispersers—and some gamebirds and songbirds devour the tender leaves of new sprouts as well. Chickweed is a well-known favorite graze of barnyard chickens, hence the plant's name; and seeds and greens of the plant were long fed to caged birds. Cottontail rabbits also graze on the plant. Livestock, including pigs, cows, sheep, and horses, will eat it, but goats are said to reject it. The plant can accumulate nitrates to toxic levels, potentially causing digestive disorders in mammal foragers.

Chickweed tea, a mild diuretic and age-old soothing treatment for coughs, also served as a wash for itches and skin irritations, and the leaves were used for poultices. "In a word," wrote 17th-century English herbalist John Gerard, "it comforteth, digesteth, defendeth and suppurateth very notably" (what more could one ask of an herb?). Chickweed water was also said to "curb obesity." Green leaves and stems, sources of vitamin C, iron, and phosphorus, can be added to salads or boiled and served as spinachlike greens.

Common Dandelion
(*Taraxacum officinale*)

RALF GOSCH/SHUTTERSTOCK.COM

Aster family. Familiar in spring on lawns and roadsides everywhere, its bright yellow flowerheads adorn single hollow stems containing milky sap; its jagged-lobed basal leaves also identify this alien perennial. When it is "gone to seed," the fluffy white, globular seed clusters become distinctive. Other names: blowball, lion's tooth, fortune-teller, puffball, Swedish mums.

Other eastern North American dandelions—of some sixty *Taraxacum* species worldwide—include red-seeded dandelion *(T. laevigatum)*, northern dandelion *(T. ceratophorum)*, and marsh-dandelion *(T. palustre)*.

Some 150 to 200 individual bisexual florets constitute the aggregate flowerhead of a dandelion. Instead of holding both ray florets and disk florets, or all disk florets, as do many aster family flowers, dandelion heads consist entirely of overlapping ray florets—a more crowded, compact version of the chicory flowerhead. Each floret displays an evolutionary fusion of five once-distinct petals, now seen only in the five tiny teeth that tip each floret and in the longitudinal lines separating them. Each floret has its own male and female organs, the style surmounting the stamens. Stamens are unnecessary, however, for the plant to produce seed;

much, if not most, dandelion seed reproduction occurs asexually, without pollen fertilization or any genetic involvement of male cells. But insect pollination (each floret produces abundant nectar in its tubular base) and self-pollination, plus vegetative reproduction via sprouting of new plants from roots and root fragments, also occur—so this plant has all reproductive fronts covered, surely an important reason for its wide abundance and distribution.

Flowerheads display only during daylight, opening about nine A.M., closing in the afternoon. They also close during wet or cloudy weather. The closing helps protect the flower parts "at times when insects will not actively visit them," as naturalist Donald W. Stokes wrote, "and the pollen and nectar from dew and rain." Strong ultraviolet reflectance, especially of the outer part of the flowerhead, makes it visible to pollinators from afar and, close-up, provides a highly conspicuous "welcome mat" to insects. Each flowerhead lasts only a day or so, then seals tight for about two days in a so-called "swine's snout," named for its shape. Bent-back green bracts beneath the flowerhead form outer wrappings, bending upward to enclose the flowerhead at night and sealing it closed during seed set. The stem lengthens during this sealed-off period, elevating the developing seedhead into the wind currents. Then the head reopens, presenting a feathery, symmetrical seedhead, a globe of one-seeded achenes, each equipped with tiny barbs and capped with a fragile "parachute" called a pappus that adapts it for wind distribution. Heat convection currents also lift seeds from the head. Each head produces about two hundred achenes. Dandelions flower most profusely in early spring; another lesser growth flush occurs in autumn—at both times when day length lasts less than twelve hours.

Dandelion leaves never rise far off the ground and remain green year-round in a circular basal rosette atop the root crown. Each leaf, grooved lengthwise at midvein, channels the rain falling on it "straight to the center of the rosette and thus to the root," according to one botanist.

Dandelion's thick, fleshy taproot, often extending many branches, may plunge a foot, sometimes much more, into the soil. In some instances, this root system may form up to half the entire plant's biomass. Younger plants have longer taproots than older plants. Most dandelion plants survive for several years.

The bitter, milky juice seen in all parts of the plant is a latex, chiefly composed of taraxacin.

One observer noted one hundred different species of pollinating insects, mainly bees and flies, frequenting dandelion flowerheads. Livestock graze dandelions, though not as a preferred forage. Deer, woodchucks, and rabbits relish the plant and are probably the foremost wildlife consumers. Grouse, pheasants, and bobwhites forage on both foliage and seeds. House and chipping sparrows and goldfinches consume dandelion seed, neatly clipping off the feathery plumes before they ingest.

The plant has much to recommend it as a nutritious food for humans. As salad or cooked greens (collected from unsprayed areas), the leaves contain high amounts of vitamins A and C, potassium, iron, and calcium. The ground and roasted roots, their bitterness baked out, make an agreeable coffee additive or substitute. Dandelion wine comes from the fermented flowers; from the flowers also comes dandelion honey, yellow and strong-tasting.

As with any ubiquitous plant, dandelions have a long history of medicinal uses, both internal and external. Traditionally the root tea was served as a diuretic for kidney and bladder ailments, also as a liver treatment, tonic, and laxative. The milky latex—which can cause contact dermatitis in allergic individuals—has been applied on pimples and warts. Probably the first North American dandelions came over with the Pilgrims in 1620, not as accidental hitchhikers but as medicinal herbs, which spread from gardens like yellow wildfire wherever forests fell and meadows grew. Dandelion's original locus was probably the Mediterranean area.

Dandelions demonstrate evolution in action on suburban lawns. Over several seasons of mowing, the only dandelions that can flower are short-stemmed plants that duck the blade. Mowing thus becomes a selective factor, and in time most of the yard's surviving dandelion flowers hug the ground.

"How emphatic it is!" noted Thoreau, "a sun itself in the grass." Yet it takes more than French hyperbole for most of us to see *dent de lion*—a lion's tooth—in the jagged leaves of dandelion (since dandelions are hardly prevalent where lions roam, the name looks like a case of imagination running as rampant as the plant itself). *Taraxacum,* the genus name, is a Persian word meaning "bitter herb"; *officinale* means "medicinal."

Common Evening-Primrose
(*Oenothera biennis*)

MELINDA FAWVER/SHUTTERSTOCK.COM

Evening-primrose family. Standing one to five feet tall, this native biennial or short-lived perennial has conspicuous, four-petaled, lemon yellow flowers up to two inches across surmounting its stem. The large, X-shaped stigma projecting from the flower center; the reflexed sepals beneath the flower; coarse, reddish, almost woody stem; and alternate, lance-shaped leaves also identify it. Other names: yellow evening-primrose, tree-primrose, night-primrose, fever-plant, night willow-herb, evening star, scabish.

All of the eighty *Oenothera* species are New World natives. Botanists believe that common evening-primrose is of hybrid origin, most likely a cross between gray common evening-primrose *(O. villosa)* and large-flower evening-primrose *(O. grandiflora)*. Because most of the flowers are self-pollinated while still in the bud, most evening-primrose populations are highly inbred and tend to remain genetically stable over many generations. Complex variations in physical features exist, however, among populations. And since insect pollination and outcrossing with other primroses—as well as hybridization with other *Oenothera* species—do occur, variations arise almost despite, it seems, the plant's own self-reproductive strategies.

Anthers of the eight stamens in each flower often fail to produce pollen, or they produce sterile pollen, so visits by insects from pollen-productive flowers are necessary if outcrossing is to occur. Yet insects transfer at least thirty-five percent of the stringy pollen on large plants—where it exists at all—to flowers on the same plant, again resulting in self-fertilization. The insect pollination that does occur is primarily by night-flying moths, since the flowers open widest late in the day, on dark overcast days, or at dusk (hence the plant's name), tending to wilt the following morning. Again, however, individual plants show much variability; many flowers remain at least partially open for a day or two. Flowering occurs over a period of several weeks, mainly in July and August. Various observers have described this flower's sudden, spectacular opening, not at all a gradual process.

The seeds occur in long, woody, cylindrical capsules—"each one a graceful vase with four flaring tips," as one naturalist wrote. Each plant produces an average of about 140 capsules, each containing about 180 seeds, though sometimes many more. During winter, those capsules not raided by seed-eating birds split their seams, releasing the seeds. Seeds germinate in spring, summer, or fall; the seedling usually overwinters as a leafy rosette, five or six inches across, atop the root crown. After producing flowers and seeds the following year, the entire plant dies. Evening-primrose semelparous—that is, it may survive more than a year in the rosette stage before conditions allow it to produce a flowering stem; once it does so, however, its life cycle is ended. Size of the rosette apparently determines whether a plant will flower. A rosette less than five or six inches across will probably delay flowering. Buried seeds may remain viable for up to eighty years, but seeds must lie no deeper than a quarter inch or so in the soil to germinate. Most seeds fall within three feet or so of the plant; others are dispersed by wind, birds, or human agency such as mud on tires or farm implements.

Evening-primrose favors light sandy or gravel soils. It commonly grows along roadsides and in disturbed dry ground, though rarely on beaches or dunes. Native to temperate North America, it probably occurs more abundantly now than in presettlement times because of agriculture and forest clearing. Introduced to Europe as a garden plant from Virginia in 1614, it now thrives there as well as in temperate regions of Asia, Africa, and South America.

The plant cannot be ranked as a major food source for birds and mammals, although I have watched hummingbirds forage on the nectar and goldfinches—probably this plant's foremost seed consumers—perch for lengthy periods on the seed stalks, raiding the capsules, leaving them ragged and torn.

Every part of evening-primrose is edible, if not tasty, to humans. The taproots, astringent but rich in potassium and magnesium, can be served as a boiled vegetable, and new leaves and flowers can be added to salads, or the leaves can be prepared as cooked greens. Seeds have been used as a poppy-seed substitute. The plant has been raised for food in Europe and is still commercially grown for its seed oil. Evening-primrose oil is a primary source of gamma-linolenic acid and tryptophan, both used in various medications, dietary fatty acid supplements, and cosmetics. Anti-inflammatory and analgesic, EPO is mainly used to treat eczema and menstrual pain. Native tribes used root teas for bowel disorders and for poultices on bruises and sore muscles.

The genus name *Oenothera* apparently stems from a Greek word meaning "ass-catcher"; at least that's one of the meanings posed—others include "donkey-chase" and "wine-imbibing."

For unconventional gardeners, evening-primrose—though not exclusively night flowering—can become a chief resident of a night garden. Night gardens, raised more for scent than color, attract some of the rarer sphinx moths that usually remain unseen and inactive during daylight.

Common Milkweed
(*Asclepias syriaca*)

RON ROWAN PHOTOGRAPHY/SHUTTERSTOCK.COM

Milkweed family. This familiar summer native perennial stands three to five feet tall, with large, oblong, opposite leaves with downy undersides. Flower clusters—reddish or purplish and highly fragrant—droop from the upper leaf axils; the large, gray-green, twinned seedpods are also distinctive. Packed with seeds on feathery plumes, the pods split open in fall, releasing the aerial sailors to the winds. All parts of the plant contain a milky latex. Other names: silkweed, wild cotton, cotton weed. Some 150 milkweed species exist, mainly in the Western Hemisphere. Of these, about 22 reside in eastern North America.

In some areas of the Northeast, common milkweed may be the most abundant summer wildflower. Wherever it grows, its features make it one of the most conspicuous plants of any season—even in winter, when its empty, twisted seedpods dangle from the dead stems. In summer, common milkweed, somewhat coarse appearing, has big felted leaves set in right-angled tiers down the stem, probably an adaptation for maximal sunlight exposure. Its sweet-smelling flowers, so attractive to insects, yet sometimes dangerous to them, and—in fall—its warty pods crammed with spilling, silk-plumed seeds also make this plant distinctive.

Individual flowers in the ball-like floral cluster droop from long stalks. Anatomy of the milkweed flower is quite complex. Each flower shows a 5-parted crown resembling petals (the actual petals are bent back along the pedicel), and each of these petal-like parts is a hood, cupping a nectary. Milkweed nectar is copious; few North American flowers produce such an abundant supply, secreted mainly in the evening and through the night. Aside from its function as a food lure, it also provides an optimal germination medium for incoming pollen.

Circling the base of the interior floral structure are five V-shaped slits, each containing a pollinium, a set of two saddlebag-shaped pollen sacs connected together by strands called translators. Each flower produces five pairs of pollinia. The insect's feet or mouthparts, slipping into the slits, entangle in the translators. A snagged insect jerks free of the trap and in so doing carries away the pollinia dangling from its feet. Insects may collect up to a dozen tangles of pollinia in the course of feeding in milkweed. When the insect lands on another milkweed flower, the pollinia twist, rotating their sacs and slipping into the stigmatic slit, sometimes breaking off and fertilizing the stigmatic chambers.

Common milkweed requires cross-pollination, rarely self-fertilizes, thus is highly dependent upon insects. Flower clusters open and mature upward on the plant, and all flowers in an umbel usually open within two or three days. Flowers may number relatively few (less than ten) in an umbel or more than one hundred. Each flower has a sexual lifespan of four to five days. Only two to four percent of the flowers eventually produce mature pods. This situation results from the fact that milkweed clones are often large; pollen deposited from a flower in the same clone, being genetically identical, will not fertilize the flower—or if it does, the young pods soon abort. Thus milkweed seeding success depends upon pollination from outside clones. One study recorded an average of four to six mature pods per milkweed stalk, the average pod containing eighty to two hundred seeds that resemble overlapping fish scales packed in the pod.

"In spite of their silk parachutes," wrote milkweed expert Douglass H. Morse, "most of the seeds do not get far." Wind carries only one to two percent of the seeds farther than a few acres from the plant. Small seeds with large plumes travel farthest, but small seeds often fail to germinate or survive. Seeds require about a year of after ripening before they germinate in moderate abundance. They can survive at least three years in the soil; stored under proper conditions, they may remain viable for ten years or longer.

A seedling does not produce a flowering plant until its second or third year or more. Common milkweed propagates not only by seeds but also by budding on lateral roots or at the subsurface stem base. Stems die back in the fall, but subsurface buds remain alive all winter, and many sprout in the spring, producing clonal colonies (though many buds also remain dormant). Thus new stems arise each year from buds on the previous year's roots.

Typically a plant of roadsides and other disturbed areas, and widely adaptable to both alkaline and acid soils, common milkweed has in recent years extended both its habitat and geographical ranges. Observers have noted its increasing shift into fertile land and cultivated fields. Common milkweed is chemically toxic to grain sorghum, its root secretions inhibiting the latter's growth. It also competes successfully with Kentucky-bluegrass in old-field swale areas. Ordinarily, however, common milkweed does not successfully compete with crop plants; its spread into grain and grass fields may be related to herbicidal weed treatments, to which milkweed is resistant, in such fields.

Milkweed latex is essentially a defensive adaptation of the plant against herbivores. The leaf, in the words of researcher D. E. Dussourd, is "a ramifying network of latex canals pressurized with a lethal brew of toxic cardenolides in a quick-setting glue." Insect foliage feeders on milkweed have evolved special physiological adaptations enabling them to tolerate these cardiac glycosides. The number of such insect species—which are themselves toxic to predators—is fairly large. Many are brightly colored in conspicuous patterns of red, orange, or yellow. A 1979 study found eleven insect species that fed exclusively on common milkweed.

Common milkweed, according to one economic botanist, "can easily qualify as the greatest underachiever among plants." Its actual usage in human enterprise has apparently never matched its potential for same. The plant's most conspicuous feature—the silky tufts that transport the seeds in late summer and fall—became the source of a brief industry during World War II. Researchers discovered that this "floss" had buoyant properties like those of kapok, a silky fiber from pods of the silk-cotton tree, cultivated in Java, that was used in life-preserver jackets. When Japanese occupation of the East Indies cut off the kapok supply, the War Hemp Industries of the Commodity Credit Corporation created a Milkweed Floss Division to manage the production and use of milkweed. From 1943 to war's end in 1945, thousands of tons of pods were harvested for floss, much of it by schoolchildren ("Pick a weed, save a life!" preached posters, offering the collectors twenty cents per bag). After the war, when kapok—and later, synthetic fibers—became cheaper to use, the milkweed floss industry wafted away. Today, however, research and field studies on milkweed floss production continue in Kansas with a view toward renewing its use for insulative and absorptive materials.

In view of the cardenolide chemistry of this plant, one would not expect milkweed to be humanly edible—yet, in sprout and bud form, and with several changes of boiling water, it is relished by many. Milkweed-root tea treated a large variety of native and frontier ailments, both external and internal. People drank the tea for laxative, emetic, and diuretic purposes, also for asthma and rheumatism, and used the latex and floss as dressings for warts and wounds.

The great Swedish biological namer Linnaeus described common milkweed for science from an alien European specimen that he thought was native to the Orient, instead of North America, thus misnaming it *syriaca*, "of Syria."

Common Mullein
(Verbascum thapsus)

STUBBLEFIELD PHOTOGRAPHY/SHUTTERSTOCK.COM

Figwort family. This common alien biennial, one of the most conspicuous wild-flower-weeds of summer, displays a clublike, sparsely flowered wand of bright yellow, five-petaled blossoms. Its large, flannel-surfaced leaves, ridged and felted stem, and height of two to six feet are also distinctive. Other names: great mullein, Aaron's-rod, Jacob's-staff, blanket-leaf, candlewick, feltwort, flannel-leaf, mullein-dock, shepherd's club, torchwort, lungwort.

All three hundred *Verbascum* species are Eurasian in origin. Other eastern North American mulleins include moth-mullein *(V. blattaria)*, white mullein *(V. lychnitis)*, and clasping mullein *(V. phlomoides)*.

Mullein's long, green flower spike looks blackish and rather greasy, as if wiped by a car under-side. One never sees this spike blaz-ing in full or even abundant flower; instead, the yellow blossoms emerge singly—two, three, or five at once, low or high on a spike—often in a loose spiral pattern. This unevenness adds to the plant's coarse, somewhat ragged appearance. Beginning in late June and continuing into fall (depending upon spike height), flowering proceeds in successive spiral patterns from bottom to top of the spike. Each spiral, as the season advances, begins slightly higher on the spike, overlapping with former spirals, sometimes densely crowding together toward season's end. Individual flowers do not last long, typically opening before dawn and closing in the afternoon. Although bisexual in form, the flowers are sequentially unisexual, undergoing a practical "sex change" during their brief tenure; they are protogynous, the female stigma maturing and bending away from the later-maturing male stamens and anthers, thus hindering self-pollination. The pollination mechanism consists of two long and three short stamens, showing a tight coevolution with insect pollinators. "Three stamens furnish a visitor with food, two others clap pollen on him," as naturalist Neltje Blanchan wrote, while the sticky stigma catches a smear of pollen from the insect's traveling underside. If cross-pollination has not occurred by the end of the day, however, the flower closes and the stigma pushes against the anthers, effecting self-pollination. This one-way-or-another, sexual backup system virtually guarantees an abundant crop of mullein seed capsules—some 200 or more, each containing 200 to 500 seeds, per plant. A single plant may produce 150,000 seeds or more.

The seeds have no dispersal mechanisms; most fall within three feet of the parent plant, creating an abundant seed bank in the soil. Seeds remain viable up to a hundred years or more; even archaeological soil samples dating from 1300 have produced viable mullein seeds. Common mullein reproduces only by seed. Its typical life cycle is biennial, with seeds germinating in early spring and forming a rosette of feltlike leaves that remains into autumn and overwinters as such. The next June, this rosette pad produces a single flower stalk (which may, however, branch into several "candelabra" stalks), and flowering continues up the stalk until the plant dies in its second fall season.

Mullein's branching taproot, usually shallow, may in some instances descend a foot or so into the soil, enabling the plant to withstand drought conditions. The distinctive velvety, whitish, frost-green leaves, clasping the stem at their bases and decreasing in size as they ascend the stem, are "so arranged that the smaller leaves above drop the rain upon the larger ones below, which direct the water to the roots," as one botanist wrote—another drought adaptation. Viewed through a microscope, the soft flannel pile on leaves and stem "consists of a fretwork of little, white, sharp spikes," wrote naturalist Anna Botsford Comstock. The branched meshwork of leaf hairs, also "a feature of the leaf-atmosphere interface," as another researcher wrote, reduces water transpiration and heat loss from the plant, as well as protects it from herbivore munching.

Common mullein often appears as one of the pioneering plants after land disturbance, clear-cutting of forest, or abandonment of crop fields. Despite its presence almost everywhere and its prolific seed production, common mullein is a here-today-gone-tomorrow sort of plant, often not regenerating beyond a sole biennial life cycle on a site.

Common mullein does not long withstand competition even by grasses. As a weak, nonaggressive contender with other plants, often leaving only dead stalks of the previous year to indicate its former presence, it typically colonizes abundantly during the second or third year after soil disruption or exposure, often becoming a dominant plant, then rapidly diminishes during subsequent years. It maintains stable populations only in worn-out soil or topsoil-sparse areas, such as old gravel pits, that cannot support other plant communities.

Colonists brought common mullein to the New World sometime in the seventeenth century as a medicinal herb and garden ornamental. It rapidly spread wherever land was cleared and ground broken and grew commonly in the East by 1820. Not regarded as a major weed pest because of its ephemeral, nonagressive habits, common mullein arouses most hostility from farmers because it hosts certain insect vectors (such as the mullein leaf bug) of crop diseases. For the gardener, however, a mulch of common mullein leaves is said to repel slugs, probably irritating their skin membranes.

Common mullein has a long history of medicinal usage since the time of Hippocrates. This plant was probably the "phlomos" that was widely prescribed as a treatment for various ailments. Primarily used as a respiratory remedy for coughs, congestion, and bronchial and lung disorders, mullein leaves were smoked in pipes for such purposes. When dried, after the fuzz disappears, the leaves, which contain soothing mucilage and anti-inflammatory properties, make a bland, mildly sedative tea. Mullein also contains coumarin and rotenone, powerful compounds with toxic effects. The latter is a well-known fish killer; pioneers in Virginia would throw the plant into water then harvest the intoxicated fish brought to surface.

Mullein also had a host of nonmedicinal uses. The ancients reputedly used the dried stalks dipped in tallow for funeral torches and the downy, rolled leaves for incendiary lamp wicks. Although native American tribes had no historic association with the plant, many adopted the pioneer habit of inserting the big, soft leaves inside footwear and clothing for effective insulation. Colonists also used it as a homemade cosmetic called "Quaker rouge"; the rubefacient, flannel-like leaves raise a red blush (that is, contact dermatitis) on the rubbed face (something to remember about mullein, advises one outdoor manual, "when you're in the woods looking for toilet paper substitutes"). Sources differ on the derivation of the name. Probably it stems from the Latin *mollis,* meaning "soft." Other sources attribute the old English word *muleyn,* meaning "woolen," from the Latin *malandrium,* that is, malanders, or leprosy, for which mullein was reputedly prescribed.

Common Purslane
(*Portulaca oleracea*)

VORANAT/SHUTTERSTOCK.COM

Purslane family. This cosmopolitan flat-sprawling, mat-forming annual with purplish red succulent stems has fleshy, paddle-shaped leaves that grow in rosettes at the ends of branches. Centering most rosettes are tiny, five-petaled yellow flowers. Other names: pressley, purslance, pusley.

Some one hundred *Portulaca* species occupy temperate and warm climates worldwide. The reddish mats of this ubiquitous weed accompany almost all human efforts to plant, till, and raise something worth eating. Purslane, itself, is worth eating; like so many weeds, however, it may be invited but is not the guest one intended. Common purslane's sprawling, fleshy stems produce up to eight degrees of subbranching, a dense mass that often shows a radial form, which may extend up to two feet in diameter. The small, spatulate leaves often crowd toward the branch tips. Purslane's thick epidermal layers and inner spongy tisues that store ample water illustrate the plant's drought-survival adaptations.

Common purslane seed cannot germinate until seasonal temperature exceeds 86 degrees F, and after rain; thus it usually emerges in late spring or early summer and continues to germinate through summer. The tiny flowers, mainly self-pollinated, appear four to six weeks after emergence of the plant, but they open only during the mornings of hot, sunny days. They last only a day and produce no nectar.

Round seed capsules, ripening some two weeks later, contain variable numbers of seeds, averaging sixty or seventy, and open with a circular lid. Seeds generally fall near the parent plant and can germinate immediately, so several purslane generations per year are possible. The durable seeds can survive temperature extremes, remaining viable for forty years or longer. This hardy little plant cannot, however, survive the cold. Most plants live for only about three months then succumb to low temperatures in September.

Broken stem pieces of the plant—resulting from a hoe chop, perhaps—can produce adventitious roots that regenerate entire plants. Uprooted plants can also ripen seed and can even reroot if in contact with the soil. Purslane knows how to live and linger; it has a thick taproot plus numerous fibrous secondary roots.

This "hot-weather weed," as one gardener called it, resides in fields, gardens, gravel pits, and waste ground almost everywhere. It grows in both acid and limy soils but thrives best in soils with high nitrogen and phosphorus levels. Vegetable gardens and crop fields—among rows of corn, strawberries, tobacco, and spring wheat—are its favored habitats.

Essayist Charles Dudley Warner probably still speaks for most American gardeners in viewing common purslane as "a fat, ground-clinging, spreading, greasy thing, and the most propagatious plant I know." Yet, for all the ardent spleen lavished on this plant for its tendency to carpet ground space in fields and gardens, little evidence exists that it causes crop losses or competes successfully with other plants. Also, purslane is one of the most nutritious of wild foods, perhaps one of humanity's earliest vegetables. No part of the plant is inedible raw, cooked, pickled, or mixed, as a salad green, potherb, or source of seed flour.

This plant has a long history of human interaction. Persians and East Indians raised it more than two thousand years ago, and popularity of the plant led to its spread throughout Europe. "It cools the blood and causes appetite," summed up sixteenth-century English herbalist John Gerard. Not only did it reputedly repel evil spirits when strewn around one's bedstead, but its use as treatment for all sorts of ailments both internal and external has made it one of the world's most popular herbal medications. One source lists seventy-five symptoms, diseases, and sores for which purslane has been recommended—from ardor in Turkey and herpes in China to palpitations in Trinidad. Whatever the factual merits of such claims, the plant is rich in iron, calcium, phosphorus, and vitamins A and C.

Purslane is one of those plants that has been cosmopolitan for so long that botanists remain unsure of its origins or native residency status. Various sources claim it as native to South America, North Africa, or the Middle East. Herbalist Euell Gibbons called it "India's gift to the world," but archaeological research into native tribal cultures indicates its presence in North America long before Columbus sailed; purslane has dwelled here at least 2,500 to 3,000 years. If it is an alien, it's a very old one indeed.

Purslane has also proven itself a useful archaeological index. American natives often raised purslane along with corn for food, and the association of its pollen and seeds with corn pollen, which the wind does not disperse for any appreciable distance, has helped identify Indian garden sites. In some Ontario archaeological sites, the presence of corn pollen in lakes, indicating Indian agriculture, may owe to the native practice of washing purslane that collected large amounts of pollen on its foliage from adjacent cornstalks.

Common St. John's Wort
(*Hypericum perforatum*)

LIANEM/SHUTTERSTOCK.COM

Mangosteen family. Recognize this alien perennial, one of our most common summer wildflowers, by its five-petaled, inch-broad, yellow flowers, the fringed petals margined by black glandular dots. Held up to the light, its small, opposite, untoothed leaves show translucent dots. Stems are two-ridged, extending down each side, making them seem flattened. (Ridges also run down branches from the base of each leaf.) The plant is often bushy and unkempt, with the flowers numerous and showy on many top branches. Other names: goatweed, klamathweed, amber, rosin-rose, tipton weed.

Almost thirty *Hypericum* species, most of them native perennials, annuals, and shrubs, reside in eastern North America.

St. John's wort flowers occur in rounded or flattened clusters called cymes, in which the terminal flower of each cluster develops and opens first. Each flower, a regular five-petaled radiating form, is bisexual, showing three bushy clumps of stamens in the center surrounding a three-parted style. Although they are insect-pollinated, these flowers do not rely exclusively upon cross-pollination for reproduction; they can also reproduce asexually and by pseudogamy, whereby a male gamete merely "knocks at the door," thereby initiating growth of an embryo, but does not fuse with the egg. Flowering usually begins in June and lasts until September. Withered flowers usually remain on the plant, giving it an increasingly scrubby appearance as the season advances. Soil moisture determines the flowering duration in these plants.

Seeds vary in number from less than 100 to 500 per three-celled capsule; a typical plant may produce some 15,000 to 30,000 seeds. The sticky seed coats attach to passing animals, shoes, and clothing. One study found that the first expansion of St. John's wort into an area reflected animal trails and movements. To germinate, seeds generally require a period of four to six months after ripening; hence few of them germinate the same year they develop. A passage of fire often produces a growth flush of St. John's wort; the brief heat exposure seems to increase germination of seeds lingering dormant in the soil seed bank. Seeds in the soil may remain viable for ten years or longer.

Seedlings may require several years to produce flowering stems (though most plants flower by age two), a period in which they become highly vulnerable to plant competition. After their first year or so, they become well equipped to compete with other plants by means of a woody taproot that may penetrate the soil to five feet. One or more root crowns per mature plant may produce up to thirty flowering stems each year. The crowns, spaced apart along rhizomes, produce colonies of the plant.

The black glandular dots on petal margins, stems, and underside leaf margins, and the translucent dots in the leaves, contain a fluorescent phototoxic chemical called hypericin, which causes abnormal sensitivity to sunlight if ingested by insects and mammals. These defensive adaptations also give St. John's wort a competitive edge.

Flowering stems die back to the perennial root crowns in the fall but often remain dead and erect for a year or so. The root crowns may produce numerous branched, prostrate rosettes in the fall. These last over winter, dying before the flowering shoots arise in spring.

Fields, roadsides, just about any moderately moist, open, sunny spot within its range hosts St. John's wort. Fairly shade-intolerant, it does not thrive in wet soils. It rapidly responds, however, to the invitations represented by overgrazed or disturbed landscapes.

Used at least since the Greek classical age as remedies for a long list of human disorders—including liver and bowel ailments plus hysteria, obesity, and insomnia—St. John's wort was primarily applied as a wound poultice for the relief of contusions, burns, and sprains, also to soothe the aching feet of Roman soldiers. The plant came into the limelight most recently in 1984, when German researchers claimed beneficial effects of the plant extract as a mild antidepressant. Sales boomed, with more than a million Americans eventually ingesting the tablets on a regular basis to ease their psychic pain. More recent and rigorous scientific work, however, has called into question the former findings, concluding that the extract is essentially useless as the highly promoted "nature's Prozac."

The plant's namesake is St. John the Baptist, whose feast (birth) day is celebrated on June 24. The summer solstice brings the peak of the flower's bloom in some of its native areas, but the exact origin of its association with the saint remains shrouded in mythology.

Since St. John's wort became the subject of possibly the first biocontrol projects in North America, the phenomenal success of that early experiment provided much impetus for subsequent biocontrol efforts against many kinds of invasive weeds, resulting in greater or lesser degrees of success (most often the latter).

In most places where it exists today as an alien, the plant was apparently deliberately imported as a medicinal herb. Pioneer botanist John Bartram not only recorded its presence as "a very pernicious weed" in 1758 Pennsylvania, but also noted its phototoxic effects. Some sources, however, say that the plant arrived accidentally in grass and grain seeds of colonists and was first recorded about thirty years later, in Massachusetts.

Wort is the old English term for "plant"; *Hypericum,* derived from the Greek, means "above a picture," that is, power over an apparition.

Common Sunflower
(*Helianthus annuus*)

CRISTALVI/SHUTTERSTOCK.COM

Aster family. Recognize this native annual by its golden yellow ray flowers radiating from a central brownish pad of disk flowers, blooming summer to fall. Its stems, often branched with several flowerheads and with toothed, heart-shaped, alternate leaves, stand up to twelve feet tall. Other names: American Mary-gold.

Some fifty *Helianthus* species all reside in North America, about half of them in the East. Species identification is notoriously difficult, since hybrids abound, and probably few taxonomists agree on the same *Helianthus* roster.

Sunflowers exist as prototypical members of the aster or composite family; that is, their flowerheads consist of multiple disk and ten to twenty ray florets. Disk florets, which make up the crowded central mass, are the bisexual and prolific seed producers, whereas the yellow, radiating ray florets, vestigially female and sterile, flag insect pollinators. A close look at a disk floret reveals the pollination mechanism. Anthers form a tube enclosing the pistillate stalk; lengthening growth of the latter pushes pollen out the top of the tube, exposing it for random pickup by foraging insects. The stalk then ruptures, exposing the stigma surface ready to receive incoming pollen brought by an insect visitor from another sunflower head. Such flowers, producing mature pollen before mature stigmas, are called protandrous. Although disk florets can also self-pollinate, the self-produced pollen seldom germinates; thus individual florets are functionally self-incompatible.

The disk florets, arranged in two spirals on the disk, appear as concentric whorls. The outside ring of florets on the disk matures first; the central ones develop last. From pollination to the existence of mature, one-seeded achenes—up to six hundred on a seedhead—requires about a month. Total florets in the bouquet of a sunflower head number one thousand to two thousand.

Flowerheads range from several inches up to a foot or more across. They exhibit a marked directional orientation toward sunlight only before they open. "The heliotropic movement of the sunflower's head results from a bending of the stem," sunflower specialist Benjamin H. Beard wrote, "and is termed nutation. After sunset the stem gradually straightens, so that by dawn the head is again facing east. When the plant reaches the stage of anthesis [the opening of the flower], nutation ceases; therefter the head faces only eastward."

Common sunflowers hybridize widely, but only with other annual sunflowers, never with perennial species, often making species identification difficult. Yet, contrary to logical expectation, such intermixture of genes does not lead to a breakdown or fusion of species but results "only in a slight blurring of the species boundaries," as Heiser wrote. The stunted reproductive capacity of hybrids plus different habitat adaptations and blooming schedules of species (albeit with much overlap) all work toward keeping the genetic lines intact if not impervious.

Sunflower roots consist of a fibrous lateral network and a taproot that may extend five to six feet deep. Root secretions of chlorogenic acids are apparently chemically inhibiting to the germination of other plants, including even sunflower seedlings. This allelopathy appears most active in sites or conditions of nutrient stress, as in a worn-out field, where it may hold back the advance of plant succession.

Gaudy resident of roadsides, dry fields, vacant lots, even trash dumps, common sunflower does not tolerate heavy shade or acidic or water-logged soils. From its original range, the western Great Plains states, clearing, settlement, and cultivation helped establish it continentally, and colonial explorers and traders also imported this economically important plant to Old World lands and peoples. Wild sunflowers often pioneer younger stages of plant succession.

Pollinating insects of sunflower probably number into the hundreds. Foremost are bees; in sunflower crop fields, a hive of honeybees per acre is considered adequate for pollination coverage. The long-horned beetle is also a common pollinator. Butterflies frequently visit sunflowers.

Sunflowers rank among the most important bird and mammal food plants, both for availability and nutritional qualities. Many birds relish the seeds, as any backyard bird-feeding platform will reveal. Almost any seed-eating bird, including most gamebird and songbird species, devour the seeds where they find them, on the sunflower seedhead itself or in a bird feeder. Mammal seed-eaters include chipmunks, squirrels, voles, mice, and pocket gophers. Several grazers, including livestock, relish sunflower stems and foliage, especially those of younger plants. Muskrats, deer, and rabbits are probably sunflower's foremost mammal herbivores.

Argentina currently leads the world in the production of sunflower seed; Russia ranks second, and the United States, native land of the sunflower, holds third place. American production did not become significant, however, until the 1960s. The chief products of value are the oil extracted from the seeds, and the seeds themselves, used as snack foods and bird feed and as a protein supplement for livestock.

Although primarily a food plant for native tribes, sunflower also provided herbal medicine for many North American peoples. Its main medicinal value, from earliest times to the present, has been claimed for pulmonary ailments—coughs, colds, bronchitis. Sufferers drank leaf teas for fevers and malaria, and poulticed leaves treated snakebite and spider bites. The plant also served decorative and ceremonial tribal uses.

Common Wintercress
(*Barbarea vulgaris*)

ARTEM AND OLGA SAPEGIN/SHUTTERSTOCK.COM

Mustard family. One of the most common mustards, this yellow-flowered alien biennial populates fields and roadsides in spring. Standing one to two feet tall, it has branching stems surmounted by end clusters of four-petaled flowers. The lobe-toothed leaves and inch-long seedpods hug the distinctively ridged stem. Basal leaves, glossy and dark green, have a large, egg-shaped terminal lobe. Other names: yellow rocket, wild mustard, bitter cress, rocket-cress, yellow weed.

About twenty *Barbarea* species occupy north temperate regions worldwide.

One of the "early yellows" along with dandelions—in contrast to most early-spring flowers, which are white or purplish—common wintercress continues blooming into summer, usually finishes by late June but occasionally flowers again later in the fall. Most of the plants germinate in early spring, producing a taproot that may extend more than a foot deep plus a secondary fibrous root system. They also produce a ground-hugging rosette consisting of about five leaves that remain green throughout the next winter. If the rosette survives frost-heaving in the early spring, from it rise one or more flowering stems that may also sprout leafy cauline rosettes on the stems before they die off in the fall. When the stems fall, these cauline rosettes may develop their own root systems and, the next spring, flowering stems. Most cauline rosettes fail to survive winter, however. Common wintercress's root crown and root branches also generate buds and rosettes in late summer and fall, and these may also sprout flowering stems the next spring. Unless a rosette root separates from its parent root branch, it usually does not survive more than three growing seasons.

Common wintercress flowers, insect-pollinated, require cross-fertilization in order to produce seed. Bisexual, they project four long, prominent stamens and two shorter ones plus a single, central stigma. Each seedpod holds an average of 13 seeds, and each plant may produce 40,000 to 116,000 seeds—though sometimes much less, depending upon habitat quality. Seeds remain viable for at least ten to twenty years, breaking dormancy and germinating when moisture, temperature, and light conditions near the soil surface become optimal. New seeds require a several-week period of cold stratification at 20 degrees F or less to break dormancy.

Yellow rocket probably originated in Mediterranean regions. Today it grows throughout most of North America. Its most abundant populations reside in the Northeast, with increasingly heavy invasion, since the 1950s, of the Midwest. Although it thrives as an opportunist in a variety of soils and open habitats, it favors moist, rich, recently disturbed soils. It often becomes a dominant plant in early spring but does not compete well against such grasses as quackgrass and bluegrasses. It does, however, invade clover, alfalfa, and wheat fields in America and abroad, becoming a particular pest in legume hay, which livestock may refuse to consume if too many stems of *Barbarea* are present.

This plant's generic name reveals its reputed connection to the early December feast day of St. Barbara, third-century virgin martyr and patron saint of architects, grave diggers, and others; for medieval farmers, fresh green rosettes of wintercress provided a winter taste treat, loaded with much-needed vitamin C. A mustard oil called sinigrin accounts for the leaves' tangy flavor. As the season progresses, the leaves become bitter unless boiled to shreds. The plant should be cautiously sampled, if at all; recent research indicates that sinigrin may cause kidney problems.

Common wintercress apparently entered North America about 1800 by unknown means but did not reach official noxious weed status for another 150 years. Homeopathic healers and, later, even some native tribes brewed teas for common ailments and used the plant for skin poultices.

Coneflowers
(*Rudbeckia* and *Echinacea* species)

OLIVIER JUNEAU/SHUTTERSTOCK.COM

Aster family. Recognize native cone flowers by their large flowerheads surmounting single stems. The dark, somewhat cone-shaped center of disk florets is surrounded by yellow rays in *Rudbeckia,* by purple to white rays in *Echinacea* species. Two commonly seen coneflowers are black-eyed Susan *(R. hirta),* with chocolate-colored center and bristly stem and leaves, and purple coneflower *(E. purpurea),* showing swept-back, reddish purple ray flowers. Other names: black-eyed daisy, brown-Betty, brown-eyed Susan, bulls-eye, yellow daisy *(R. hirta);* black Sampson, comb-flower, Indian-head, purple daisy, snakeroot *(E. purpurea).*

Some sixteen *Rudbeckia* species exist in North America, about half of them eastern residents. They include the eastern coneflower *(R. fulgida),* three-lobed coneflower *(R. triloba),* sweet coneflower *(R. subtomentosa),* and cutleaf coneflower *(R. laciniata).* Only five *Echinacea* species exist, all in North America; the prairie coneflower *(E. pallida),* a paler flower that is mainly a western species, has been introduced in the East.

Alien weeds are not the only plant pests that infest native croplands. Sometimes it is a native plant that invades agricultural fields. Such is the case with black-eyed Susans, the commonest coneflowers of all, which sometimes gain colorful pesthood status in summer fields.

Black-eyed Susan stands about two feet tall, with flowerheads about two inches across. As in many radially symmetrical flowers of the aster or composite tribe, two sorts of florets inhabit the flowerhead: the central disk florets, blooming inward from the outside rim in successive circles of pollinating florets, a progression easily seen by close inspection; and the ten to twenty long, petal-like ray florets radiating from the central disk. Only the disk florets have bisexual parts; the ray florets in this species are reproductively neutral, lacking stamens and pistil, and tend to curl backward as they age, thrusting the central disk outward. The insect-pollinated disk florets develop into four-angled seedcases, and reproduction occurs mainly by seed. In most places, black-eyed Susans are biennials—that is, they sprout a leafy rosette that overwinters the first year; then they flower, produce seed, and die in their second year. This plant's complex genetics manifest in several intergrading varieties, some of which (such as the so-called gloriosa daisy) have become popular garden ornamentals. Black-eyed Susan has a spreading, fibrous root system and tough, minutely grooved stems that resist breakage.

Purple coneflower has much the same biological characteristics as black-eyed Susan, except that it usually stands a foot or so taller. It also has a larger flower (two to three or more inches wide) with a very chaffy, almost spiny, cone-shaped central disk (a thicket for pollinating insects). The flowers also can self-pollinate. The fifteen to twenty drooping rays, neutral or with sterile pistils, are notched and often pale gray at their tips. Purple coneflower is a native perennial.

Both *Rudbeckia* and *Echinacea* originated in the western prairie regions. Forest clearing and settlement encouraged their invasion eastward. Both are sun-loving, shade-intolerant species. They like space at their bases and also at the tops of their stalks. Vigorous grass growth usually outcompetes them. Black-eyed Susan thrives in dry, sandy habitats. Although it is quite drought-tolerant, it also grows in wetland fens and sedge meadows. Purple coneflower requires moister sites than the dry habitats that *R. hirta* tolerates.

Pollinating insects are numerous. Pollen-collecting bees of various species land in the central disk "thickets," and long-tongued bumblebees and butterflies seek nectar in the tubular, brown disk florets. Two brush-footed butterflies commonly seen on black-eyed Susan are the pearl crescent and the great spangled fritillary. Native solitary bees are the chief pollinators of purple coneflower in prairie areas.

Although it is a New World native, black-eyed Susan received its scientific name in 1753 from a type specimen given to the Swedish father of taxonomy, Linnaeus. He honored two professors named Olaf Rudbeck, father and son, by naming the foreign plant after them; the specific name *hirta* means "rough hairy" in Latin. His original type specimen resides today in a museum at Bognor Regis, England. In 1720, English poet John Gray wrote a love ballad titled "Sweet William's Farewell to Blackey'd Susan"; the flower name probably followed from the poem rather than vice versa.

No part of Susan is palatable to humans, even if nontoxic (some persons do show allergic sensitivity to the bristly stems). American natives used root teas of *Rudbeckia* as a bitter drink to eliminate intestinal worms and a skin wash for sores and earaches.

The purple coneflower name *Echinacea* comes from the Greek term meaning "hedgehog" or "sea urchin" (the bristly "cone" of the coneflower), the same root as for "echinoderm," a spiny marine invertebrate. This flower has had much more usage than Susan as an herbal remedy. According to some sources, purple coneflower was the most widely used medicinal plant by Plains tribes, who applied the root tea to a variety of internal and external ailments and also used it in sweat lodge rites. The Lakota Sioux, among others, still harvest purple coneflower roots for medicinal uses. Modern research has confirmed the validity of many traditional uses, also finding that extracts of purple coneflower stimulate the immune system. As salves or tincture treatments for wounds, sores, and insect and spider bites, so popular and profitable has *Echinacea* become in the herbal industry that the plant faces depletion in some areas.

Curly Dock
(*Rumex crispus*)

MARTIN FOWLER/SHUTTERSTOCK.COM

Smartweed family. Recognize this tall (up to four feet), alien perennial by its greenish terminal flower clusters on ascending branches and its long leaves with wavy, crumpled margins. Other names: curled dock, bitter dock, yellow dock, sour dock, sorrel.

Some two hundred *Rumex* species exist worldwide. About eighteen of them reside in eastern North America.

Many plants require close observation and paging through manuals and field guides for positive identification, but curly dock's distinctive leaves—resembling the lolling tongues of dogs—make this plant instantly recognizable. Another way to recognize docks, as well as many other plants of their family, is by the sheath circling just above the base of each leaf stem.

The valentine-shaped bracts that back the bisexual flowers are stemmed, greenish, and veiny; they later provide wings for the dry fruits. Flowering proceeds upward from the base of the flower stalk, so that (in vertical progression) seeds, flowers, and flower buds may all occur on the same stalk. The entire stalk may extend up to two feet long. Growth of this panicle ceases just before pollen production begins. Usually the flowers, producing no nectar, are unisexually sequenced, liberating pollen before the stigmas mature. The wind-pollinated flowers are mainly cross-fertilized, but self-fertilization may also occur. Curly dock's dangling flower clusters, at first greenish yellow, turn reddish, then reddish brown. The flowers have no petals but a prominent tubercle or wartlike swelling is prominent on each "valentine" bract. Each flower produces one reddish brown, triangular, one-seeded fruit. The entire plant, in fact, turns reddish brown at seed time in summer and fall. Sources differ on how many seeds a single plant may produce; figures range from 160 to 4,000. Seed dispersal occurs mainly by wind and bird excreta. The tubercle on each achene also helps float the fruit in water.

Curly dock reproduces entirely by seed, which may germinate anytime during the growing season. Often, though, it germinates in late summer or fall, producing only a basal rosette of leaves that remains green over winter. Then the plant flowers for the first time the following spring. Curly dock exhibits, however, a high frequency of germination polymorphism; that is, seeds from separate plants in the same habitat—and often even seeds from the same plant—show variable sprouting capacities. Some germinate soon after maturing, while others may not sprout for weeks, months, even years. Deeply buried seeds of curly dock have been found viable for up to eighty years. This variability probably gives the plant greater adaptability for colonizing new areas in both space and time dimensions. Most individual plants survive at least three years, many longer.

The plant's thick, fleshy taproot, somewhat branched, anchors it firmly. Several stems may rise from a single root crown, though a single stem per root is typical. The root may extend five feet deep. They have a radishlike taste and odor. Fragmented roots can sprout new plants.

Curly dock thrives in disturbed ground, moist or dry, often favoring sandy and rich loam soils but able to survive in all but the most acid soils. Typical sites include roadsides, irrigation ditches, pastures, fields, and vacant lots. The plant often invades gardens and croplands, in some areas has become a pest of alfalfa. Curly dock typically occurs in small patches, reflecting seed drop near the parent plants.

Although curly dock flowers rely on wind rather than insects for pollination, bumblebees collect pollen from them, probably pollinating some of the flowers. Regarding curly dock's usage as mammal forage, few plants have inspired such contradictory information. According to one source, cottontail rabbits favor the leaves over those of carrots or lettuce. Other sources claim that curly dock is "rabbit resistant," that rabbits as well as livestock avoid it. (The best way to circumvent botanical and herbalist misinformation is to trust one's own observations.)

Curly dock has a long history of medicinal usage. Homeopaths and herbalists prescribe the dried root tea for rheumatism, liver problems, and sore throat, among other ailments. It "may cause or relieve diarrhea, depending on dose," states one source. Externally, root teas were applied as a wash for skin sores, ringworm, and "spongy gums." Active ingredients include rumicin, anthraquinone glycosides, and tannins. Rich in protein, zinc, and vitamin A, curly dock leaves taste too bitter to eat without long boiling. Fresh young leaves, however—mildly bitter and lemonlike in flavor—can add interest to salad greens. Curly dock is one of the few alien plants that native Americans quickly adopted into their own medicine troves.

Swedish botanist-explorer Peter Kalm described this plant in 1749 as a resident in New Jersey; Linnaeus named it for science a few years later, in 1753. *Rumex* is the Latin name for docks; *dock* itself derives from the Old English *docce,* which may mean "a dark-colored plant."

Eastern Prickly Pear
(*Opuntia humifusa*)

SARI O'NEAL/SHUTTERSTOCK.COM

Cactus family. This prostrate cactus, a native perennial, forms mats or colonies of flat, green, oval, leathery pads up to three inches long, tufted with hairy bristles. In summer, buds rising from the pad margins produce showy yellow flowers, often with reddish centers. Other names: Eastern cactus, Indian fig, devil's tongue, beaver-tail cactus.

Some 150 *Opuntia* cacti exist (some botanists identify almost 300), all occurring in the Western Hemisphere and most in semiarid regions and the tropics. Other *Opuntia* sometimes resident in eastern North America include the plains prickly pear *(O. macrorhiza)* and little prickly pear *(O. fragilis)*.

Always an exotic find when encountered in a sandy field or roadside, prickly pear seems out of place in our green Northeast. Yet the same adaptations that allow cacti to survive in dry areas allow them to exist in other places too. These adaptations are mainly water-conservative. They include the spines, which serve as heat-radiating points; the tough, rindlike skin of the pads, which protects the succulent, spongelike inner tissue; and the plant's process of dehydration in the fall, triggered by cold weather, concentrating its sap into an antifreezelike solution that withstands subzero temperatures. Shade-intolerant, prickly pear remains green and flabby, flat under the snow, during winter.

Specialized prickly pear anatomy includes small, cushionlike organs on the pad surface called areoles, containing the buds from which develop new stem growth, spines, flowers, and fruit. Spines, if any (this *Opuntia* species usually bears few), rise from the base of the areoles; also from the areoles arise glochidia, short, fuzzy, multibarbed bristles that provide this porcupine of plants its defense against munching herbivores.

Prickly pear begins flowering in its second year. The sunburst of waxy yellow flowers opens in June along the marginal tips of the previous year's pad joints. Each flower measures up to three inches across and consists of eight to twelve petals. As in most cacti, the male parts of the flowers mature before female parts, thus deterring self-pollination; they are probably self-sterile as well. Insect-pollinated, the bisexual blooms produce a spiny knob that ripens into a reddish or purple, somewhat pear-shaped fruit—actually a pulpy, sweet-flavored berry—containing numerous seeds. The fruits may remain on the plant over winter but are usually consumed by an animal before spring.

Most successful prickly pear reproduction, however, is a vegetative rather than sexual procedure. Root growth can occur from any joint surface in contact with the ground, and the typical clumped and matted form of the plant indicates this mode of reproduction. Roots, a shallow meshwork, quickly absorb water and nutrients from even a quick rain shower.

Open sandy areas—fields, roadsides, dunes, shores—are this cactus's favored habitats. A common pollinating insect visitor to the flower is the spring rose beetle, related to the Japanese beetle. Bees, wasps, ants, and other beetles also visit, and some of them pollinate. Many birds and mammals relish prickly pear fruits. In the East, cottontail rabbits are probably the plant's most important seed dispersers. White-tailed deer and livestock also eat the pads and fruits without apparent injury from spines and areoles.

Almost every part of prickly pear makes a nutritious, tasty human food if properly prepared (with gloves; sticky tape or tweezers will remove the barbs from careless fingers). The peeled pads can be cooked like green beans, and the fleshy pulp of the fruit (bristles removed with a damp cloth), when chilled, makes an excellent sweet jelly ("tastes like pink lemonade," wrote one sampler). Even the seeds, ground when dried, can be used as flour or a thickener. Prickly pear is not so abundant in the East, however, that it can survive collection for food or other purposes.

Native Americans and homeopathic healers applied the plant's pads as poultices for wounds and joint pains and drank a tea made from the pads for lung and kidney ailments.

Prickly pear fruits, cultivated and relished in Mexico, are called *tunas* and sold there in market stalls. Prickly pear fruits also enjoy popularity in Italy, where the plants were introduced in the sixteenth century.

into the visible flowerhead surface. Female flowerheads continue to elongate after pollination, elevating their pappi to the wind.

Pussytoes usually grows in unisexual clonal patches, with cross-pollination by insects virtually guaranteed as a result. Occasionally male and female plants mingle their clones by intruding stolons among their separate stands.

The one-seeded achenes, each encircled by long hairs of the pappus, are dispersed by wind. Pussytoes reproduces both by seed and by stolons that extend from a plant and sprout a new clone at their ends. Sprouting plants produce a leafy basal rosette, from which rise solitary flowering stems, each of which may produce three to ten clustered flowerheads. The one-ribbed, wedge-shaped, basal leaves have pointed tips, are densely silvery-woolly beneath (as is the entire grayish green plant to a lesser extent); these rosettes remain green beneath the snow in winter. Crowded rosettes often form a matlike growth on the ground. Pussytoes roots are shallow and fibrous.

Field pussytoes favors dry, sandy ground in open fields, grassy hillsides, often in woodlands. Not as spectacular a wildflower as the colorful spring ephemerals, their silver-gray, silken tufts may clothe acres of open ground alongside trout lilies and spring beauties.

One division of plant endeavor common in English-speaking countries may be labeled "the botany of cute." It finds greatest expression in the vernacular naming of plants, especially wildflowers. It is related to the antique doctrine of signatures belief, which attempted to correlate plant shapes and forms with their human usages. The botany of cute endeavors to correspond plants with human sentiments (forget-me-not), with names of persons or other creatures, or with anatomical portions thereof—as in ladies'-tresses, jack-in-the-pulpit, blue-eyed Mary, and many others. Once primarily a garden botany and associated mainly with maiden aunts and Sunday school outings, the botany of cute has long since crashed those borders. Thus flowers named after feet, a subdivision of this weird anatomical botany, are not uncommon. Pussytoes is, of course, a standard bearer in the botany of foot-cute, a plant so named from the woolly floral branches that supposedly resemble furry cat digits.

Like most aster family plants, *Antennaria* has no gastronomic palatability or value for humans. These plants found some usage as a treatment for diarrhea and lung ailments by herbal practitioners, also as a poultice for sprains, festers, and snakebite.

The name *Antennaria* derives from a Latin word meaning "like antennae," referring to features of the female flowerhead.

Fireweed
(*Chamerion angustifolium*)

MAX SUDAKOV/SHUTTERSTOCK.COM

Evening-primrose family. Recognize this native perennial wildflower by its elongated spike of magenta-pink or rose-purple flowers, each with four roundish, lobed petals; its long, vertically erect seedpods; its narrow, willowlike, alternate leaves; and its three- to seven-foot height. Other names: great or spiked willow-herb; rosebay, blooming Sally, wickup.

Some twelve *Chamerion* species reside in eastern North America. The genus, consisting of about two hundred species, occupies temperate and arctic regions worldwide.

This plant reproduces mainly by subsurface stems creeping horizontally in the top couple inches of soil cover. Its four-petaled flowers—up to fifty on a spike—splay at right angles from the tip of the long ovary. Flowering begins at the bottom and proceeds up the spike. Three-inch-long, gracefully curved seedpods stand erect behind the flower progression.

The insect-pollinated flowers, measuring about an inch across, contain a small, green, nectar-secreting disk. The eight purplish, pollen-producing anthers mature and decline a day or so before the pistil matures, thus promoting cross-pollination. Another aspect that promotes cross-pollination is the behavior of pollinating insects: Typically they visit the lower, more mature flowers first, working spirally upward along the flower spike to the upper, male-phase flowers. Then they move to the bottom of another spike, depositing pollen on new female-phase flowers. Thus the pollen reaching a receptive stigma has usually originated from either a different plant or a different flower on the same plant. Fireweed is also self-compatible, however, and can self-fertilize. Since most fireweed patches consist of cloned shoots of genetically identical plants, the practical distinctions between cross- and self-pollination become rather obscure.

The seedpods, which split open lengthwise in late summer, release masses of seeds (300 to 500 per pod) attached to feathery down, giving the plant "a wild and disheveled appearance," as one observer wrote. A single plant may produce up to 80,000 seeds—though about half that number is typical—through a season. The silky plumes can carry seeds far on wind currents; wind becomes the only efficient distributor for a plant that must establish itself on bare mineral soil. Air humidity is an important aspect of this distribution—an increase in humidity causes the seed plumes to decline in lifting efficiency, thus increasing the chances for the seed to drop in areas with adequate moisture for germination. A 1987 study demonstrated that twenty to fifty percent of fireweed seed plumes cruise on air currents at altitudes higher than three hundred feet, and that they may travel for hundreds of miles. The plant's continuous production of seeds over a season means that dispersal occurs during most of the summer and fall. Seeds can germinate almost immediately and up to two years following deposition.

Broadly tolerant of diverse climates and soils, fireweed can also tolerate light shade and low, damp ground. Frequently a dominant pioneering species, fireweed often appears as one of the first plants to rise in profusion following fire or other site disturbance. Favored habitats include open ground bearing little plant competition. In addition to burns, it also favors such disturbed sites as forest clear-cuts, river sandbars, gravel pits, roadsides, and old fields. It frequents mountainous areas in its southern range, often colonizing avalanche scars, and it clothes tundra in the North. Yet, depending on the ecosystem, fireweed also appears in smaller colonies and much thinner abundance, such as in dunes and woodland clearings. Its adaptability makes fireweed "one of the most completely circumpolar of all plants," wrote one botanist.

Fireweed's young shoots (especially the stem pith) and tender leaves make edible fresh or cooked greens, and the dried older leaves make a decent tea. All were used by native peoples; some tribes established fireweed clans in their social systems. They made poultices of the peeled roots for burns and skin sores, drinking leaf and root teas for abdominal ailments and using the tea as a mouthwash for sore gums. They also smoked the leaves as a tobacco substitute and used tough, fibrous peelings from outer stems in making twine for fishnets and other needs.

Fireweed contains high amounts of beta carotene and vitamin C, and leaf extracts are anti-inflammatory on the skin. Fireweed's main contribution to the human palate is its rich honey; the plant makes "excellent bee pasture," according to one source.

Fleabanes
(*Erigeron* species)

Aster family. These native annuals, biennials, and perennials display numerous small, daisylike flowers that strongly resemble asters in appearance. Unlike asters, however, fleabanes begin flowering in spring, and the ray flowers radiating from their central disks are much more numerous (up to 150) than in most (though not all) asters. Flowerheads are flat, about a half inch across, and delicate in appearance. Fleabanes stand one to four feet tall. The most common species are Philadelphia fleabane *(E. philadelphicus)*, a biennial or short-lived perennial with wide-rayed, pinkish or magenta flowers and stem-clasping leaves; rough fleabane *(E. strigosus)*, annual or sometimes biennial with narrow-rayed, white, sometimes pinkish flowers and mostly untoothed leaves; and eastern daisy fleabane *(E. annuus)*, also narrow rayed and white flowered, hairy, and with many toothed leaves. Other names: daisy, tall daisy, horseweed, sweet scabious; Philadelphia daisy, skevish *(E. philadelphicus)*; whitetop *(E. strigosus)*.

Some two hundred *Erigeron* species exist in north temperate regions worldwide; about nine reside in eastern North America.

ZPRECECH/SHUTTERSTOCK.COM

The floral biology of fleabanes is much the same as for asters. About a hundred tubular florets make up the central disk, and varying numbers of petal-like ray florets radiate from it. In Philadelphia fleabane both ray and disk florets are sexually functional, but the rays are pistillate only, whereas the disk florets are perfect, and the plant is insect-pollinated.

The reproductive situation is different in *E. strigosus* and *E. annuus*. Both are entirely asexual, reproducing without a fusion of sexual gametes (thus even self-fertilization does not occur), a system called apomixis. The flowers nonetheless produce large amounts of pollen, which is sterile. Since all progeny are clonal, apomictic reproduction has long been viewed as disadvantageous to a plant's capacities for evolutionary change and adaptation, thus to its long-term survival success. Experiments with fleabanes, however, have demonstrated that a wide variety of adaptations exist in these clonal populations—so wide that a literal plant succession, not of different species but of differentially adapted biotypes among separate *Erigeron* clones, may sequentially appear in a single field habitat.

Fleabanes reproduce only by seed; an annual fleabane plant may produce some 10,000 to 50,000 one-seeded achenes, all of them genetically identical. The plants are shallow rooted. Those that germinate in late summer or fall may last over winter as low sprouts, then flower in the following year. Most fleabanes, however, germinate in spring from seeds of the previous year. The flowers close at night, as if to shelter their supply of impotent pollen.

Fleabanes primarily colonize open, disturbed sites; they commonly appear in overgrazed pastures and are regarded as indicator species of mismanaged range. Weedy gardens and roadsides are also typical habitats. These plants adapt well to dry conditions and to various soils throughout most of North America. Eastern daisy fleabane, however, seems more prevalent in cultivated (that is, more disturbed) land than daisy fleabane; and Philadelphia fleabane adapts to somewhat moister habitats—swamps, ditches, beaches, riverbanks—as well as to field and roadside areas.

A bane of existence for our Old World ancestors was the near-constant presence of biting mites and insects. This plant's name derives from its supposed repellent powers against fleas, a claim much overstated if not totally false. If fleas plague you, reach for something other than fleabane. The "bane claim" is supported only by those experts who have not actually used them dried, powdered, or "sprinkled in kennels, from which, however, they have been known to drive away dogs," according to one botanist. Nevertheless, the ugly and descriptively inaccurate name stuck, ill serving these lovely and delicate asters. *Erigeron* stems from a Greek compound meaning "early old man," supposedly a reference to fleabane's spring-blooming habit and the hoary appearance of some species.

These are not plants that provide tasty nibbles of any sort, but their astringent properties led to medicinal usages among many native tribes. Ailments as diverse as diarrhea, kidney stones, diabetes, internal bleeding, fevers, bronchitis, and tumors—plus many more—were treated by drinking the bitter tea. The distilled oil treated external wounds and sores as well. Some allergic individuals may develop contact dermatitis from handling fleabane.

Garlic Mustard
(*Alliaria petiolata*)

HARTMUT MORGENTHAL/SHUTTERSTOCK.COM

Mustard family. Recognize this invasive Eurasian biennial by its triangular, sharply toothed alternate leaves; its white flower cluster surmounting the stem; and the strong garlic odor of crushed leaves. Other names: hedge-garlic, hedge-mustard, poor-man's-mustard, garlic-root, leek cress, European wild mustard.

A mustard that smells and tastes like garlic! Some mustards adopt astonishing characters, and this mustard is one of them. Like all mustards, however, its flower is four-petaled—and like most, its elongate seedpods stand erect beneath the terminal flower cluster.

Garlic mustard's two-year life cycle begins as a leafy rosette hugging the ground; it remains green beneath winter snow and provides the greenest greeting of late winter when the snow melts. The flowering stem rises one to three feet from the rosette in the spring of the plant's second year, with peak of flowering from mid-April to mid-May. Although insect-pollinated, the bisexual flowers are also completely self-compatible and do not require cross-pollination in order to produce seed. They open in ascending progression up the flower spike; most remain open two or three days, but sexual action typically occurs on the first day of flowering.

Each plant produces, on average, four to sixteen seedpods, each containing ten to twenty black seeds. When the pods split open in the fall, thousands of seeds are forcibly ejected; you can hear the seeds popping out if you walk through a patch at the right time. Seeds genetically identical to the sole parent plant can colonize large areas, producing essentially clonal stands. New seeds usually remain dormant eight to twenty-two months in northern areas, requiring a period of freezing in the soil to break dormancy—thus a seed is often at least a year old by the time it germinates. Seeds typically fall near the plant; they are dispersed by rodents, birds, and (especially) people, on clothing, footwear, and machinery.

This taprooted plant (an S-curve at the top of the root is distinctive) reproduces entirely by seed, dying at the end of its second season. Axillary buds on the root crown may, however, produce one or more additional stems, especially if the primary stem is cut or damaged.

Garlic mustard favors moist, partially shaded soils of all kinds except highly acidic ones. It thrives on disturbed land. Open forest, forest edges, riverbanks, and shaded roadsides are its foremost North American habitats; it also adapts to drier, more open locales such as fields and railroad embankments. Seedlings, however, are vulnerable to drought. Many die in this first-year stage of growth. Garlic mustard's spread across the continent has been rapid; most weed manuals of only a few decades ago did not even list it. Studies have revealed that once it invades a site, it usually becomes a permanent part of the plant community—but unless soil disturbance becomes repeated or continuous, its population gradually declines to a level of low stability. "This strategy of increased presence and low but continuous abundance," wrote one researcher, "allows garlic mustard to rapidly expand when disturbance occurs."

In its native Europe, garlic mustard lurks modestly in the hedgerows and is not a terribly aggressive plant. It first appeared in North America on Long Island in 1868. Thoreau in New England never saw it. By the year 2000, garlic mustard had spread to thirty-four states.

A substance called allicin gives the distinctive flavor to garlics and garlic mustard alike. Garlic mustard's odor and taste gradually dissipate during the plant's later growth stages in summer and fall. In Europe, the plant has long been used as a potherb, salad green, and garlic substitute in cooking. Its vitamin A and C contents rank higher than in spinach and oranges, respectively, on a weight basis. As a homeopathic medicine, the leaves found use as a sweat inducer, for treating edema and dropsy, and as poultices for sores and boils. Colonists probably brought the first plants into areas other than North America for use as garden potherbs and herbal remedies, and the plants soon overran the garden walls, widely escaping.

Probably the best, most effective control method for garlic mustard is to prevent its initial establishment. Eradication efforts, where undertaken, should focus on the early rosettes. Garlic mustard's total eradication from areas where it is well established becomes extremely difficult, given the plant's prolific seed bank. Probably the most effective means of eradication from such areas, combined with the least amount of soil and habitat disturbance, is repeated mowing over a period of years.

Goldenrods
(*Solidago* species)

PETER RADACSI/SHUTTERSTOCK.COM

Aster family. Probably the most common flowers of summer and early fall, these native perennials adorn fields, open woods, and roadsides almost everywhere. Their bright yellow flower clusters surmounting straight, leafy stems, and their alternate, mostly linear leaves identify them. Among the most commonly seen species are early goldenrod *(S. juncea)*, late goldenrod *(S. gigantea)*, and Canadian goldenrod *(S. canadensis)*. Other names: yellow-weeds, yellow-tops, flowers-of-gold.

Almost one hundred *Solidago* species exist, mainly in North America; about half of these reside east of the Mississippi.

Yellow flowers predominate in summer, and of all the yellow flowers, the goldenrods are the most showy and abundant. The species vary in form of the flowering clusters—some are bushy and plumed, some gracefully spread or pyramidal and nodding like elms, some clublike, some wandlike; a few are flat-topped and zigzag stemmed. All three of the common species have dense, plumelike flowers and bloom from July through September. Canadian goldenrod's flower branches often appear somewhat arched and bent back. Early goldenrod has untoothed upper leaves; all leaves of the other two are toothed.

Look closely and you will see that a tiny, apparently individual flower of a goldenrod cluster actually consists of aggregate flowers arranged in the typical daisylike form—that is, with central disk florets and with spreading but irregular ray florets, the main source of goldenrod's yellow appearance. Both sorts of florets are relatively few in number—a pocket magnifier reveals them clearly. Common goldenrod has two to seven disk florets, six to twelve ray florets; early and late goldenrod florets range from eight to fifteen and three to seven disk florets, respectively, and seven to twelve and ten to fifteen ray florets. Disk florets are all bisexual, having both stamens and pistils, whereas ray florets are pistillate only. Most goldenrods require outcrossing via insect pollination from another cloning goldenrod and cannot self-fertilize. Both ray and disk florets produce one-seeded achenes, wind-dispersed by means of the attached fuzzy tuft called the pappus atop the achenes.

Each flowering stem typically produces more than ten thousand achenes. Thoreau described the fluffy seedheads in early November as "richly and exuberantly downy . . . They cover our clothes like dust. No wonder that they spread over all fields and far into the woods." Seeds of the previous year germinate in June or July, but those shoots usually do not produce flowering stems until the next year.

Reproduction also occurs by cloning. In any field of goldenrods, you are not seeing large numbers of individual plants but of individual stems from considerably fewer numbers of clonal groups. Cloning stems rise from the nodes on rhizomes, which spread horizontally outward from the parent plant. The rhizomes with their sprouts form a circular clone that tends to expand in diameter each year. Clones that extend ten feet across are not uncommon. Very old clones may completely die off in their central areas, become replaced by other plant species, and thus form a surrounding "fairy ring" of goldenrods like a circular ripple on a pond.

Rhizomes, extending mainly in late fall after seed production, lie dormant over winter. In the spring, a new shoot rises from the tip of each rhizome, producing a rosette of scale leaves, then a rapidly rising, upright stem. Each shoot may produce two to six daughter rhizomes, and each rhizome can potentially produce a single shoot from its tip in the following spring. Stems do not grow from the same rhizome nodes in successive years but always from the tips of new rhizomes; these underground connections may persist for six years. Flowering stems typically rise only from rhizomes, not as seed sprouts. The plant roots are shallow and fibrous.

Early, late, and Canadian goldenrods are probably the most widely distributed of all goldenrods. All reside in fairly dry, open areas—old fields, roadsides, disturbed soils. They are shade-intolerant, though many survive in light shade, but they show wide tolerance for various soil and fertility conditions.

Once established on abandoned farmland, they become successful plant competitors, often the dominant herb species, sometimes persisting as such for several decades. This situation may owe considerably to the plant's chemical allelopathy. Goldenrods also thrive, however, on native tallgrass prairie, coexisting with more than three hundred species of prairie forbs and grasses. Some evidence indicates that critical population sizes of certain goldenrod species exist, below which the plants do not produce abundant seed crops.

The most conspicuous insect associations with goldenrods are those involving stem galls, created by a stem-feeding larva and reacting plant tissues. The three most common galls, readily identifiable by shape, result from the activities of two fly larvae and a moth caterpillar. Most conspicuous is the goldenrod ball gall, a spherical bulge in the stem caused by the fruit fly *Eurosta solidaginis,* called the goldenrod gall fly.

Their astringent oils gave goldenrods wide usage for native tribal medications that served a roster of curative purposes. The flower tea was said to quell fevers and ease sore throats; externally, the infusions treated boils and burns. Thomas Edison seriously pursued the idea of creating an ersatz rubber from goldenrod sap. Through breeding and cultivation, he produced a goldenrod almost twelve feet tall that yielded up to twelve percent rubber. The tires on the Model T given to him by Henry Ford were made from goldenrod rubber.

Goldenrods have achieved an undeserved reputation as "pollen plants," anathema to hay fever and allergy sufferers. The blame is misplaced, for goldenrod pollen is heavy and sticky, and it does not readily disperse into the air. (The sneeze culprit is usually common ragweed.)

Most goldenrods are native to North America, though a few species reside in Central and South America. Eurasia has only a single native species, but S. *Canadensis* and a few other American goldenrods have become popular garden flowers in Europe, where horticulturists have developed many hybrid forms for ornamental planting.

Hawkweeds
(*Hieracium* species)

DOUWEVRS/SHUTTERSTOCK.COM

Aster family. Resembling yellow or orange dandelions but with much different leaves, most hawkweeds are coarse, bristly perennials—some native, some alien—that often grow colonially on poor ground. The most commonly seen ones, all aliens, have hairy stems and basal rosettes of tongue-shaped hairy or woolly leaves. They include mouse-ear hawkweed *(H. pilosella)*, a short (four inches to a foot high) lawn and field weed with a solitary yellow flowerhead and cordlike runners forming mats over the ground; orange hawkweed *(H. aurantiacum)*, one to two feet high, having up to thirty red-orange flowerheads; yellow hawkweed *(H. piloselloides)* and meadow hawkweed *(H. caespitosum)*, both with several yellow flowerheads clustered atop the stem. Most native hawkweeds, by contrast, have leaves ascending the stem rather than clustering in basal rosettes. Other names: devil's-paintbrush, orange-red king-devil, lungwort, tawny hawkweed *(H. aurantiacum)*; glaucous king-devil, king-devil hawkweed *(H. pilosel-*

loides); field hawkweed, yellow king-devil *(H. caespitosum)*.

Some eighteen *Hieracium* species, about half of which are Eurasian natives, reside in eastern North America. Mouse-ear hawkweed, flowering in May, often blooms the earliest of this mainly summer- and fall-flowering genus. Orange hawkweed is easily identified, but the many alien yellow hawkweeds often hybridize and are highly variable.

Hawkweed florets, yellow or orange atop the crowded aggregate flowerhead (up to an inch across), are all petal-like or strap-shaped with square, fringed tips and have bisexual flower parts. In mouse-ear and probably most other hawkweeds, the individual florets are protandrous, sequentially unisexual, with male pollen-producing parts maturing before female parts. All stages of sexual development may simultaneously occur on a flowerhead with, however, the younger florets located toward the center. Yet all of the usual sexual processes in most plants essentially amount to vestigial systems in hawkweeds, for their reproduction is asexual; the flowers of most North American hawkweeds are apomictic—that is, the seeds develop without pollination. The offspring are thus clones, genetically identical to the parent plant, and large colonies of such clones are typical in hawkweeds.

Most reproduction in these plants, however, occurs vegetatively. Nonseedling clones originate from creeping stolons in mouse-ear and orange hawkweeds; the latter hawkweed also extends elongate rhizomes. Only plants in flower produce stolons, which spread like tentacles, some four to twelve in number, across the ground surface. Stolons (hawkweeds' main means of reproduction) elongate throughout summer, reaching up to a foot long, developing new rosettes and roots at their tips. These rosettes survive over winter; each may or may not produce several to thirty flowering stems the following summer. If the plants do flower, both stems and rosettes die in the fall; if not, the rosettes sometimes survive for a year or longer, usually producing more stems. Flowering occurs mainly near the outside edges of a colony; density of plants in the center inhibits the growth of flowering stems.

Hawkweed roots are shallow and fibrous, and the plants have a milky latex sap. Each ridged, one-seeded achene—twelve to fifty on each flowerhead—has a hairy crown that aids in wind distribution. Most ripe seeds, however, fall within the hawkweed colony. Seedlings that develop outside a colony have low survival rates, though a colony can only originate from one or more seedling hawkweeds. Seeds can germinate immediately or may remain viable in the soil for up to seven years.

Hawkweeds grow almost anywhere on moist or dry ground, favoring open or lightly shaded areas. In June, I frequently note how the shape of a dense hawkweed colony follows the edge of a tree or shrub shadow. Such "shadow colonies" can sometimes be quite sharply marked. Whether this sun-shadow preference reflects a possible soil moisture gradient or simply a favoritism for light shade remains unknown.

Most hawkweed flowers don't need pollinators, but insects in abundance still fly to them. Orange hawkweeds, especially, are good sites to watch for various butterfly nectar feeders. Despite the attraction to insects, the nectar rewards are small. "To get even the tiniest droplet visible to the human eye," wrote researcher Bernd Heinrich, "the whole inflorescence with its dozens of tiny florets must be squeezed at the base, and even then one is rarely rewarded with the sight of nectar. . . . It barely matches the energy the bee expends in collecting it." Yet insects need only small amounts to keep going, and the flowers' magnetic brilliance testifies to its reliable if not lavish rewards.

No part of these plants is palatable to humans; yet the name *hawkweed,* it is said, derives from the folklore that eating the plant will sharpen eyesight. The Greek word for hawk is *hierax,* whence emerged *Hieracium.* The Roman scholar Pliny—first of a long line of wrong botanical experts—reported that hawks themselves ate the plants to aid their vision. Exactly how the idea of keen vision came to be associated with these plants remains an enigma perhaps based on a long-ago not-so-keen observation.

Hoary Alyssum
(*Berteroa incana*)

KRIS LIGHT

Mustard family. Common in summer, this white-flowered alien grows a foot or two high. Its four-petaled flowers surmount the two or more erect branches that rise atop the main stem. The small petals are deeply notched, and the hairy seedpods, oblong with a beak at one end, stand erect close to the stem. A whitish bloom covers the plant. Other names: hoary false alyssum, hoary alison.

Five *Berteroa* species exist, all in temperate Eurasia. Hoary alyssum shows close resemblances to other mustards, notably the peppergrasses and false flaxes. More than forty mustard genera occur in eastern North America.

Its frosted appearance—a gray-green coat of downy, star-shaped hairs, easily seen with a hand lens—immediately identifies this hardy mustard. Reproductively, it covers the gamut from annual and biennial to short-lived perennial life cycles, spreading mainly by seed.

Numerous stems rise from alyssum's deeply plunging taproot, which gives the plant drought resistance.

Hoary alyssum favors dry, sandy, or gravelly ground along roadsides and in old fields, pastures, gravel pits, disturbed ground. Drought and winter-kill in hayfields are said to increase invasive occurrences of this plant. It readily competes with crop alfalfa during conditions of drought.

Seeds of hoary alyssum are not widely consumed by wildlife. Probably some ground-feeding sparrows and finches occasionally eat them. Mammals rarely graze this plant. While hoary alyssum does not rank as harmful in livestock forage as some other plants, it can cause toxic symptoms, especially in horses, when consumed in large quantity. Horses may suffer swelling of the lower legs. Cattle and sheep usually reject the plant.

The word *alyssum* originates from a Greek word for similar plants meaning "rabies cure." It doesn't and won't. The plant's native home is Europe. When or how it came to North America remains unknown.

Indian Paintbrush
(*Castilleja coccinea*)

MONA MAKELA/SHUTTERSTOCK.COM

Figwort family. Green, three-lobed bracts topping a short terminal spike dipped in scarlet paint is the visual impression of this one- to two-foot-tall native biennial. The undivided basal leaves form a rosette; upper leaves show deeply cleft linear segments. The unbranched stems are hairy. Other names: painted cup, Indian pink, fire pink, prairie-fire, bloody-nose, wickawee, election posy.

About 150 *Castilleja* species exist, mainly in western North America. Two eastern residents besides *C. coccinea* are downy paintbrush *(C. sessiliflora)* and northeastern paintbrush *(C. septentrionalis)*.

"It is all the more interesting," wrote Thoreau of this plant, "for being a painted leaf and not a petal, and its spidery leaves, pinnatifid [featherlike] with linear divisions, increase its strangeness." Not only are the lobed terminal bracts red—scarlet too are the tips of the outer part of the flower, collectively the sepals. The inner flower is greenish yellow, hidden inside the bracts. These garish bracts (occasional plants display yellow instead of red bracts) attract numerous insect pollinators to the flower; yet the lack of a flower lip landing place for insects may indicate reliance on hummingbirds as pollinators. Each shoot produces five to twenty flowers. The resulting two-chambered capsules hold up to three hundred seeds apiece, shaken out of the capsules by wind. Some seeds may germinate immediately, producing a leafy rosette that survives winter under the snow and raises a flowering shoot in spring. Most seeds, however, germinate in spring, producing only rosettes the first year and a flowering stem the following spring.

Indian paintbrushes favor open, sandy areas and limestone soils, often shores and damp meadows. Some five hundred figwort species, including this Indian paintbrush, are classified as hemiparasites—partial parasites not exclusively dependent on another plant host (they commit "petty larceny" in the words of one botanist). Although paintbrushes are green and perform photosynthesis like most plants, they also take water and mineral nutrients from the roots of adjacent plants. They tap into these root structures from their own roots by means of connecting structures, penetrating to the vascular channels of the host roots. No painted cup plant grows to maturity without tapping into a root host. This hemiparasite is blindly nonselective, the connectors even attaching to pebbles, sand grains, and organic debris at times, as well as to almost any plant roots in the vicinity, herb or tree. Grass roots are common hosts, as are those of Virginia strawberry, oxeye daisy, and tall lettuce. Host suitability, however, apparently depends more upon the density of neighborhood root distribution than on host identity.

Indian paintbrush seems especially adapted for ruby-throated hummingbird pollination, not only in its tubular floral anatomy, but also in its early-May flowering (through July), which coincides with hummingbird arrival. The hummingbirds seek it for nectar; wild columbines, flowering at the same time, also attract these bird pollinators.

Chippewa tribes used a weak tea steeped from *Castilleja* flowers for "diseases of women" and for rheumatic aches. It was said to be good for both "paralysis and a cold," according to one report. The Menomini used it as a love charm in food, "the scheme being to try to secrete some of the herb upon the person who is the object of the amour," wrote ethnobotanist Huron H. Smith. On dubious authority, the plants are also said to be potentially toxic.

Knotweeds
(*Polygonum* species)

Smartweed family. Recognize *Polygonum* by the swollen, papery sheath covering each joint of the stems. Botanists define knotweeds as *Polygonum* species that bear small, greenish flowers in the leaf angles on the stem, whereas smartweeds have spikelike clusters of pink or white flowers. Other biologists define knotweeds as upland *Polygonum* species and smartweeds as lowland or wetland plants. Three common species residing on drier ground are prostrate knotweed *(P. aviculare)*, small and matlike, sprawling in sidewalk cracks and disturbed ground, with tiny, greenish, pink-tipped flowers in leaf axils; erect knotweed *(P. erectum)*, much like the latter except standing mostly erect from a few inches to three feet tall; and lady's thumb *(P. perscaria)*, with fringed sheaths on the reddish joints, pink flower spikes, reddish stems, and blackish, triangular smudge marks, like a fingerprint, on the top surface of leaves. Lady's thumb is an alien, erect knotweed is native, and prostrate knotweed is ubiquitous worldwide. All three are annuals. Other names: common knotweed, knotgrass, doorgrass,

IVASCHENKO ROMAN/SHUTTERSTOCK.COM

bindweed, stoneweed, wiregrass, wireweed, many others *(P. aviculare)*; redleg, redweed, redshanks, heart's-ease, black-heart, willow-weed, common persicary, goose grass, heartspot, heartweed, spotted knotweed *(P. persicaria)*.

Some two hundred *Polygonum* species range worldwide, mostly in temperate climates. Almost forty, many favoring marshes and wet ground, exist in eastern North America. *Polygonum* plants display so many variants that botanists puzzle whether certain of them are indeed true species, as labeled, or mere forms and varieties of other species. Even within the identified species, variations appear common and puzzling.

The flowers, emerging in summer and often lasting into fall, are bisexual and insect-pollinated. Lacking petals, they show colored sepals in lady's thumb, greenish or tinged sepals in the two others. *Polygonum* stamens and pistils are homogamous, maturing at the same time, and self-pollination often occurs. The flowers produce little pollen and nectar yet seem to attract numerous foragers.

Polygonum species can grow in almost any spot of disturbed soil. The three common species thrive especially in the compacted soil of footpaths, driveways, trails, barnyards—routes of frequent passage by people and other animals. Thoreau noted the typical frequency of prostrate knotweed's occurrence "where the earth is trodden, bordering on paths," and he was "not aware that it prevails in any other places." What were the original habitats of these plants? One botanist labeled lady's thumb an "archaeophyte," a plant invariably associated with human disturbance of the ground; perhaps it originally occurred most frequently on pond margins.

Erect and prostrate knotweeds will often be found growing in close association, the latter flowering and reaching maturity before the later-emerging erect knotweed. One older text on weeds pointed out that prostrate knotweed is "very frequently the first plant to spring up where a heap of stable manure has stood"—a hostile habitat for most plants, owing to the high temperature that kills most seeds.

Polygonum provides a rich seed supply for ground-feeding birds. Mammal seed-eaters include least chipmunks, ground squirrels, and white-footed mice. White-tailed deer and probably rabbits also consume the plants.

The beauties of *Polygonum* are subtle and easily overlooked. As with so many relatively harmless weeds, "familiarity alone breeds contempt," as naturalist Neltje Blanchan wrote. Their low hues and tinges present an appearance (as well as a taxonomy) full of ambiguity, good medicine for the either-or mind-set of the obsessively orderly among us.

As actual medicine, *Polygonum* is strong stuff; even native healers used it sparingly. These plants provided astringents for external poultices and internal bleeding. Rutin, a glycoside ingredient found also in tobacco and buckwheat leaves, strengthens blood capillaries, acting as a coagulant to prevent or stop bleeding. Juice from stems and leaves can cause skin irritation in allergic individuals. The leaves have a peppery taste ranging from mild and pleasing to acrid and inedible, depending on the species. Young leaves and shoots of lady's thumb make an acceptable salad green. The name *smartweed* comes from the plants' tongue-burning taste, the name *knotweed* from their swollen stem joints.

Lamb's-Quarters
(*Chenopodium album*)

KRIS LIGHT

Goosefoot family. One of the commonest weeds of roadside and garden from May to October, lamb's-quarters stands one to three feet tall. Small, greenish, dense flower clusters develop on short stems rising from the leaf axils and atop the main stem. A native annual, it has broadly toothed leaves with powdery white undersides. Stems are ridged, sometimes purple striped. Other names: pigweed, fat-hen, white goosefoot, wild spinach.

Almost twenty of the hundred or so *Chenopodium* species that exist worldwide reside in eastern North America. Some of these, such as Jerusalem-oak *(C. botrys)*, are aliens—but many, including Mexican tea *(C. ambrosioides)* and strawberryblite *(C. capitatum)*, are New World natives.

The bisexual flowers, occurring in dense, green clusters resembling tiny broccolis, lack petals. They are wind-pollinated, and the female parts mature before the male pollen matures, thus abetting cross-pollination. Self-pollination also occurs as the flowers age. Lamb's-quarters reproduces exclusively by seed. Fruits are tiny, bladderlike, one-seeded structures called utricles, and a typical plant may produce almost 75,000 of them. Seed dispersal is probably effected mainly by birds. Seeds germinate early in the season but also throughout, sometimes in even-aged seedling groups. Seeds may remain viable up to forty years, though one study found only twenty-three percent seed survival from twenty-year-old buried seeds. The plant produces a short, branching taproot that dies in the fall.

Lamb's-quarters thrives in both acid and alkaline soils but favors limy soils and cultivated habitats. As with most annuals, this plant favors disturbed open habitats—gravel pits, construction sites, roadsides, weedy fields. Being a reliable indicator of rich soil, it also frequents compost heaps and manure piles, accounting for two of its less pleasant names: mixenweed and muckweed. It associates with humans, their sites and traffic routes. Nobody knows where the plant would (or originally did) appear without man's activities. Since lamb's-quarters is often a strong crop competitor, humans have become weed-killing competitors of the plant as well.

Seeds of lamb's-quarters provide choice nutritious, late-season food for many bird species. Almost all ground birds seem to relish them. Studies indicate that *Chenopodium* seed passage through birds increases germination of the plant by a considerable percentage. Least chipmunks and ground squirrels also consume the seeds, and white-tailed deer graze the plant, though it is toxic in large amounts to sheep and swine (and possibly other grazers).

Lamb's-quarters, by statistics and consensus, is one of the world's most abundant and noxious weeds. It competes with some forty crops, is especially invasive in tomato, potato, sugar beet, soybean, and corn fields. The plant accumulates high levels of nitrates and pesticides in addition to its oxalic acid content. Yet it also ranks high in vitamins A and C, calcium, potassium, and phosphorus, plus other vitamins and trace minerals.

Harvested from a nonpolluted soil source, the young leaves and shoots make a nutritious cooked green. The flowers are also edible, as are the seeds. Harvested *Chenopodium* seeds helped relieve a Russian famine in 1891, and they were also used in crafting the granular-surfaced leather called shagreen.

Native Americans used this plant for food, as treatment for scurvy and digestive upsets, and in burn poultices. Homeopathic healers also used lamb's-quarters for treating vitilago skin pigmentation. The plant contains ascaridole, an anthelminthic oil that can be extracted from the leaves that is useful for treatment of intestinal worms.

It was once a popular botanical gospel that all noxious or abundant weeds in North America arrived from far shores to corrupt our native flora. A 1964 archaeological investigation of a Michigan Indian village site, however, established the common presence of *C. album* seeds dating from the years 800 to 1320. Sites in Ohio and Ontario indicate usage of the plant many centuries prior—so if indeed the plant first appeared as an introduced species, it probably came with prehistoric migrations from Asia.

Chenopodium, from Greek words meaning "goose foot," refers to the supposed shape of the leaves in some species (another sign, some would say, that plant people make wretched bird-watchers). The name *lamb's-quarters* probably refers to the woolly leaf coating.

Oxeye Daisy
(*Leucanthemum vulgare*)

Aster family. The familiar summer field daisy with white radiating ray florets and a depressed, yellow hub of disk florets is an alien perennial. It stands one to three feet tall. Other names: marguerite, field daisy, big daisy, whiteweed, white daisy, bull's-eye daisy, Dutch-morgan, herb-Margaret, maudlin daisy, moon daisy, moonflower.

Some one hundred *Leucanthemum* species exist; most are Old World natives. The half dozen eastern North American residents are introductions or garden escapees.

Hardly a pasture or roadside lacks daisies in summer. They beautify poor land, vacant lots, and waste places, yet they can be aggressive pests of agriculture. Entire fields once whitened the landscape with what was termed "the snows of June," acres of daisies that sometimes took over crop fields and gardens alike. Today daisies survive in nowhere near their former abundance, as much of eastern North America reverts to woodland or sprouts urban subdivisions.

KATHY CLARK/SHUTTERSTOCK.COM

Oxeye daisy bears a solitary flowerhead up to two inches across. This flowerhead, like that of most composites, is an aggregate bouquet consisting of many individual florets. Fertile bisexual florets occur only in the central disk, crowded with hundreds of the tiny tubular structures. In each floret, "as the pistil within the ring of stamens develops and rises," wrote botanist Neltje Blanchan, "two little hair brushes on its tip sweep the pollen from their anthers. . . . Now the pollen is elevated to a point where any insect crawling over the floret must remove it." After the anthers stop producing pollen, the closed central pistil opens and spreads its sticky surfaces, receiving pollen brought from other daisies. The twenty to thirty radiating, petal-like ray florets are female but sterile, apparently having evolved as attention-fetchers for pollinating insects.

Oxeye daisy reproduces mainly by prolific seeding; a single healthy plant may produce up to 26,000 (more typically, 1,300 to 4,000) seeds. Wind disperses most of its seeds near the parent plant, though animals may disperse some. The seeds remain viable for years; in one study, more than eighty percent germinated after six years, one percent after forty years. Most seedlings emerge in the fall, though germination may occur continuously throughout the growing season. An individual daisy plant may consist of one to many rosettes on the soil surface, each of which produces a single flower stem and which together may form a dense mat of rosettes. Most oxeyes begin flowering in their second year (that is, their first summer after germination) and continue flowering in subsequent years. Oxeye also reproduces by budding from shallow, branched rhizomes. The plant has a small taproot and a shallow, fibrous root system.

Neither as human food nor medicament does oxeye daisy glow on the menu, though both uses are occasional. The young leaves can make an "interesting" addition to salads, according to one herbal source. A nightly daisy wash is said to aid the complexion. Oxeye's polyacetylenes and thiophenes are insecticides. English farmers mixed the dried plant with raw bedding as insect repellent for livestock and hung it inside their houses as flea repellents. Many hikers and anglers know that crushing and rubbing daisy flowerheads into the clothing provides good natural protection from blackflies, mosquitoes, and deer flies. (Some people react allergically to the plant sap on the skin, however.)

In religious iconography, oxeye daisy became associated with Artemis, Greek goddess of women, owing to its medicinal usage for menstrual complaints. Christians transferred the association to St. Mary Magdalen—the plant thence became known as the maudelyn or maudlin daisy. It was also dedicated to St. John.

Oxeyes appear to be among those alien plants that—for various reasons—have lost vigor and potency during their long acclimation to New World ecologies. Although they can still summon ample hostility from livestock and crop farmers, the plants seem, in many areas, less aggressive than they once were. This phenomenon follows the typical pattern of invading plant and animal species, the gradual process of naturalization by which ecological balance tends to reassert.

A daisy epiphany once occurred in Philadelphia. This flower, it is said, inspired the career of North America's foremost pioneer botanist, John Bartram—and indirectly, that of his prolific botanist-naturalist son William Bartram. While plowing his fields near Philadelphia one day, the sight of a daisy stopped the uneducated Quaker farmer in his tracks. The vision prompted Bartram's subsequent lifework of exploring, collecting, and naming much of North America's plant bounty. It seems ironic that a colorful alien "weed," rather than a charming native wildflower, birthed Bartram's devotion to American flora.

Pearly Everlasting
(*Anaphalis margaritacea*)

PHOTO_JOURNEY/SHUTTERSTOCK.COM

Aster family. Recognize this native perennial, which stands one to three feet tall, by its gray-green, somewhat downy foliage; its narrow, linear leaves; and its white, globular flowerheads in flat-topped clusters, the flowers with dry, overlapping, scalelike bracts. The flowers bloom in summer and fall. Other names: cudweed, cottonweed, silverleaf, silver button, immortelle, life everlasting.

Some twenty-five other *Anaphalis* species exist in north temperate climates, mainly in eastern Asia. Pearly everlasting is the only eastern North American *Anaphalis.* Its silvery foliage and papery, scaly flowerheads sometimes give this plant the appearance of an artificial bloom—"a truly elysian flower," Thoreau called it, "suggesting a widowed virginity." Although its appearance may not suggest so much to most of us, it has a biological feature rare in both composites and wildflowers generally: The yellow flowers in the densely packed central disk are mainly unisexual, with male and female flowers appearing on separate plants. Male plants are always exclusively so, but female flowerheads often show a central pit in which a few bisexual florets exist. One must look closely to detect which sex one is viewing: Pistillate florets have a divided stalk whereas staminate stalks are undivided. Female florets have been likened to miniature lotuses or waterlilies in appearance, male florets to white nests with a central yellow clutch of eggs spilling out. The surrounding scaly, overlapping bracts are not ray florets but highly modified leaves.

Each short branch near the stem top bears four to eight flowerheads, the clusters forming a flat-topped array. These "dry bouquets" are, however, nectar producing and insect-pollinated, the female florets producing one-seeded achenes. Reproduction occurs mainly by seed, but the plant also extends rhizomes anchored by roots, producing cloned patches that are likewise unisexual. Even rhizome fragments can reproduce the plant.

Pearly everlasting favors open sun or light shade. Dry, sandy fields, dunes, rocky shores, open woods and thickets, and roadsides are common habitats. It often emerges on recently logged land or following fire.

Insect foliage feeders are not numerous on this plant, owing to its protective downy "gloss." This does not deter at least two spring butterfly caterpillars, however: the American and painted lady are probably pearly everlasting's most spectacular foragers. The first is velvety black with yellow crossbands, the second yellowish green with black markings. Both butterflies construct simple compact nest shelters of plant fragments, leaves, and silken webbing on the plant, sometimes enclosing flowerheads in the web.

This plant has a long tradition of medicinal usage among numerous native tribes. Peoples as diverse as Cherokee, Montagnais, Mohegan, Cheyenne, Chippewa, Menomini, Potawatomi, and Mohawk—plus early European settlers and pioneers—brewed tea from the plant for colds, coughs, diarrhea, and other ailments, also using it as a sedative. Its astringent properties also made it useful for poultices on skin ailments and contusions. Flowerheads were apparently widely used as a smoking tobacco substitute, and herbalists also recommended the dried flowers "as a quieting filling for the pillows of consumptives." Some tribes attributed strong mystical power to this plant; it was used in rites for purification, for protection from witches and evil spirits, and in sorcery.

Pearly everlasting is a plant seemingly made for dried ornaments and bouquets. Its winter appearance doesn't change much—even while still alive and flowering, it looks already dried and preserved. Some observers have found its aspect funereal, "the most uncheering of winter bouquets," wrote one naturalist. It is "stiff, dry, soulless," like a wreath "made from the lifeless hair of some dear departed." The plant's name "everlasting" refers to this long-lived proclivity. "Pearly," of course, refers to the white chaffy bracts. Some botanists postulate that the generic name *Anaphalis* may be an anagram of a closely related genus *Gnaphalium*. The species name *margaritacea* derives from the Latin word for "pearl."

Almost all pokeweed flowers seem to set fruit; such high frequency of fruiting often indicates primarily self-fertilized species. Each flower produces a ten-seeded, inky purple berry, the clusters resembling grapes as they heavily weigh the now-drooping racemes. Seeds, distributed mainly by birds, can remain viable in the soil for forty years or longer.

Pokeweed reproduces exclusively by seed. "I personally believe that it is a frustrated tree," wrote weed-lorist Pamela Jones. The plant's thick, succulent, trunklike stalks springing from an old root may achieve a diameter of four inches, yet they all die back to the root in autumn. The taproot is itself imposing, fleshy and white, sometimes six inches across at the crown. Pokeweed roots produce allelopathic chemicals that deter germination of its own seeds, and possibly those of other potential competitor plants as well.

Pokeweed often suggests its close association with birds by the sites it frequents—along fencerows, beneath power lines, around shrubs, anywhere that fruit-eating birds perch. Pokeweed provides at least thirty species of birds a major food resource, offering an important transient food in late summer and fall for bird migrants as they stop to rest and feed en route. It "never invades cultivated fields," observed naturalist John Burroughs, "but hovers about the borders and looks over the fences." The plant also favors barnyards, roadsides, vacant lots, in open land or shade, usually in fairly rich, moist soil. Pokeweed "is bound to disturbed sites," wrote researcher Jonathan D. Sauer, "and nowhere does it seem to belong to a stable plant association." Sauer believed that its foremost habitat before pioneer land settlement was "open stream-bank woods," where shifting streams constantly created new open ground. Research has not yet established whether pokeweed's allelopathy works to delay its seed germination until the spring following its production, thereby increasing its survival chances.

Many plant manuals note pokeweed's unpleasant odor. My own observations indicate that writers have much exaggerated this characteristic—many plants smell worse, and pokeweed's odor is, if not fragrant, fairly innocuous. Toxic chemistry does abound in this plant, however—foremost in the large rootstock and the seeds, also in the foliage and berries. Even the plant juice on one's skin can raise a rash and invade cellular tissue, causing chromosomal damage and mutations. One should always wear gloves when handling this plant. Poisonous not only to humans, pokeweed is also toxic to horses, sheep, cattle, and pigs.

Despite the plant's toxicity, gourmands relish (after two boilings) pokeweed's young tender shoots and the leafy tips for asparaguslike greens. Delaware and Virginia native tribes, among others, collected the sprouts for food. Collectors, however, are advised to discard any shoots tinged red and never to harvest any piece of the root. Cooking destroys many toxins, and pokeweed's ripe berries, though sour tasting, have also been used for pies. Yet, as Pamela Jones remarked, "Why should I run even the slightest risk to my safety and health when there are so many other far safer weeds for my veggies and herbal teas?"

Pokeweed berry juice found frequent use as a fabric coloring agent. As a dye for woolens, however, the deep purple stain fades fairly rapidly. Native tribes used the dye for clothing and other items, as well as for horse and skin painting. The juice "makes a better red or purple ink than I have bought," wrote Thoreau. (In a journal entry of September 24, 1859, he wrote the word "poke" in the ink of the berry itself; by 1906, the word had faded to a light brown stain on the paper.)

The name *pokeweed* apparently derives from the Algonquin Indian name for the plant, *pokon,* from a word meaning "bloody," alluding to the plant's berry stain. The generic name *Phytolacca,* from the Greek, means "crimson plant."

Puccoons
(*Lithospermum* species)

KRIS LIGHT

Borage family. Recognize these yellow spring and summer wildflowers by their branching, somewhat flat-topped or curled-over flower clusters atop the stem. Each flower radiates five petals from a central tube that hides the sexual parts. Leaf shape and hairiness vary among species, but leaves in all species are alternate and untoothed.

About seventy-five *Lithospermum* species exist worldwide, seven of which reside in eastern North America. Our most common species is probably hoary puccoon *(L. canescens)*, with softly hairy leaves. Hairy puccoon *(L. caroliniense)* has roughly haired foliage, while narrowleaf stoneseed *(L. incisum)* has fringed petals and narrow, grasslike leaves. All three are native perennials and grow a foot or more tall. Other names: Indian paint *(L. canescens)*; yellow or plains pucoon, plains-stoneseed *(L. incisum)*; narrow-leaved, fringed, or Carolina puccoon *(L. caroliniense)*.

Puccoons hide their sexual organs inside the flower's central corolla tube, from the top of which the yellow petals flare outward. The flowers of hoary and hairy puccoons have two different forms based on differing lengths of sexual parts. One form bears flowers with long styles and short stamens; the other has short styles and long stamens. This heterostyly reduces the likelihood of self-pollination because only the pollen of long-styled forms is compatible with short-styled forms, and vice versa. Successful reproduction requires both forms. These puccoons depend upon insects for pollination, but an imbalance exists in most populations of the species mentioned: the short-styled forms outnumber the long-styled.

Narrowleaf stoneseed is not heterostylous; its stamens and styles are of equal length. Also, in addition to its showy visible flowers, it produces yellowish green self-fertilized flowers in the leaf axils that produce an abundance of single-parent seeds. Such plants also occur in *L. caroliniense* populations. Most researchers view self-fertilized flowers in puccoons as a complementary reproductive strategy, since this cleistogamy frequently produces more seed than cross-pollination.

Puccoon seeds are ivory-white nutlets, four from each flower, but sometimes only a single nutlet matures. Seed distribution appears passive, with most seeds falling near parent plants. Puccoons reproduce exclusively by seed, but the stony seeds do not germinate quickly and can remain viable but dormant for many years in the soil.

The three common puccoon species frequent dry, sandy, unshaded ground. *L. caroliniense* frequents dunelands, whereas *L. canescens* more often resides in prairie remnants and openings; *L. incisum* favors disturbed ground as well as prairie patches.

Sparse information exists on puccoon insect associates. Pollinators, mainly bumblebees, also include some smaller bees and butterflies. Look for small blue butterflies called spring azures and Juvenal's duskywings, dark brown skippers, feeding on the flowers. According to one study, short-styled forms of the flower, owing to their longer, more extrusive anthers, deposit pollen on both face and proboscis of the insect; whereas long-styled forms tend to deposit pollen only on the proboscis.

Apart from the fascinating examples of heterostyly they exhibit, puccoons have received relatively scant attention from plant researchers. Even many wildflower manuals give them short shrift. These attractive native wildflowers illumine many dry summer landscapes, especially in combination with the blue of lupine. Perhaps the name puccoon repels some "serious" observers? This word derives from the Algonquian word *poken,* for plants that yield red or yellow dyes, the same root word as for pokeweed.

Native tribes used puccoons—the pulverized small, dried taproots—for dyes, producing various red shades for body and garment decoration. Facial painting and hair dying functioned as important elements of many tribal rites, and the equally native puccoons supplied these colors of tribal identity. A leaf tea from *L. canescens,* used as a skin wash, treated persons suffering fevers and convulsions. Pioneer herbalists, noting the stonelike seeds, prescribed the plant as a remedy for kidney stones.

Queen Anne's Lace
(*Daucus carota*)

KEVIN H KNUTH/SHUTTERSTOCK.COM

Carrot family. An alien biennial or short-lived perennial and one of our most familiar summer wildflowers, Queen Anne's lace stands two or three feet tall. Its white, umbrellalike flower clusters form a lacy pattern, often centered by a tiny, dark purple floret. Flower clusters curl up into a nestlike cup shape as they age. Leaves are lacy, fernlike, and finely subdivided. Other names: wild carrot, bird's-nest, devil's-plague.

Some sixty *Daucus* species range worldwide. Only two (including *D. carota*) reside in eastern North America—*D. pusillus* is the other. The familiar garden carrot, with its enlarged orange taproot, is a race of *D. carota*.

Flowering stages of Queen Anne's lace can be easily traced by noting the progressively varying shapes of the flowerhead, called the umbel. A flowering plant may produce five to ten umbels at once, up to one hundred umbels from July to September. Each umbel flowers from ten to fifteen days. The disklike umbels, two to four inches in diameter, consist of numerous smaller clusters, each of which terminates a stalk that rises from a central point atop the main stem. Stiff, three-forked bracts underlie the umbel, clasping it closed during later phases of development. As the florets (more than one thousand in an umbel) mature, the umbel assumes a flat-topped or convex shape. When fertilization occurs and seeds begin developing, the umbel sinks in the center and becomes concave. Soon it closes, the cupped bracts bending upward to form the closed seedhead "nest," inside which the green fruits ripen. The double-seeded fruits ripen first on the outer edges of the terminal umbels. They soon split apart, forming one-seeded mericarps. As the mericarps mature and become dry, the cup opens outward again, flattens, and empties the seeds (which may number tp to 40,000 per plant). Or mericarps may remain in the dry umbel until winter winds shake them loose or they attach to a passing coat or pelt by means of their tiny hooked spines.

Inspecting closer, one may observe that each white floret has five petals. Each floret is bisexual, but the male parts develop and decline before the female parts mature, making it sequentially unisexual. Lacking insects to pollinate the florets (owing to weather conditions or low insect populations), they are also capable of self-fertilization via the long anthers of adjacent florets.

Botanists have long puzzled the over significance of the red or purple central floret in Queen Anne's lacy umbel. Many have assumed that the color contrast of the white-backed floret provides a long-distance visual signal that attracts pollinating insects. Experiments do not corroborate this assumption, however; a 1996 study confirmed earlier findings that most insects do not show a preference for umbels with a purple central floret over those with none. Thus the floret's function, if any, remains a mystery.

Flushes of seed germination often occur following rainy periods, not only in spring but also in summer and fall. Queen Anne's lace can and often does occur as an annual, flowering six weeks after spring germination and completing its life cycle within a single growing season. In shady conditions, the plant can also linger as a short-lived perennial, not flowering until its third or fourth year after germination. Typically, however, these plants are biennials, germinating in summer or fall, then wintering as a six- to eight-inch-long whitish taproot surmounted by a leafy, ground-level rosette. Once having flowered (however long it takes), the plant dies. All reproduction is by seed—Queen Anne's lace does not extend itself by adventitious sprouts or rhizomes.

A worldwide resident of temperate regions, Queen Anne's lace probably originated in Afghanistan and adjacent areas. It had spread to Mediterranean Europe before the common era. Highly adaptable to many soil types and moisture conditions, it favors clay and limy soils and open, sunny locales but is not limited to them. Almost every weedy field and roadside displays abundant *Daucus* populations. In some areas, the plant competes with native grasses and forbs.

Some two hundred or more insects are said to pollinate Queen Anne's lace. These include a large variety of flies (including mosquitoes and gnats), beetles, bees, wasps, and ants, also butterflies and moths.

Nobody knows, at this date, what kind of carrots the colonists imported. Although Queen Anne's lace and the domestic garden carrot are the same species, they differ much in appearance, mainly of the roots; their physical appearances show much more variety than their almost identical genetic makeup. The Queen Anne's lace taproot resembles a parsnip more than a carrot. Current consensus among researchers is that the modern cultivated carrot is a hybrid cross between *Daucus carota* and the giant carrot *(D. maximus)* of the Mediterranean region. Queen Anne's lace and garden carrot can and do hybridize where they grow in proximity. The former can also host pests of the latter, so commercial carrot farmers do not relish the sight of Anne's medallions decorating any field near their crop rows.

Several carrot family plants (most notably poison hemlock, fool's parsley, and water-hemlock) are deadly toxic, and the leaves of some look similar to those of *Daucus,* so food harvesters of the wild carrot need to carry awareness along with the trowel. Only the first-year roots of *Daucus* are tender enough for cooking like regular carrots—older ones become too woody and fibrous.

The root tea of Queen Anne's lace, herbalists discovered, has beneficial effects. Scientists have confirmed its properties as an antiseptic, diuretic, and vermicide. It also enjoys some repute as a remedy for flatulence. Almost any health benefit to be derived from carrots can likewise be had from Queen Anne's lace. Both are rich sources of vitamin A.

Accounts vary regarding the name of this plant. Queen Anne, arriving on the British throne ninety-nine years after Elizabeth, brought the plant to legendary status—the purple floret centering the flowerhead was said to symbolize a drop of royal finger blood while she tatted lace. Other accounts state that Queen Anne liked to wear lacy medallion patterns resembling the flowerhead disk of *Daucus,* thence the flower's name. Whatever the name's origin, in America, at least, it remains almost the sole reminder of this queen's long reign.

Ragweeds
(*Ambrosia* species)

LIANEM/SHUTTERSTOCK.COM

Aster family. The two most abundant ragweeds, both native annuals with greenish flowers on long spikes, differ mainly in size and leaf shape. Common ragweed *(A. artemisiifolia)* stands one to five feet tall and has dissected, fernlike leaves. Great ragweed *(A. trifida)*, with a woody, bamboolike stem, grows up to fifteen feet tall and has large, three-lobed leaves. Both ragweeds flower in summer and fall. Other names: short or small ragweed, Roman or wild wormwood, bitterweed, hogweed, hayfever-weed *(A. artemisiifolia)*; giant or tall ragweed, kinghead, horseweed *(A. trifida)*.

About forty *Ambrosia* species, all in the Western Hemisphere, include six that reside in eastern North America.

Male and female flowers occupy separate sites on the same plant in both common ragweed species. The conspicuous racemes seen at the ends of stems and branches consist of all male flowers; female flowers, much more sparse and inconspicuous, occur singly or in small clusters at the bases and forks of upper branches. Female flowers probably mature before the male flowers, thus increasing chances of cross-pollination. Ragweed flowers are wind-pollinated and can also self-pollinate. They produce two-seeded achenes.

These plants reproduce only by seed. Seeds of common ragweed number from 3,000 on a small plant to more than 50,000 on a large one. Common ragweed seeds that do not germinate in the spring following their production may enter a secondary dormancy period that can last for forty years or more. Giant ragweed produces fewer seeds, three hundred or less per plant. Both plants have fibrous roots and relatively short taproots.

Ragweeds are known as short-day plants because they begin flowering only after day length begins to shorten in midsummer. Common and giant ragweeds sometimes hybridize, producing a plant with intermediate characteristics.

A 1973 study discovered a common ragweed adaptation that could account in some degree for its success. Experiments demonstrated that the plant collects and channels rainfall and nightly dew condensation down its slightly grooved stem to its root system, providing "a competitive advantage," wrote the researchers.

Common ragweed grows in open, disturbed sites of almost any sort—roadsides, railroad embankments, fields, vacant lots, and erosion channels and gulleys. It favors loamy, low-acid soils and grows less vigorously on acid soils. Land clearing and agricultural settlement brought episodes of abundant ragweed growth that followed the farmer's plow throughout the East and Midwest.

Great ragweed favors moister disturbed ground—river floodplains are among its foremost habitats. It often grows in dense stands along ditches and streambanks and in lowland fields. Its early emergence in spring and its height usually make it the dominant plant where it grows.

The two common ragweed species differ markedly in their seed use by wildlife. Common ragweed, for all of its despised reputation among farmers, gardeners, and allergy sufferers, is bird manna, sustaining resident bird populations over winter and helping fuel many a fall migration. Great ragweed, by contrast—with its tough seed coats—is relatively little used. Mammal seed-eaters of common ragweed include least chipmunks, ground squirrels, deer mice, and voles. Cottontail rabbits and white-tailed deer feed at times on the foliage.

Although common ragweed ranks as one of North America's most valuable wildlife food plants, its allergenic effects on humans are well known. It is probably the dominant hay-fever plant, operant as such during its flowering season from mid-August sometimes to the October frost. Each plant, it is said, can produce a billion pollen grains during this period, and the microscopic, windblown grains can travel up to four hundred miles. What makes ragweed pollen such an insidious enemy of human respiratory membranes is not a pollen chemical but the simple fact of mechanical abrasion—these grains are ragged and spiny, irritating sensitive nasal passages like fine-ground glass and evoking defensive responses from the tissues—swellings and histamines that produce the allergic reactions.

"Perchance some poet likened this yellow dust to the ambrosia of the gods," speculated Thoreau on ragweeds' generic name, which signifies immortality (or the food of the gods who gave it). The "rag" in ragweed is said to derive from the ragged pattern of the leaves in some species.

Windblown ragweed pollen in archaeological sites has proven a useful tool and indicator for dating and analyzing regional environmental conditions of the past. Since ragweeds so often accompany agricultural plantings, a ragweed pollen deposit can and often does indicate a historic or prehistoric tribal settlement site—as well as records of later pioneer settlement.

Salsify
(*Tragopogon* species)

DANI VINCEK/SHUTTERSTOCK.COM

Aster family. Recognize these alien biennials by their grasslike leaves; summer-blooming, yellow, dandelionlike flowerheads atop one- to three-foot-tall stems; big, fluffy, puffball seedheads; and milky sap. Two species are most common in eastern North America: meadow salsify *(T. pratensis)*, with curled leaf tips and slightly enlarged flower stalks, and yellow salsify *(T. dubius)*, with straight leaf tips and thick, inflated stalks. Other names: goatsbeard, noonflower, star-of-Jerusalem, Johnny-go-to-bed-at-noon.

Some fifty *Tragopogon* species occur, mainly in Eurasia and North Africa; no native North American species exist.

Salsify follows the sun, opening toward the sun in the morning and closing by midday on bright days (often closing later on cloudy days). All the florets in the flowerhead are ray florets, and all are bisexual and insect-pollinated. They occur, however, in two distinct belts, inner and outer. As in many aster family flowers, a progression of development occurs on the flowerhead, with the outer ones opening and maturing first; the unopened inner florets resemble the central disk florets on daisylike flowers. Each plant may produce several flowering stems—six is about average.

The plant's fluffy seed ball is a grand example of radial symmetry. Each plant produces 100 to 850 one-seeded achenes, each crowned with a bristle (somewhat resembling radiating porcupine quills) and a feathery umbrellalike pappus, an adaptation for wind dispersal. The seeds are of two types, with the peripheral or outer-belt florets producing heavier, darker seeds than the central florets. These outer seeds also float on wind with a terminal velocity about 1.3 times greater than the central seeds, which have smaller pappi. Both morphs, however, germinate at equal frequency.

Tragopogon seeds are relatively slow-moving, creating much air-drag. Probably few of these seeds disperse much beyond a quarter mile. The plants reproduce entirely by seed, but seeds are short-lived. One study found that less than three percent of buried seeds remained viable after thirteen months; thus a large, persistent seed bank for these plants does not exist. The surfaces of *T. dubius* achenes contain fluorescent compounds, perhaps protective against fungous parasites.

Upon germination in spring or fall, salsify produces an erect rosette of grasslike leaves, enabling the plant to emerge through ground litter. It rapidly develops an extensive root system with a fleshy taproot. Salsify are usually labeled binennials because of their typical two-year life cycle, but "they are better described as monocarpic perennials," as other botanists suggest; that is, the rosette may produce flowering stems during the current growing season or—depending on local habitat, temperatures, and plant competition—may survive for several years without flowering; once it flowers and produces seed, however, the plant dies. Ideal habitat conditions encourage faster life cycles, whereas more competitive sites may lead to prolonged vegetative phases, hence longer occupancy in successional stages of plant growth.

Adaptable to a broad range of cover types throughout temperate North America, salsify can establish themselves in bare soil, amid grasses and old-field vegetation, and in heavy ground litter. Such adaptability permits them to thrive across a range of early plant successional stages, though they favor open, unshaded areas. Occasionally they may form dense colonies, excluding less competitive species, but typically they occur in scattered, thinly dispersed stands.

The seedheads are choice food sources for goldfinches. Most species of deer, squirrels, and rabbits graze the plants, especially the young rosettes; deer also consume the flowering stalks, and livestock relish the young plants. Mice and goldfinches may collect the seedhead down for nesting.

Fairly recent plant immigrants from northern Europe, salsify are absent from some of the older American plant and wildflower manuals. Probably early settlers in the West brought them as food plants for their gardens, but they rapidly escaped cultivation, spreading eastward—*T. dubius* became established in eastern Canada only in the 1970s. Certain native tribes adopted the plants for food and medicine (chewing the milky stems was said to cure indigestion), but the plants have never been widely used by humans in North America.

Tragopogon—the name literally means "goat beard," referring to the fuzzy pappus tufts on the seedhead—has proven a useful genus of plants for genetic and evolutionary researchers. The great Swedish taxonomist Linnaeus crossed *T. pratensis* and *T. porrifolius* in 1759, thus producing the first plant species hybrid created for scientific purposes. Hybridization in this genus has been studied extensively since then, especially as it relates to species with multiple chromosome sets.

Self-Heal
(*Prunella vulgaris*)

Mint family. Recognize this blue-flowered native perennial mint by its square stems; opposite, almost toothless leaves; and violet, hooded flowers with fringed lower lips crowded among densely leafy bracts. (Pinkish or white-flowered plants also occasionally appear.) The square-shaped or oblong spike surmounts a three- to twelve-inch-tall stem. Flowering from early summer into fall, the plant tends to sprawl on the ground, raising only its flowering branches erect. Unlike most mints, self-heal has no aroma. Other names: heal-all, allheal, blue curls, blue lucy, brownwort, carpenter weed.

Only four *Prunella* species exist worldwide. Cut-leaved self-heal *(P. laciniata)*, a white-flowered, much hairier herb, occasionally appears as a waif plant.

Mint family flowers usually appear in one of two distinct forms—in leaf angles along the stem, or atop the plant. Self-heal exhibits one of the latter forms. It produces one to ten flowering stems from a root, each stem bearing up to six paired, flowering branches. Self-heal's blue flowers appear closely packed in tiers on the thick flower spike. Each tier—some six to twelve total—consists of sets displaying three stalkless flowers that emerge in

PETER RADACSI/SHUTTERSTOCK.COM

the angles of green, hairy, closely set bracts. Flowering on the spike is irregular, with entire tiers seldom blooming all at once, so the spike usually looks somewhat ragged and only partially flowered. Tiers begin flowering from the apex toward the base, however, and on any given spike, flowers may occur in all stages of development—in bud, in bloom, or setting seed. The spikes continue to elongate as flower tiers develop and may finally extend more than three inches.

Each flower consists of five petals fused into two lips. The upper lip forms a wide, flat hood with a peaked roof that shelters two pairs of stamens and a long pistil extending between them. The lower lip, shorter and three-lobed, forms a landing platform for visitors to this bisexual, insect-pollinated flower. In entering the corolla tube, at the bottom of which pools the sought-after nectar, the furry heads and thoraxes of bees become dusted with pollen that, in flowers of subsequent visits, rubs off onto the jostled stigmas, thus effecting cross-pollination. Self-heal flowers are also self-compatible and can produce abundant seed without cross-pollination.

Four one-sided nutlets develop from each flower; the spike now somewhat resembles a stubby ear of corn. Seeds usually remain viable no longer than a year. In the meantime, the plant extends prostrate leafy stems in every direction. These stems produce new roots at their nodes, often forming clonal colonies, the green rosettes of which survive over winter and raise new flowering stems in the spring.

Adaptable to just about any habitat—wet or dry, disturbed or pristine, along streams and roadsides, in shaded woods, open fields, and suburban lawns—self-heal adds a touch of blue almost everywhere. In my own observation, it favors low-lying, dampish spots along forest roads or in fields.

Few fungi or insects parasitize this plant. Most insect activity focuses on the flowers. Bumblebees are probably its chief pollinators; they also collect large quantities of pollen from this plant, combing it from their fur and packing it into their enlarged hind tarsi or pollen baskets.

Chippewa, Mohegan, and Delaware tribes, among others, brewed teas from self-heal to treat fevers and dysentery. "There is not a better wound herb in the world," wrote English herbalist John Gerard in 1633. Between its functions of chemistry and suture, self-heal was truly viewed as a miracle plant, according to all the old herbalists (not to say hyperbolists), literally a cure-all for just about any human pain or unpleasantness. But "these uses have not withstood the rigorous testing of modern medicine," according to researcher Laurence J. Crockett. Its popular name heal-all reflected the plant's ample uses in Europe for a roster of human ailments. According to the doctrine of signatures belief, self-heal's throatlike corollas suggested it as a remedy for mouth sores and sore throat. Today the plant's main recognized medicinal benefit is probably as an effective astringent, useful for stopping blood flow from a cut or wound as well as for poulticing sores and, taken internally, for treating diarrhea. It contains ursolic acid, an antitumor and diuretic compound, and the plant also possesses astringent antibiotic qualities plus possible capacities of lowering blood pressure and blocking genetic mutations.

The name *Prunella* apparently stems from the German label *Brunella* for this plant, in turn deriving from the word *bruen,* "brown," the plant's final color in the fall.

Sheep Sorrel
(*Rumex acetosella*)

TAINA SOHLMAN/SHUTTERSTOCK.COM

Smartweed family. Identify this slim, four- to twelve-inch-tall alien perennial by its halberd-shaped leaves with lobed, pointed bases, and by its loose, spikelike clusters of tiny greenish flowers that turn to brownish red seed stalks. Other names: common, red, field, or wild sorrel, sour dock, sourgrass.

A thin, reddish ground cover on poor land in summer is probably sheep sorrel, which often colonizes large tracts that other plants don't want. Sexes occur separately on different plants in this species (with occasional instances of male, female, and bisexual flowers appearing on the same plant), an uncommon system in flowering plants. Flowers of sheep sorrel display no petals but have six tepals, in two circles of three (outer and inner); they are wind-pollinated. On female flowers appear three red, feathery stigmas, the entire flower turning red when mature. ("I feel well into summer when I see this redness" in the fields, wrote Thoreau.) The six stamens on pollen-producing male plants, by contrast, tend to turn orange-yellow.

Its fruits, one-seeded achenes, show no special distribution mechanism. Seeds can germinate in three or four weeks and may remain viable but dormant in the soil seed bank for up to twenty years. Typically two germination flushes occur, one in spring and one in early fall—often the latter seedlings never survive to flower.

The slender, yellowish roots, fibrous and branching, may penetrate to a depth of five feet, producing an underground tangle that "can be a gardener's nightmare," wrote one busy weeder. The entire root system can produce buds; even a tiny fragment can regenerate a new shoot, and unless every particle of the easily broken root is weeded, the plant will likely sprout again. The roots also extend horizontally and rhizomelike, sending up erect clones from their tips. Sheep sorrel's root extensions, rather than its seeding, probably account for most of its colonial spread. Both seedlings and root sprouts produce leafy rosettes, from which may arise several flowering stems. Individual root crowns probably last about eighteen months, by which time their creeping roots have produced several other crowns. Thus a given patch of sheep sorrel may be decades old.

Sheep sorrel favors dry, sandy, disturbed soil in open areas. It thrives on acidic soils of low fertility. Although long regarded as an acid-soil indicator, sheep sorrel hardly restricts itself to such soils. Its presence there may not necessarily owe to its inherent preference for low pH, but being acid-tolerant, it may simply encounter less plant competition in such sites.

Sheep sorrel provides a major food resource for many birds, mainly ground-feeding seedeaters. Meadow voles and white-footed mice also eat the seeds. Poultry, cottontail rabbits, and deer readily graze the plant. This plant is, however, potentially toxic to livestock, which do not feed on it if other forage is available. Sheep sorrel's nutritional values as well as energy and protein contents are generally ranked poor to fair. Its sour, pungent taste, similar to that of the unrelated wood sorrels, emanates from potassium oxalate acid crystals in the foliage. The leaves do make a pleasant-tasting salad, cooked green, or trail-nibble, but its oxalates make it toxic to mammals in large quantity.

Despite its poor forage ranking, sheep sorrel is rich in vitamin C and several other vitamins, as well as carotinoids. Herbalists and practitioners of folk medicine have long cherished the plant for its reputed curative qualities—in poultices for tumors and as teas for diarrhea, fevers, and other ailments.

Although of Eurasian origin, sheep sorrel has apparently resided in North America for a very long time. Cree writer-historian Bernard Assiniwi wrote of this plant, "No Algonquin Ojibway child can ever forget 'jiwisi' the sour leaf." Many native tribes readily adopted the plant into their medicinal troves and lore.

The word *sorrel* stems from the French *sur*, meaning "sour." The sheep association probably refers to the plant's usage as forage in poor pastures. *Rumex* is the Latin word for *docks*. *Acetosella*, the species name, means "slightly acid."

Showy Tick Trefoil
(*Desmodium canadense*)

JOHN HILTY

Pea family. Showy tick trefoil, a native perennial standing two to six feet tall, bears loose spikes of magenta, pink, or lavender (rarely white) pealike flowers above cloverlike trifoliate leaves. Hairy, flat, jointed seedpods consisting of three to five segments ("sticktights") adhere to clothing or fur. Other names: Canadian tick trefoil, sticktights, beggar's-lice, beggar ticks, devil's-thistle, tick-clover.

About three hundred *Desmodium* species exist globally, most in warm regions. Northeastern tick trefoils number about twenty-two species, many of them woodland residents. Showy tick trefoil, the commonest of this colorful spindly genus, attracts attention both in flower—a spectacular, elongated plume or raceme, progressively flowering up the stalk in July and August—and in its adherent seed, matted souvenirs stuck on one's clothing after a walk in the autumn fields. When not in flower or seed, however, this plant is easily overlooked.

Bisexual *Desmodium* flowers, irregular in form as are the flowers of most legumes, consist of a rooflike banner or standard petal, two oblong wing petals at the sides, and a keel of two fused petals that enfold ten stamens and a pistil in its horizontal length. When an insect probes between the wing petals, the motion snaps down the keel, jerking the stamens loose and exploding a puff of pollen on the insect's underside. Those wing-petal triggers only function once—the flower dusts but a single time—which usually proves more than enough to paste ample seeds onto any passerby.

Probably the differing sex organs of individual *Desmodium* flowers are sequentially timed as to readiness, thus promoting cross-pollination among plants. The green, slightly curved, inch-long fruit, a modified pod called a loment, consists of a chain of several one-seeded oval or triangular segments that ultimately tear apart as separate units—"like a piece of a saw blade with three teeth," as Thoreau wrote. Tiny, hooked hairs on the loment give it a Velcro adherence; hairs also cover the ridged stems, making insect approach via lower routes difficult. The hard seed coats require time or a scratch, break, or cut, often by means of freezing or fire, in order to germinate.

Tick trefoil stems, as they lengthen, tend to tilt over, sometimes against other plants, sometimes almost to the ground. Perhaps this "lodging" is an adaptation that brings seeds down to the pelt level of passing mammals. It's why loments often encrust one's socks after an autumn hike.

Showy tick trefoil favors open, sandy ground, dry or moist. Common sites include fields, clearings, roadsides, even wet prairies and fen edges. These plants often sprout quickly after a ground fire. "They love dry hillsides," wrote one observer; in some areas, tick trefoil growth seems to favor north-facing slopes.

Like most legumes, tick trefoil exists by means of a vital symbiosis. It creates nitrogen in a form available for its own and other plant use by means of root nodules containing nitrogen-fixing bacteria.

Despite making its presence thickly "felt" in the fall, this native tick trefoil is not much of an invasive or noxious weed. Moreover, it improves the soil wherever it grows, and it feeds a few creatures besides. (Some *Desmodium* species, though not this one, are indeed planted as forage crops in some parts of the world.) Like most legumes, the plant ranks high in protein and palatability. No part of *Desmodium* is humanly edible, though people chewed the roots as a treatment for mouth sores in some tribal cultures.

The name tick trefoil originates from the loment's ticklike adherence and from the three-part leaf form. The Greek word *desmos* denotes "chain," descriptive of the linear loment.

Speedwells
(*Veronica* species)

ROBERT BIEDERMANN/SHUTTERSTOCK.COM

Figwort family. Recognize these low, creeping, mostly alien perennials by their opposite leaves and tiny, four-petaled, violet or lavender flowers (the bottom petal smaller than the three others) on loose spikes atop branching stems. Some species display solitary flowers in leaf angles. The most familiar species include common speedwell *(V. officinalis)*, downy with shallow-toothed, stalked leaves; germander speedwell *(V. chamedrys)*, also woolly with unstalked, toothed leaves and a widely spaced raceme; and threadstalk speedwell *(V. filiformis)*, with larger flowers on thin stalks. Other names: fluellin, ground-hale, gypsy-weed, Paul's-betony.

Some twenty *Veronica* species, of about three hundred worldwide, reside in North America, but few are native. Several wetland species exist.

Speedwells form dense patches and mats, erecting their flower stalks only a few inches above their prostrate creeping stems. Floral biology of all the species is similar except that several of the less common species are annuals, completing their life cycles within a year.

Inconspicuous in the grass, speedwells' tiny flowers attract attention only when masses of them appear from spring through summer. Colorwise, naturalist John Burroughs called *Veronica* "a small and delicate edition of our hepatica, done in indigo blue." The plant's colonial habit plus its clustered racemes help make it visible. Its insect-pollinated flowers are sequentially unisexual, the female parts maturing and declining before the male parts. Two hornlike stamens stretch outward from either side of the top petal. Grasped by an insect visitor probing for nectar, they dust the visitor's underside with pollen, thus furbishing the insect for a subsequent visit to a flower still in female phase, the flower's sticky stigma projecting over its dwarf lower petal, its stamens not yet ready. The flower's corolla (all the petals collectively) "is so lightly attached," wrote one observer, "that the least jarring causes it to drop." Speedwell flowers close at night and remain closed in the rain. At least some speedwell species can self-fertilize inside the closed flower during lengthy periods of wet weather.

Flattened, heart-shaped capsules contain numerous seeds. Speedwells reproduce not only by seed, but also by rooting where the prostrate stems touch the ground. The stems of germander speedwell show two fuzzy lines of long hairs descending from each pair of leaves, perhaps defensive barriers against crawling insect herbivores.

Speedwells occupy north temperate regions worldwide, generally favoring open areas, though habitat preferences exist among species. Common speedwell favors dry fields and upland woods, especially along trails or in clearings. Germander speedwell invades woodland as well, also resides along roadsides and trails and in lawns. Threadstalk speedwell often appears in lawns and gardens.

Some sources claim that common speedwell may indeed be a native North American as well as European resident. The Cherokee, it is said, used it for treating various ailments. Most sources, however, identify this species as an import that probably arrived in grains and hay forage with the first colonists. Also, many a settler's shoe boarded ship, no doubt, with a speedwell seed stuck to its sole. Indeed, the sister ship of the *Mayflower* was christened the *Speedwell*, reflecting a tradition of handing bouquets of the blue flowers to departing travelers with the blessing "Speed well."

The plants' English name, apparently associated with farewells, may also refer to the flower's easy dislodgment, or to its familiar presence along roadways and paths, its color bidding travelers a cheery "Godspeed." But "the most entertaining explanation," wrote one observer, is that English peasants brewed an expectorant from the plant's leaves to treat colds, earning it the good name "spit-well." The genus name *Veronica* stems from St. Veronica (Greek words *veron* and *ikon*, meaning "true image"), a Jewish maiden who, in Roman Catholic hagiography, wiped the face of a cross-bearing Jesus with her towel, thus preserving the sacred image on the linen relic.

Too insubstantial and too bitter to use as food plants, speedwells have a long history of usage in "the-bitterer-the-better" folk medicine. Stems, leaves, and roots, boiled for tea or packed into poultices, treated coughs, stomach and urinary ailments, gout, rheumatism, and skin diseases, among other ills. As astringents and tonics, they "purified the blood" and also eased breathing for asthmatics. Speedwell herbal remedies apparently found particular usage among Welsh peasantry. Modern herbalists still prescribe the plant. Common speedwell, used in the manufacture of some vermouths, also adds some bite to absinthe.

Popular greenhouse varieties of *Veronica* rarely need replacement as border plantings once established. Of threadstalk speedwell, one botanist wrote that "if a person once puts it on his property, he will always have something growing there." This species may completely take over a lawn—which may not be all bad if one seeks a colorful ground cover or erosion control on a terrace or bank.

Spotted Knapweed
(*Centaurea steobe*)

Aster family. Spotted knapweed's thistlelike flowerheads—pink or white but most often purplish—also resemble those of blazing stars. Its rough, wiry stem, branching above the middle, and deeply cut leaves also help identify this alien perennial, biennial, or short-lived perennial as a knapweed. This species shows fringed black tips on the bracts below the flowerhead, hence its name. It stands up to three or four feet tall. Other names: star-thistle.

Some five hundred *Centaurea* species, mostly Old World natives, exist. Eleven of these aliens reside in northeastern North America. Probably spotted knapweed is the most abundant of these, but tumble knapweed *(C. diffusa)*, mainly white flowered, is also well established. Bachelor's button *(C. cyanus)* is a bright blue garden escapee.

Summer fields and roadsides are largely taken over by these thistlelike tufts on wiry, gray-green stems. Naturalists and farmers alike loathe them for their aggressiveness, but of course—like all plants—they go mainly where invited by land disturbance and other prepared habitats.

BRIAN LASENBY/SHUTTERSTOCK.COM

Some twenty-five to thirty-five tubular flowers exist in each inch-wide flowerhead, about sixteen of which develop, on average, for each plant. The flowers often bear a subtle honeylike fragrance (though the nectar is said to be bitter). Unlike many aster family flowers, knapweed has no outer ray florets, only disk florets. The stiff, spine-fringed bracts beneath each flowerhead provide a vaselike enclosure. Although the bisexual flowers are insect-pollinated, they are also sexually self-compatible. The single-seeded achenes bear a short tuft of bristles at one end; dispersal usually occurs in August, two or three weeks after the achenes mature. Movement of the stem by wind or jostling causes the achenes to shoot forth up to a yard distant from the seedhead; they also attach to feathers or fur (or trousers or socks) that may brush against the plant. In September, when most knapweed stems are dead, some of the plants still flower but at a lower level.

Spotted knapweed reproduces mainly by seed, which germinates in the fall (less than six percent) or spring (twenty to forty percent); germination in two seasons increases chances of seedling survival. Although experts claim that seed germination while still on the seedhead does not occur in this species, I have witnessed that it does; one early October after a spell of warm, rainy weather, I could see minute green leaves sprouting vigorously from knapweed seedheads. Seeds in the soil may remain viable for five or more years.

Seedlings form a stout taproot, a root crown, and in the fall, a leafy basal rosette that lasts over winter and produces one to six (sometimes more) flowering stems in spring. The "biennial" designation for this plant applies only to a fall-germinated rosette that produces a flowering stem the next year, then dies (probably a minority of knapweed plants). Most knapweed plants spread lateral shoots an inch or so from the root crown, producing another rosette at their tips; these become mature plants in the following year. The root crown of a single plant may survive up to nine years, though five years or less is probably a plant's typical lifespan. Spotted knapweed populations thus enlarge mainly by means of peripheral expansion, via seed and lateral shoots, of existing stands. Knapweed roots also exude a natural herbicide, found mainly in the leaves and shoots, that inhibits the germination of nearby plants.

Disturbed ground—whether by cow, plow, fire, axe, or bulldozer—invites spotted knapweed to come stay awhile. Occasionally knapweed also invades ground undisturbed by grazing or human activity. It thrives in open land and sandy or gravelly soil and is quite shade-intolerant. Spotted knapweed favors moister, more northern and mountainous environments than most other knapweed species.

Just how it competes has been the subject of recent investigation. As with most plants, knapweed roots maintain a symbiotic association with mycorrhizal fungi, which aid the absorption of nutrients by the plant. Researchers have found that where spotted knapweed has invaded native bunchgrass or fescue, knapweed's mycorrhizae have indirectly enhanced its competitive vigor; the fescue thrived much more abundantly in the experimental absence of mycorrhizae in knapweed roots. A similar coaction that bears on knapweed competitiveness may also involve insects, so that herbivory in combination with mycorrhizal action may actually stimulate knapweed growth.

Some fourteen Eurasian insect and fungous species have been released as potential knapweed biocontrol agents since 1970. Recent studies on the effects of knapweed biological control seem to indicate that *Agapeta* moths and perhaps other insects feeding on the plant may increase allelopathic secretions from the roots or induce compensatory growth, perhaps both—thus actually increasing rather than diminishing knapweed's competitive success. Perhaps "the biocontrols we are releasing all over the place," stated researcher Ragan M. Callaway in 1999, "are having no effect, or worse, they might be giving knapweed more of a competitive advantage."

The name *knapweed* is said to derive from the German word *knobbe,* meaning "bump" or "button." As "bachelor's buttons," the flowerheads decorated the clothing of eligible young women, according to folklore. The *Centaurea* connection—with the Greek centaur, the mythological beast with man's head and arms and horse's body and legs—remains uncertain but probably stems from Charon the centaur, who taught Achilles healing herbal knowledge for his warriors before the siege of Troy.

No part of knapweed is palatable to humans. Even herbalists and homeopathic practitioners (who often seem to value the bitter as best) have scant use for it.

Spurges
(*Euphorbia* species)

RALF NEUMANN/SHUTTERSTOCK.COM

Spurge family. Recognize these plants, which bloom in spring and summer, by their small flowers that, in common species, occur in branched, flat-topped clusters atop the leafy stems, and by their milky sap. Species otherwise vary to such an extent that a completely inclusive generic description is difficult.

Three of our most common spurges are leafy spurge *(E. esula)*, an alien, green-flowered perennial with pairs of yellow-green bracts and linear leaves and few lateral branches, standing up to two feet tall; cypress spurge *(E. cyparissias)*, an alien perennial with small, densely crowded, cypresslike leaves on many lateral branches, also green-flowered, but with paired floral bracts, standing six to twelve inches high; and flowering spurge *(E. corollata)*, a white-flowered native perennial with five petal-like bracts, standing one to three feet tall. Other names: wolf's-milk, Faitour's grass *(E. esula)*; graveyard spurge *(E. cyparissias)*; prairie baby's breath *(E. corollata)*.

More than 30 Euphorbia species—of about 1,500 globally—reside in northeastern North America. Carpeting open country with canopies of bright yellow-green in early summer, leafy spurge gleams with shiny nectar droplets in its flowers and a sweet fragrance that bathes the air around its colonies. Cypress spurge emits likewise, its denser foliage and branches identifying it. The two species seldom occur together; where they do, hybrids often occur.

Spurges share with aster family plants some optical illusions concerning the "flower." What appears to be a tiny flower arranged in a cluster of them is actually a structure called a cyathium, consisting of a cup-shaped involucre. Inside the involucre, some eleven to twenty male flowers surround each three-part pistil, producing orange, sticky pollen masses that clump together. The pistillate stalk elongates as it ages; male flowers last only two to five days. Around the involucral rim lie four large, crescent-shaped glands that secrete copious nectar. The central cyathium, which is oldest and usually aborts, stands surrounded by twenty-five to sixty other ciathia; the entire mock inflorescence, mimicking a cluster of single flowers, is termed the pseudocyme.

A whorl of small leaves circles the base of the stem-top floral branches. All of the tiny unisexual flowers crowded together at the tips of radiating branches are insect-pollinated, though leafy spurge—and probably others—can also self-pollinate. Female flowers in the centers of the cyathia usually mature and invert themselves on their stalks before male flowers develop, hindering chances of self-pollination.

Seeds ripen about thirty days after pollination occurs. Spurge fruits are three-chambered capsules, each chamber producing a seed with a yellowish caruncle at one end. These seed capsules are audibly explosive; when mature, they shoot their contents outward with great force, up to fifteen feet away. Once hurled, the seeds may be further dispersed by birds, mammals, insects, or farm machinery, or in hay and fodder. Look for seedling plants mainly on the outer edges of a colony; a patch of spurge in optimal habitat may expand almost three feet in a year. Seeds may remain viable for five to eight years, germinating best after a period of freezing or cold stratification. Individual plants of leafy spurge may produce up to three hundred seeds; cypress spurge plants may shoot nine hundred or more.

Also complex are spurge root systems, consisting of vertical plus long and short horizontal roots. Taproots, with thick, corky bark, contain abundant starch reserves. They commonly extend six feet downward but sometimes more than twice as far, enabling the plants to survive long periods of drought. The horizontal short or feeder root system usually lasts only a single growing season, but the long, lateral, rhizomelike roots produce buds that give rise to cloning shoots in spring. Spurge colonies more frequently expand by these spreading roots rather than by seed. Root fragments can also bud and produce new plants. Root buds, whether from the root crown, a horizontal extension, or a fragment, develop most readily in the spring; they slow when the plants flower in June and July, increase development again in late summer, and virtually cease by fall. Spurge stems all die back to the soil surface in the fall. Leafy spurge leaves often redden before dropping.

Apparently originating in the Caucasus steppes of Eurasia, leafy spurge first arrived in North America about 1827, probably as a contaminant in ship ballast. It was subsequently reintroduced many times from different regions of its native range, probably accounting for the variability it shows.

Cypress spurge, more uniform in physical appearance but with varying chromosomal makeup, originated in Mediterranean and western European regions.

Both spurge species occur in dry to moderately moist, disturbed, open sites—old fields, roadsides, woodland clearings. They often favor light, sandy soils. Leafy spurge appears more aggressive than cypress spurge in cultivated crop fields, can become a dominant plant in mixed-grass prairies and the main source of pollen and nectar for local insect populations. Root secretions and the decayed litter of spurge plants apparently exert allelopathic effects on the germination and growth of certain other plants.

By far the largest number and variety of insects on spurges are attracted by the plants' abundant nectar and pollen, as well as by the insects that seek them. Birds also disperse spurge seeds; one study suggested that mourning doves, which are major spurge seed feeders, may account for much of the plants' dispersal. Cattle and horses cannot eat spurges—the acid latex blisters their mouths, also causes acute diarrhea, which may kill the animals. Sheep and goats, however, seem usually unaffected by the plants' chemistry.

Leafy spurge (and probably cypress spurge as well) "appears to be a serious problem only in the continental climate of North America," reported one research team. Leafy spurge currently infests at least five million acres of prairie rangeland. Spurge not only "eats up" land quickly, but once established, it does not easily relinquish hold; it resists fire, flood, drought, mowing, and herbicides.

Any plant that tastes bitter is likely to have found numerous medicinal usages, and the spurges are no exceptions. The latex, though harsh on the skin, astonishingly was used to treat and supposedly alleviate skin irritations, one more apparent spurge paradox. Known for its purgative effects on cattle, spurges were also widely used as strong laxatives (an Indian name for flowering spurge translated as "go-quick").

The genus name *Euphorbia* refers to a royal physician of ancient Numidia. The word *spurge* derives from the Latin *expurgare,* meaning "to purge," indicating the plants' laxative nature.

stands surrounded by upcurved, pronged bracts, some of which extend above it. Flowers do not appear all at once. The first ones open in a ring about midway up the oval head; thence rings of flowers move both upward and downward from the middle over a period of weeks from July to September. The top and bottom of the inflorescence become the last areas to produce flowers and seed.

The flowers themselves, consisting of four fused lilac or dark pink petals, four stamens, and one pistil, are protandrous, thus making them sequentially unisexual and promoting cross-pollination by insects from teasels with flowers in other time phases. Self-pollination and self-fertilization occasionally occur, but the resulting seeds often show low viability.

A single plant may produce three thousand or more one-seeded achenes, which mature on the head and simply drop off in the fall. Teasel's seeds float in water; the plant's dispersal in North America has mainly proceeded along creeks and rivers. Most of the seeds germinate from April to June, producing ground-hugging rosettes of crinkled leaves that increase in size until late fall, then overwinter. If, by autumn, the rosette reaches a critical size of about a foot in diameter, it produces a flowering stem from its center the next May; then the entire plant dies after producing seeds. Teasel exhibits this two-year life cycle, however, only in optimal conditions and habitats. It is a semelparous plant, often surviving three or more years until the rosette achieves the critical size for flowering. Thus some botanists prefer to call this plant a monocarpic perennial (that is, a plant that lives until it bears seed only once) rather than a biennial.

Teasel's taproot, often exceeding two feet in length, gives it a drought-competitive edge over shorter-rooted plants found in its habitats. The plant reproduces only by seed and does not sprout vegetative clones. Yet despite its noncloning habit, common teasel often forms dense, slow-spreading colonies and thickets. Teasel's habit of providing its own optimal seedling sites—relatively large patches of bare ground, formerly covered by a teasel plant's basal leaves and newly exposed when an old plant dies—probably accounts for its often populous colonies.

Teasel leaves, a study unto themselves, occur in pairs, spaced at right angles to each other down the stem, thus receiving maximum sunlight. Often spiny on their underside midribs, the leaves and prickly stems discourage munchers. Also, the united opposite leaf bases form small receptacles or cups next to the stem itself; these hold rainwater, acting as traps and providing microhabitats for various organisms. Some botanists believe that teasel shows us the evolutionary beginnings of plant insectivory, as seen in pitcher-plants.

Widely adapted to many sorts of soils, common teasel favors moist, open, low-lying ground, as along drainage ditches and in floodplain meadows. It also resides in old fields, vacant lots, dumps, and other disturbed-soil areas. A prominent roadside weed, in recent decades it has colonized many areas along interstate highways. The plant tolerates road salt. Its large leaf rosettes shade out many competing seedlings such as grasses, though it emits no known allelopathic chemicals. Teasel ranges across the continent in areas of local abundance, perhaps reflecting multiple introductions from its native Eurasia.

Teasel has no widely known human medicinal or food usages (except for its tasty honey), but its spiny seedheads once served admirably as combs for carding wool and making mohair fabric, both in the home and in textile factories. From its nap-teasing function for wool fabric comes the plant's English name. Teasel seedheads have long been popular in flower or dried bouquets, wreaths, and decorations. It is said that teasel's frequent spread in cemeteries owes to such arrangements placed on graves.

Vetches
(*Vicia* species)

Pea family. Vetch leaves, divided into numerous oblong, opposite leaflets along the midrib, terminate in tendrils, by which these plants climb and sprawl upon other plants or supports. Flower stalks and color, as well as life cycle duration, vary among the species. The three most familiar vetches are common vetch *(V. sativa)*, an alien annual with four to eight pairs of notched leaflets and pink or purple flowers that are single or paired; hairy vetch *(V. villosa)*, an alien annual or biennial with hairy stems and leaves and six to eight leaflet pairs with ten to forty usually bicolored (blue and white) flowers on densely crowded spikes; and bird-vetch *(V. cracca)*, perennial natives and aliens with eight to twelve leaflets, each with a pronounced spiny tip, and twenty to fifty blue-violet flowers crowded on one side of long-stalked flower spikes. All three species may stand one to three feet tall, but they often sprawl horizontally over surrounding vegetation. Other names: spring or pebble vetch, tare *(V. sativa)*; sand, winter, woolly or woolypod, Russian, or Siberian vetch *(V.*

MARKMIRROR/SHUTTERSTOCK.COM

villosa); blue, tufted, or cow vetch, cat pea, tinegrass *(V. cracca).*

Some 140 vetches exist worldwide. About 15 species, many of them alien, reside in northeastern North America.

Resembling small, sprawling locust trees, vetches mat over the ground and upon other plants in summer, their flowers producing colorful hues of blue in fields and along roadsides. Most vetches bear racemes, long spikes with flowers that open in sequence from the bottom up; an exception is common vetch, which typically bears no raceme but only a pair of flowers in the upper leaf angles. Vetch racemes and leafstalks often curve, unlike those in similar pea family plants.

The form of the three species differs somewhat. Common vetch straggles or climbs, attaining tallest height only if supported by a tall grass such as rye or another tall plant; its taproots typically extend more than two feet down. Hairy vetch stems may reach twelve feet in length, but the plant's viny, sprawling habit seldom lets it rise more than three or four feet; it has a fibrous root mass with a taproot that extends to a depth of one to three feet. Bird-vetch, most distinctive because of its one-sided flower and seed stalk, may form twining mats and tangled patches; it has wiry, spreading roots.

The vetch flower exemplifies the classic pea family type of five irregular petals: the topmost banner or standard, a wing petal at either side, and two fused keel petals that enclose the sexual column consisting of ten stamens and a pistil. Keel parts slip aside as an insect lands to forage nectar at the base of the stamens, which dust the insect's underside with pollen at the same time that the top of the pistil, a sticky tongue, "licks" an arriving insect's belly for incoming pollen. This mechanisim adapts the flowers for cross-pollination. Vetch species differ in sexual strategies, however. Common vetch produces both aerial and cleistogamous flowers, creating most of its seed by self-fertilization. Hairy vetch is often protogynous. It can also self-pollinate but requires insects to rupture the stigmatic membrane, releasing its stickiness; insect pollination thus produces much more seed than self-pollination in this species. Bird-vetch is mainly cross-pollinated. Vetches typically flower from June into September.

Vetch fruits, called legumes, are flat pods an inch or more long that split into 2 twisted halves, releasing several seeds. At the right time, as one walks through a stand of vetches, the rustling explosions of rupturing pods are audible. Common vetch germinates in spring and dies in fall; hairy vetch germinates in the fall, overwinters as a seedling, flowering and dying the next summer; bird-vetch may germinate in either spring or fall, with individual stems dying after they flower, but this species can also reproduce vegetatively by budding clones from its spreading roots.

Vetches' hard, impermeable seed coats require a period of freezing or chemical abrasion (as achieved in passage through animal intestines) in order to germinate. All vetch reproduction, except in the perennial bird-vetch, is by seed only.

At the base of each compound leaf in common vetch projects a pair of small stipules, each of which bears on its underside a reddish purple nectary, which secretes a thick, sugary fluid said to be more attractive to bees than the floral nectaries.

All three common vetches occupy similar habitats throughout most of North America—roadsides, vacant lots, old fields, pastures, cropland. Hairy vetch, probably the most widespread, is also resistant to drought, is shade-tolerant, and is the most adaptable to cold climates.

Like most legumes, vetches improve the soil by means of a symbiotic relationship with nitrogen-fixing bacteria, which occupy nodules in the roots. Some studies indicate that vetch roots may release allelopathic compounds into the soil, but apparent effects are slight.

Vetches, via their curling tendrils at the ends of their compound leaves, grow non-parasitically on other plants. Those tendrils indicate their reliance on plant species with taller, stronger stems—often cereal grasses—a coaction known as a commensal relationship, in which the vetches benefit and the host plants neither suffer nor benefit.

Vetches provide mixed blessings to farmers. On the one hand, they produce a soil-improving green manure and cover crop as well as nourishing, palatable hay, silage, and pasture forage for livestock. On the other hand, vetches may infest cereal crops, their twining growth causing leaning grass stalks, increasing likelihood of disease and difficulty of harvest. Hairy vetch can be a serious pest weed in wheat. Bird-vetch, the perennial, appears the most persistent and difficult to control in grain and berry crops.

Common and hairy vetches produce excellent honey, the only humanly edible product of most vetches. Hairy vetch plantings are found useful for highway medians and borders. The thick growth stabilizes the soil, needs scant mowing and maintenance, and provides a cost-effective, attractive alternative to spraying with herbicides.

Long grown in their native Europe as forage and cover crops, vetches probably originated in the Near East and arrived in the New World repeatedly at unknown dates; some came as seed contaminants in grain, some as crop seed.

The word *vetch* stems from the Latin *vencire,* "to tie" or "bind," referring to the tendrils of these plants.

Viper's Bugloss
(*Echium vulgare*)

DABJOLA/SHUTTERSTOCK.COM

Borage family. Identify this coarse alien biennial by its stiff, bristly, spotted stem; rough, hairy leaves; and down-curved, one-sided flower spikes on which a single blue, tubular flower blooms at a time. It stands one to three feet tall. Other names: blue-weed, viper's herb, snake-flower, blue-thistle, blue devil, blue or wild borage, Our Lord's flannel.

Some fifty *Echium* species exist, all Old World natives. Purple viper's bugloss *(E. plantagineum)*, a shorter species, often decorates gardens. Often mistaken for a thistle because of its bristling appearance, viper's bugloss extends a deep taproot. It produces only a flat basal rosette of leaves the first year (or sometimes in several successive years if disturbed or in unfavorable conditions) and the erect flowering stem the second. The insect-pollinated flowers may range in color between lilac, sky blue, blue-violet, even purple (rarely white or pink), usually all the same color on a single plant and typically appearing from June to September. The tightly coiled flower spike gradually unfurls, opening a single flower that runs a sex-change course from male to female. As it opens, it projects four conspicuously red, pollen-abundant stamens upon which insects alight. Then, after the stamens are spent, the pinkish pistil elongates, the stems dividing into two small horns that stickily greet the incoming, pollen-bearing insects. Then another flower opens on the spike, repeating the progression, and flowering continues through summer.

Viper's bugloss reproduction occurs only by seed. The seeds are flattened, angular nutlets, occurring in tangled groups of four. Bugloss produces prolific seed—five hundred to two thousand per plant—and seeds may remain viable for several years.

Bugloss favors dry, rocky habitats where dense stands may occur. It is a calciphile—a plant favoring limestone soils. Often, though, it stands solitarily in disturbed, infertile areas—gravelly roadsides, railroads, fields—where it often seems to function as a vegetative dust-catcher; its fibrous coating seems to attract windblown silt, sometimes giving the plant a grayish appearance.

Bugloss's abundant pollen and nectar production attracts many insects. These include several species of bees. Bugloss is also a good place to look for pipevine swallowtail butterflies, which feed on the nectar. The plant's bristled surfaces preclude its use as forage by mammals and even discourage ants from exploring this plant.

Since viper's bugloss only reached North America about 1683 from England, little usage of the plant by native Americans occurred. A substantial Old World medicinal lore exists, however, much of it based on the doctrine of signatures theory. Thus, because bugloss stems are "speckled like a snake or viper," according to William Cole's *Art of Simples* (1656), and the seeds resemble the shape of a snake's head, the plant revealed its God-ordained purpose as a remedy for snakebite. Probably some unfortunates have died believing this.

A decoction of the seeds in wine was also said to "comfort the heart and drive away melancholy" (a treatment less effective, probably, without the wine). A leaf tea promoted sweating and calming and reputedly relieved everything from fevers and headaches to the nervous nellies. Bugloss roots contain allantoin, an oxidation product of uric acid that indeed promotes cell proliferation and healing. The roots also produce a red dye. The only humanly edible part of this plant is the flowers, which, crystallized, may be added to salads. Examine the plant's bristly hairs; many of them have blisterlike bases, as if "loaded"—they are, with a toxic alkaloid that may cause a rash on skin contact.

The unappealing word *bugloss* derives from the Greek word *bouglossus,* meaning "ox-tongued," referring to the leaf shape.

Virginia Strawberry
(*Fragaria virginiana*)

OLENAA/SHUTTERSTOCK.COM

Rose family. Recognize Virginia strawberry, a native perennial, by its low growth (three to six inches high); hairy, dark green leaves divided into three leaflets; five-petaled white flowers in flat clusters on a separate stalk; long, reddish runners threading over the ground surface; and red fruits with one-seeded achenes embedded in surface pits. Other names: wild, common, scarlet, meadow, or thick-leaved strawberry.

About thirty *Fragaria* species exist in north temperate regions and in South America. Only two species—*F. virginiana* and *F. vesca*, the woodland strawberry—reside as wild plants in eastern North America.

The white, insect-pollinated flowers of Virginia strawberry, one of the most familiar and conspicuous low plants of April and May, seem almost as common as dandelions, especially in open, grassy areas. I always wondered at the fact that the abundance of strawberry flowers in April seemed to outnumber by far the plants that held actual fruits in June. Perhaps part of the answer is that some wild strawberry populations consist of both bisexual and unisexual plants. The female flowers, which produce most strawberry fruits in wild populations, have twenty to thirty vestigial stamens but produce no pollen. Cultivated strawberry varieties are mostly bisexual, but original native Virginia strawberry populations produced mainly unisexual flowers. Of the minority bisexual flowers, "on the average not one in ten flowers set fruit," according to an 1854 observer. Today exclusively male flowers are rare, perhaps extirpated by the selection pressures of cultivation and genetic migration from cultivated hybrids to Virginia strawberry populations. Only bisexual flowers produce pollen, but the frequencies of female and bisexual forms vary among populations. The species thus exhibits what researchers call "a transitional breeding system."

Flower clusters are cymes, in which the primary or terminal flower matures first, is likeliest to set fruit, and produces the earliest, largest fruit. Two secondary and up to four tertial (plus sometimes more) flowers produce smaller, later-ripening fruits. Typically about ten flowers occur in each cyme, with usually only a single one opening at a time and lasting about a day. Many of the later flowers never develop fruits. Primary fruits may hold one hundred or more achenes.

Typical bisexual flowers of Virginia strawberry exhibit numerous yellow stamens encircling the tiny, greenish yellow, spirally arranged pistils on the conelike receptacle. The receptacle becomes increasingly fleshy as it matures. Red strawberries are actually the swollen stem ends, the fruit holders rather than true fruits themselves. In common with apple and some other actual fruits, however, the strawberry may function as a nutrient sink or collector for other parts of the plant, a vitamin-rich microhabitat for achene development. Insects as well as wind pollinate strawberry flowers, and self-pollination readily occurs. Pistils remain receptive for several days. Thus, between its variably sexed flowers and its mimic fruits, strawberry is a plant whose most conspicuous structures are both more and less than they seem, all apparently adaptive to its own survival.

Virginia strawberry also reproduces vegetatively, cloning itself by means of its horizontal runners, called stolons. One to four stolons per rooted plant shallowly arch one to three feet along the ground surface, rooting new strawberry plants where they touch soil. By means of this strategy, large, genetically identical strawberry populations may cover many yards of ground, the entire spread basically consisting of one plant with many separate stems, roots, and flowers. In the stolons, "food and water may be carried freely in either direction," wrote strawberry scholar George M. Darrow, "and the parent plant may support, or be supported by, a large clone of runner plants for months." Stolons wither and die in winter, after cloned plants have rooted.

Strawberry's dense, fan-shaped networks of fibrous roots tend to turn woody and dark with age. Many roots are biennial, dying at fruiting time, though some may survive many years. They remain fairly shallow, seldom penetrating more than a foot, making the plant vulnerable to drought. Lengthwise curled strawberry leaves are familiar sights during such periods.

Strawberry's versatile reproduction, life cycles, and adaptiveness render its presence possible and its survivability assured in just about any land habitat except extremes of drought or wetness. Regional populations develop special tolerances; far northern populations, for example, can withstand cold below minus 40 degrees F, whereas southern plants are much less cold-hardy. And Virginia strawberry proves much more adaptable to various habitats than cultivated varieties, ranging from woodlands to fields, roadsides, lawns, shores. Although shade-tolerant, it favors open, sunny clearings where competing vegetation is not dense.

Cultivated strawberries may host numerous viral and fungal parasites, most of which can also infect wild strawberries. These parasites, however, seem much less invasive in wild populations, which apparently have evolved effective genetic defenses against them. Virginia strawberries may, however, act as reservoirs for various plant viruses that severely affect strawberry crops, which is why strawberry growers try to avoid planting new stocks where the wild plants abound.

The Virginia strawberry invariably "makes up in flavor what it lacks in size," as botanist Edward G. Voss wrote. Yet the unique tang of its flavor, unduplicated by any cultivated strawberry, does not last long once plucked off the plant; it rapidly turns "red delicious" and loses its distinctive soul. Wild strawberries are best consumed, aficionados agree, in a single motion from plant to hand to mouth. Eaters who defer their gratification to a later mealtime will seldom know this flavor. Although native Americans commonly dried and preserved them for winter food, these fruits do not refrigerate or freeze well.

In addition to Virginia strawberry's long usage as a food by native cultures, root and leaf teas of the plant were commonly dosed medicines. The mildly astringent tea, sometimes steeped with thimbleberry leaves, treated gout, bowel disorders, sore throat, bladder and kidney problems and was also used as a nerve tonic. The fresh leaves are high in vitamin C.

The name *strawberry* supposedly derives from the European practice of bedding the plants with straw, in which they sprouted. Botanist Neltje Blanchan, however, suggested another theory: "In earliest Anglo-Saxon it was called *streowberie* and later *straberry,* from the peculiarity of its straying suckers lying as if strewn on the ground." *Fragaria* comes from the Latin *fraga,* "frequent."

Wild Bergamot
(*Monarda fistulosa*)

SHARON DAY/SHUTTERSTOCK.COM

Mint family. Its coarse appearance; roundish flowerhead of pink, magenta, lavender, or pale lilac tubular flowers; opposite leaves; square stems; and pungent odor identify this summer native perennial. It stands two to three feet tall. Other names: purple bee-balm, lemon-mint.

Of the fifteen native *Monardas* that exist in North America, seven reside in the East.

Variable in hue but consistently displaying color shades on the subdued edge of the red-blue spectra, bergamot florets bloom separately; part of the flowerhead often looks spiky or vacant. Past, present, and future florets may exist on any given head. Florets progressively develop from the center of the cyme outward, the color moving about the flowerhead as individual tubes "blink" on and off. The final stage is a bald central cyme ringed by a fringe of florets. Each cyme produces twenty to fifty florets over the July-August season, and each floret is bisexual, its color attracting long-tongued pollinators, especially butterflies. One problem experienced by many long-tubed flowers is that placement of the nectar reward deep within the tube summons insect entry and efficient pollination but also makes the floral tube vulnerable to nectar robbery by certain insects that chew through the petals into the nectaries from outside the floret, thus circumventing the pollination route.

Close inspection of a floret reveals the lower of its two lobed lips as spreading and platformlike—an insect "landing stage." Note also the densely hairy interior of the inner floret and the protruding stamens and pistil, which not even a slender butterfly proboscis can avoid brushing against. The seeds are four small nutlets embedded in the base of each inner floret.

Much of bergamot's strong odor—as in all mint-family plants—emanates from a system of hairlike epidermal cells called trichomes, which contain volatile oils.

Bergamot's root system is shallow, making the plant vulnerable to winter-kill by intense cold. Where well established, bergamot reproduces mainly by vegetative cloning from the roots. Over time, the plant spreads outward from the central root mass, which sometimes dies out, leaving its clonal progeny to encircle the parent plant site.

Wild bergamot favors open sandy ground, roadsides, and forest and thicket edges, tolerating light shade. It also tolerates a range of soils, from moist to moderately dry. Bergamot's chief pollinators are bumblebees and butterflies; among the latter are pipevine swallowtails. Spectacular sphinx moths—notably the hummingbird and snowberry clearwings—also visit bergamot flowers. Examine the floret bases for punch holes, where solitary bees or wasps may have tapped the nectaries from outside. Other insects also come to feed at these wounds. An occasional pollinator is the ruby-throated hummingbird, whose needlelike bill easily inserts into the deep nectaries.

As attractive as this plant is to some insects, the oils that give the plant its characteristic odor apparently repel others. The dried and powdered leaves, sprinkled over meat or food, reputedly keep away flies. Few records exist of seed consumption by larger wildlife, but field sparrows and goldfinches perch on swaying stems and pick out the seeds.

As with most mints, a decent tea may be brewed from bergamot leaves, or they may be mixed with other tea leaves. It is said that New England colonists used bergamot leaves as a tea substitute after the 1773 Boston Tea Party deprived them of the Asian brew. Bergamot has a long history of medicinal uses among native Americans, who drank the leaf tea for many ailments—colic, flatulence, colds and bronchial complaints, fever, stomachaches, nosebleeds, insomnia, among others. Bergamot is also diaphoretic, inducing sweating, and physicians once prescribed it to expel worms and gas. Bergamot became a popular yard flower in colonial gardens, also in England, where it was imported in 1637.

The name *bergamot,* applied to the plant by pioneer collectors in North America, originated from its supposed aromatic similarity to the unrelated Italian bergamot orange, a source of perfumes and cosmetics. Wild bergamot itself is grown commercially for a modest market; its aromatic and antiseptic oil is used in perfumes, soaps, cosmetics, and as a source of oil of thyme.

Wild Lupine
(*Lupinus perennis*)

LIANEM/SHUTTERSTOCK.COM

Pea family. A spike of spectacular blue, pealike flowers and radiating basal leaves of seven to nine segments identify this one- to two-foot-tall native perennial of spring and summer. Other names: wild lupine, blue lupine, sundial-lupine, wild pea.

Some two hundred lupine species, mostly North American natives, exist. These include white lupine *(L. albus)*, silvery lupine *(A. argenteus)*, and garden lupine *(L. polyphyllus)*.

"It paints a whole hillside with its blue," waxed Thoreau, likening a lupine meadow to "the Elysian Fields." Yet he also noted that lupine's color seemed to disappear with distance—"a third of a mile distant I do not detect their color on the hillside." The reason for this has to do with the fade-away property of blue, a color produced not by pigments but by optical angles and reflections of light.

Lupine's bisexual flowers (usually blue but occasionally pink or white) are two lipped, the upper one double-toothed, the lower one unlobed. As with most pea family flowers, sex organs and nectar lie concealed inside the bottom keel petal. The pollen-bearing stamens thrust forward in a pistonlike action, likened to a grease gun, when an insect alights and depresses the side wing petals, thus depositing pollen on the nectar-seeking forager. Nectar is actually sparse or lacking in most lupines; the flowers attract insects by color, fragrance, and pollen. Flowers often self-fertilize, though cross-pollination apparently produces more seed.

The pods contain an average of four to nine seeds. As the pods dry, they suddenly twist and pop open, tossing the seeds several feet. The hard-coated seeds require a period of stratification or freezing in the soil before moisture can penetrate and break their dormancy. Seeds remain viable for at least three years. Lupines also form colonies by reproducing vegetatively from buds on subsurface stems. Over several years, clonal groups may become so densely established that individual plants cannot easily be distinguished. A long taproot enables the plant to reach soil moisture in its often dry habitats. Like most legumes, lupines improve soil fertility by hosting bacteria that convert atmospheric nitrogen into a form usable by plants. Sites of this activity are nodules that form on the roots.

"Its leaf was made to be covered with dewdrops," wrote Thoreau. Lupine leaflets, with their wedge shapes and grooved midribs, are said to channel dew and rainwater into the root crown, thus aiding the plant's irrigation in its dry habitats. The leaflets are also said to track the sun throughout the day, accounting for one of its names, sundial plant.

Lupine thrives in dry, sandy, nitrogen-poor soils that contain, however, sufficient phosphorus. It favors open land and lightly shaded clearings, frequently associates with oaks and pines in savanna habitats. These are fire-maintained complexes, today increasingly rare as fire control, plant succession, and habitat loss continue to alter these unique areas. Heavy shade and competition from such plants as hawkweeds, Pennsylvania sedge, spotted knapweed, and others tend to suppress lupine growth. Lupine populations today exist mainly as isolated, discontinuous stands in patchy though sometimes extensive clearings.

Best known of the butterfly species that depend on lupine is a subspecies of the Melissa blue, called the Karner blue. The Karner blue has received much attention and study because it feeds exclusively on *Lupinus perennis*—and also because, despite areas of local abundance, the Karner blue has been listed, since 1992, as a federally endangered species owing to the decline of lupine habitat.

The lupine seed, though high in protein, also contains toxic alkaloids, which may be removed by soaking or, in recent years, by genetic tinkering. The Latin poet Virgil noted lupines as commonplace crops, and Roman youngsters used the seeds for play money. Spanish explorers in the Andes found lupine crops "as we have in Spain." Lupine cultivation probably began in Egypt. Today these large-seeded, low-alkaloid species mentioned continue to be raised as forage and grain legumes in Russia, Poland, Germany, and Australia, as well as in the American Midwest.

In North America, botanists believe that *L. perennis* arrived in the East from the West during the hypsithermal interval (ca. 7000 to 600 B.C.E.), a postglacial arid period. One North American lupine *(L. arcticus)* produced what are reputedly the oldest known viable seeds: An ancient burrow of a collared lemming in frozen silt, discovered along a Yukon creek in

1954, contained a trove of the seeds that were dated at least 10,000 years old; in 1967, some of them were germinated in a laboratory, and one of the plants even flowered.

Seeds of most legumes, many of which produce agricultural crops all over the world, are edible and relished by humans. Lupine, however, is another story. The alkaloid toxicity of the various species—and of individual plants within species—seems to vary greatly enough that the pealike seeds should not be eaten.

Lupinus is Latin for "wolfish." The plant is said to be so called from the peasants' belief that lupine's barren habitats were the result of the plant's "wolfing" of nutrients from the soil. Rather, the opposite is true: Lupine root nodules help increase soil fertility.

Yarrow
(*Achillea millefolium*)

ZPRECECH/SHUTTERSTOCK.COM

Aster family. This perennial, both alien and native races, stands one to three feet tall and exhibits a dense, flat-topped, usually white (sometimes pinkish) flower cluster and soft, finely cut, fernlike leaves that alternately ascend the somewhat hairy stem. Yarrow smells pungently aromatic when crushed or bruised. Other names: milfoil, western yarrow, yarroway, old-man's-pepper, nosebleed, sneezefoil, staunchweed, soldier's-woundwort, green arrow, thousand-weed.

About seventy-five *Achillea* species, mainly Eurasian natives, exist in the Northern Hemisphere. Besides yarrow, which shows many variations in color and chromosomal identity, a few others also reside in North America.

Probably as common as dandelions in many areas, but taller, yarrow is one of those ubiquitous weedy wildflowers that define summer in North America. Most American yarrow populations are probably native, being distinguished from historical European introductions of the plant by their difference in chromosome number. The entire species consists of many hybrid variations of both native and alien forms. Some sources say that native varieties show rounder-topped flower-heads than the aliens.

As in some other aster family plants, the flowers of yarrow are deceptive in appearance. What looks like a small individual flower in the flat-topped cluster atop the stem—a regular, radially symmetrical flower complete with five petals radiating from a central hub—is actually an aggregate flowerhead made up of many flowers. Clusters may contain several hundred flowerheads. A flowerhead's three-toothed "petals," five in number, are actually pistillate ray flowers; the ten to thirty tubular disk flowers in the center are bisexual. Self-incompatible and producing a sucrose-rich nectar, flowers must be cross-fertilized and insect-pollinated to produce the one-seeded, nonplumed achenes. Typically, about twelve or thirteen achenes per flowerhead develop, and each plant may produce five hundred to two thousand achenes (many of the flowers remain unpollinated). Simply blown off the seedhead in fall and winter, yarrow seeds may remain viable for years.

Many seeds, however, germinate the following spring, most forming only leafy rosettes that dormantly survive the next winter and produce flowering stems the second year; a few, however, may flower in their first year. The plants typically flower in July and August, producing seed in August and September. Yarrow stems die back to new-grown rosettes in the fall. Yarrow rosettes may, however, be seen at almost any time of year, since the seeds may germinate in any season except winter.

Yarrow usually occurs in colonial stands owing to its extensively branched rhizomes, which may spread horizontally up to eight inches per year, producing clonal aerial stems. But unlike many clonal groups, which soon decay their subsurface connections, yarrow rhizomes apparently remain intact, leading botanists to assess that "vegetative growth would appear to be exploitive [for the parent plant] rather than reproductive," as one report stated. Yet, as studies demonstrate, dense clonal stands produce many fewer seeds than thinner stands, also less flowering, less seed production from flowering stems, and more plant die-off. The limiting density appears about three hundred stems per square meter.

Yarrow has a shallow but extensive fibrous root system, enabling the plant to survive dry spells. Roots typically extend two to five inches deep. Root and rhizome fragments do not readily propagate this species. Yarrow's finely cut leaves, with their small surface area, result in relatively modest transpiration rates, further conserving available moisture.

Yarrow favors open land and abundant sunlight; it also tolerates shade and can persist on many soil types, including sandy and unfertile sites. Rare is the North American roadside, old field, or vacant lot without a stand of yarrow. Generally the plant's presence indicates poor soil, overgrazing, or land abuse or disturbance.

Remnants of yarrow, its bitterness beloved from ancient times as medicine and magic for almost any physical or spiritual ailment that human flesh bears, have been found in 60,000-year-old Neanderthal burial caves. The plant contains more than one hundred biologically active compounds—among them, thujone, the alkaloid achilleine, lactones, ethanol, resins, tannins, gums, and the essential oil known as oleum millefolii. The name old-man's-pepper for the plant derived from its supposed aphrodisiac powers. In ancient battles—and up to the American Civil War—yarrow served as standard medical treatment for stopping bleeding, thus one of its names, soldier's-woundwort. American colonists and many native tribes applied yarrow to more than twenty-five ailments. Modern medicine uses a yarrow compound in the treatment of acute viral hepatitis and *Staphylococcus* bacterial infections.

Planted in gardens, yarrow is said to repel destructive insects; and fleas and lice reputedly go away when they find it as a dried plant in animal bedding. Other uses of yarrow have included yellow and olive green dyes made from the flowers, hair shampoos, tobacco substitute, refreshing herbal baths, and dried floral bouquets.

Foodwise, yarrow offers not much to humans, the leaves being too bitter and unpalatable even for most salads. "The differences between food, medicine, and poison," as one naturalist wrote, "are a matter of dosage," a statement that certainly applies to yarrow. As an exceedingly bitter tea or tonic, it is harmless, perhaps even beneficial, if not precisely refreshing. Large or frequent doses, however, should be avoided; the toxic substance, though less than in common wormwood, is thujone. Yarrow's lactones make the plant allergenic to some individuals, causing skin irritations and rashes if handled.

Wetlands

TATIANA VOLGUTOVA/SHUTTERSTOCK.COM

Arrow-Arum
(*Peltandra virginica*)

KRIS LIGHT

Arum family. Herb in swamps, fens, shallow water, along pond margins. Its large, arrow-shaped leaves; its erect, pointed sheath (called a spathe) enfolding the green, tapering flower spike (called a spadix); and its cluster of greenish-brown berries in the fall identify arrow-arum. Other names: green arrow-arum, tuckahoe, poison-arum, Virginia wake-robin.

Arrow-arum leaves are easily confused in size and shape with those of broad-leaved arrowhead. Note, however, that arrow-arum leaves are feather-veined while arrowhead leaves have parallel veins. Both male and female flowers occur on the largely enclosed spadix, which may be seen through a vertical gap in the spathe. Male flowers occupy most of the spadix; the female flowers occupy the lower fourth or fifth of it. They are insect pollinated.

The fleshy base of the spathe swells as the berry cluster grows inside it, and the seed stalk bends toward the ground. Usually the top part of the pointed spathe dries and falls off, leaving a roundish green pod full of seeds enmeshed in a jellylike mass. Sometimes, however, the now-inverted spathe point remains and serves as a kind of drill or auger into the soft mud, thus "planting" the seed packet. Released seeds also float, dispersing the plant. Cloning from the thick, fibrous roots, however, probably accounts for most plant colonies.

Like arrowheads, this plant is often a shore-line emergent, growing in several inches of water. It also thrives on muddy banks.

In spring and summer, shallow emergent vegetation including arrowheads, wild calla, bur-reeds, and pickerel-weed are frequent arrow-arum associates. Arrow-arum berries are especially relished by wood ducks. Other consumers include mallards and king rails.

Raphides—acrid, needlelike calcium oxalate crystals—are found in all parts of most arums. They are intensely burning and irritating if eaten and will actually create numerous tiny wounds in mouth membranes. Only thorough drying renders the rhizomes harmless and edible. American natives collected them for making flour.

Blue Vervain
(*Verbena hastata*)

Vervain family. Herb in swamps, low spots, along water margins, as well as in less moist habitats. Blue vervain displays several erect, pencil-like spikes of blue flowers like candelabra atop a four-angled stem; its narrow leaves are toothed and opposite. This is the most common of some dozen blue-flowered and white-flowered vervains in east-central North America. Other names: false or American vervain, wild hyssop, purvain, ironweed, simpler's-joy.

Blue vervain begins flowering in midsummer and continues through early fall. Like many plants with flowers on spikes, the flowers come into bloom from the bottom up. On any given spike, you can usually see seeds on the lowermost portion, a circular fringe of flowers midway up, and unopened flower buds at the top. The nectar-rich flowers are bisexual and insect pollinated, producing linear nutlets. The flowers often self-fertilize as well.

Vervain's stalk dies in the fall but often remains standing throughout winter, dispersing seeds. In late summer, the thick, spreading rhizome produces small reddish buds just

KRIS LIGHT

beneath the soil surface; from these, new stalks arise the following spring.

Although blue vervain adapts to almost any fairly moist, open, acid-neutral or alkaline habitat, it usually favors wetter sites than its close relatives, white and European vervains, which generally prefer drier ground.

Plant companions of blue vervain include boneset, Joe-Pye-weeds, meadowsweet, reed canary grass, great lobelia, and jewelweeds, among others. On drier sites, blue vervain sometimes associates with other vervains as well. The twining, threadlike, parasitic dodder often enmeshes blue vervain in its yellowish, matted strands, tapping into the stem and not infrequently killing it.

Bumblebees, honeybees, and other bees are the chief pollinators. At least two broods of a noctuid moth caterpillar, the verbena moth, feed on the leaves beginning in spring. The verbena leaf miner, a midge larva, produces large blotch mines near the leaf margins. Vervains have only slight value as wildlife food plants.

American natives used blue vervain leaves and roots for making various medicinal teas and tonics that were emetic in large doses. The Mohawks had a further use: "For refreshment, cut the root into pieces, place on top of the head with a little cold water, and sit in a current of air" (the beneficial effect was said to result with or without the root topping!). The only humanly edible part of the plant is said to be the seeds, which can be soaked, roasted, and ground for flour.

Related European vervain, also common in North America, has a long Old World history associated with the occult: Druid rites, Roman sacrifices and love potions, and witches' incantations (the Latin word *verbena* means "sacred herb"). Virgil and Pliny referred to the plant in their writings, and the ancient Greeks also considered it a holy herb and aphrodisiac, a general cure-all for sicknesses of soul and body. One source marvels that the plant has survived extinction, so abundantly was it once collected by herbalists and folk practitioners.

Boneset
(*Eupatorium perfoliatum*)

KRIS LIGHT

Composite family. Herb in wet ground, along marsh and pond edges. Identify boneset by its flat-topped clusters of dull white flowers that bloom all summer; and by its opposite, crinkly leaves united at their bases to enclose the hairy stem. Other names: thoroughwort, ague-weed, Indian-sage, crosswort, feverweed, sweating-plant.

More than twenty *Eupatorium* species reside in various habitats of east-central North America, but boneset is the most common one. This plant is so frequent along open shorelines and marshy spots that its absence is more remarkable than its presence.

The flowers, as in most composites, consist of multiple bisexual florets that are insect pollinated. Flower heads usually contain fifteen to twenty florets, which secrete abundant nectar. Occasional purple-flowered and three-leaved forms occur. Like many plants in this family, the seeds come equipped with a hairy pappus, or "parachute," a more efficient device for wind distribution than the seed wings seen in maple and ash trees. This plant sometimes hybridizes with upland boneset *(E. sessilifolium)*, a woods dweller. Boneset frequently dwells among its close relatives, the Joe-Pye-weeds, and also with wetland sedges and grasses, jewelweeds, and other typical edge plants of swamps and fens.

The name boneset probably refers to this plant's historic usage as a tea treatment for break-bone fever (now identified as the viral disease dengue), characterized by severe pains in the joints. The plant's fused, opposite leaves may also have suggested it as a treatment for mending bone fractures. Boneset tea was one of the most widely used folk remedies for general aches and malaise by American natives and pioneers alike. It reportedly became one of the most effective relief medicines during nineteenth- and early twentieth-century flu epidemics. Today, boneset tea, a bitter brew indeed, remains a popular herbal drink to induce sweating, as a tonic for colds, and, still, as a medicine that supposedly promotes bone healing. Larger doses have emetic and laxative effects.

Modern medical research verifies some of boneset's reputed benefits; some of its compounds apparently stimulate the immune system. Its potential for producing anticancer chemotherapeutic drugs is also being explored.

Cardinal-Flower
(*Lobelia cardinalis*)

SARI O'NEAL/SHUTTERSTOCK.COM

Lobelia family. Herb in wet soil, along stream and pond margins. Its spike of large, brilliantly scarlet flowers in summer makes cardinal-flower impossible to misidentify. Other names: red lobelia, slinkweed.

"It is not so much something colored as it is color itself," wrote naturalist John Burroughs. Cardinal-flower probably shows the reddest red of any American wildflower. Though not a rare plant, it is hardly abundant even in prime habitats. Except for flower color, it closely resembles the great lobelia, which grows in similar habitats. The color difference between these close relatives probably stems from their very unalike pollinators, which may also explain the cardinal-flower's lack of a landing platform for insects. Examining a cardinal-flower closely reveals its conspicuous sexual part: a red tube projecting above the brilliant petals. The petals are gaudy flags for attracting ruby-throated hummingbirds, the flower's chief pollinators. This sexual tube is at first "male," displaying pollen-bearing stamens at the tube tip. As the stamens decline, the sticky, Y-shaped pistils extend from the tube, which is now "female" and ready to receive pollen from a cardinal-flower still in the pollen stage. The sequencing proceeds from the bottom to the top of a flower spike. Thus a single plant may show flowers in both stages of development, plus new flower buds at the top and developing fruits below. The flowers grow somewhat one-sided on the spike.

Hummingbirds pollinate the plant by brushing their foreheads against the tube tip as they plunge their needlelike bills into the "flag tube" below, where the nectaries are located. They do all this on the wing, so the flower needs no landing platform.

The dry fruit capsules split open in the fall, spilling hundreds of small seeds, which are dispersed by wind and water. The plant dies back to clusters of green, basal rosettes of leaves lasting all winter. From these arise the single flower stalks in late spring.

Cardinal-flowers often occur in sparse, patchy colonies, frequently in light shade, which may partially account for their brilliance. An occasional plant with pink or white flowers also occurs. I have often found cardinal-flowers in the company of boneset, though the latter is a much more common wildflower. Without hummingbirds, their main pollinators, cardinal-flowers would surely be far fewer than they already are.

"Thy sins shall be as scarlet. Is it my sins that I see?" pondered Thoreau as he viewed these flowers, which also reminded him of "red men, war, and bloodshed." But he could not resist plucking them; they grew by the thousands in the Concord ditches. Since his day, however, the wild plant has drastically declined in occurrence. Today, cardinal-flower is a legally protected species and should never be picked or removed from the wild. It can be obtained from seed suppliers by those who want to attract hummingbirds to the garden.

Native Americans used root and leaf teas of cardinal-flower as remedies for stomachache, fever, headache, and colds. The teas were believed to expel worms, soothe the nerves, and cure syphilis and typhoid fever to boot. Some tribes used the dried, ground-up plant as a ceremonial powder to dispel storms, strew into graves, and mix into love potions. The plant, however, contains potentially toxic pyridine alkaloids. New England farmers believed that cows miscarried from eating the plant, and some people are allergic to the sap on their skin. If you're not a shaman (and even if you are), you might want to leave it alone.

Wetlands Cinquefoils
(*Potentilla* and *Dasiphora* species)

PHASUT WARAPISIT/SHUTTERSTOCK.COM

Rose family. These genuses includes many flowering herbs, but both wetland species are low, woody shrubs. Purple marshlocks *(P. palustris)* has a sprawling stem and maroon flowers. Shrubby cinquefoil *(Dasiphora fruticosa)* grows in dense, hip-high thickets, displaying shreddy bark and yellow flowers in summer and fall. Both show the characteristic five-to-seven-fingered compound leaves of this genus. Other names: five-finger (all cinquefoils); marsh or purple cinquefoil, cowberry, purplewort, meadownuts, bog strawberry *(P. palustris)*; prairie weed, bush cinquefoil *(D. fruticosa)*.

Both wetland cinquefoils favor mineral-rich swamps and fens; don't look for them in bogs. Both species also flower at about the same time, but purple marshlocks is lower, more solitary and inconspicuous. It often occupies wetter ground than the bushy and colonial shrubby cinquefoil, which seems to prefer higher and drier portions of fens.

Both species have bisexual, insect-pollinated flowers that may also self-pollinate if no insect lands at the right time. Marshlocks flowers share certain characteristics with such unrelated white-flowered species as anemones and flowering dogwood: The conspicuous color resides not in the flower petals (which, in marshlocks, are small and pointed), but in the larger, underlying sepals or bracts. This arrangement does not occur in most other cinquefoils.

Shrubby cinquefoil is also unusual. It is one of the few woody plants that begins flowering in summer and continues to do so into late fall. From June or July onward all stages of floral development are visible on the plant as individual flowers open, mature, and set seed. Flowering, especially in woody plants, requires a huge energy expenditure, good nutrition, and ample resting periods. Shrubby cinquefoil, however, has refined this biological process so that the plant requires no respite once flowering begins. Repeated growth "flushes" occur throughout the season, resulting in frequent branching, which produces a very bushy shrub. The hairy, pear-shaped seeds, often held on the flower head long into winter, are achenes. Shrubby cinquefoil, highly intolerant of shade, is also very cold tolerant.

Cinquefoils and Virginia strawberry are so closely related that they sometimes hybridize. Note the similarity of their disk flower forms. But this form also frequently appears in unrelated plants such as buttercups and frostweeds. Some botanists pose this similarity as an example of Müllerian mimicry—certain flowers have independently evolved the shallow bowl or disk form because of its general efficiency in hosting nonspecialized insect pollinators.

Still, because of their unlike flower colors, purple marshlocks and shrubby cinquefoils probably attract different insect pollinators at least some of the time. Many yellow flowers are not yellow to insect eyes but rather reflect ultraviolet "bee purple," invisible to human eyes.

Marshlocks, characteristic of pioneer sedge mats, often associates with the sedge *Carex lasiocarpa*, three-way sedge, cattails, and buckbean in such habitats. Shrubby cinquefoil occupies more advanced fen habitats in company with the moss *Campylium stellatum*, various sedges, speckled alder, shrub willows, and tamarack, among others. Because shrubby cinquefoil can also colonize drier, rocky uplands and is not grazed by cattle, it is often treated as an invasive nuisance weed. Elsewhere, however, its long flowering season and compact growth form have made it a popular yard ornamental. This usage dates back to the eighteenth century in Europe, and many horticultural varieties of the plant have been developed.

Cinquefoil's astringent roots and leaves achieved popularity as a folk medicine for such ailments as diarrhea, sore throat, and catarrh. The roots can be made edible by boiling or roasting. Steeped, the dried leaves of shrubby cinquefoil make a decent, harmless tea.

Cottongrasses
(*Eriophorum* species)

TTPHOTO/SHUTTERSTOCK.COM

Sedge family. Herbs in bogs and fens. Recognize cottongrasses by their grasslike form and tufted, cottony seed-heads, solitary or clustered at the top of the plant. About 8 species occupy mainly bogs in our area, though green-keeled cottongrass *(E. viridicarinatum)* also resides in rich fens. Three of the most common bog species are tall cottongrass *(E. angustifolium)*, tawny cottongrass *(E. virginicum)*, and dense cottongrass *(E. spissum)*. Other names: cotton-sedge; sheathed cotton-sedge *(E. spissum)*

A pleasing aspect of many bogs is the "cotton field" vista of these white-tufted plants rising above the sag-and-swell surface of the sphagnum-moss ground layer. Various species of cottongrass flower and fruit from spring through fall. The downy "cotton" actually consists of soft, persistent bristles that develop on the bisexual flowers, which are wind pollinated. The seeds are also dispersed by wind.

In many northern bogs, cottongrasses form tussocks—round, bunchy, sodlike clumps bearing many stems of the plant. Tussocks are the result of the simultaneous growth and restraint of new shoots on a single plant. Buds at the leaf bases develop into new shoots, but the persistent leaf bases of old shoots slow the plant's lateral spread. The result is a sort of pot-bound growth form without the pot. Each shoot produces new shoots and a new pair of leaves annually. Leaves die back in the fall but may remain intact on the plant for years, eventually producing the tussock's bushy appearance. In undisturbed bogs, individual tussocks may survive for a century or more. Often they assume a crescent shape; as winds bend the old, bushy growth permanently to the leeward side, tussock expansion occurs mainly on the unshaded windward side.

Their sequential leaf growth apparently enables cottongrasses to recycle nutrients. As old leaves age, many of their mineral constituents translocate into the new leaf growth, thus reducing the plant's dependence on soil nutrients in the unfertile bog environment. Young flowering shoots contain high levels of phosphorus and potassium.

This is one of the few plants that can invade disturbed habitats as well as colonize undisturbed ones. Dense cottongrass thrives especially well following a passage of fire. Cottongrass "cotton" was apparently used by pioneer families for pillow stuffing. But its collection for such purposes must have been even more laborious than picking regular cotton; poultry feathers were much more efficiently gathered.

Gentians
(*Gentianopsis* and *Gentiana* species)

MARY TERRIBERRY/SHUTTERSTOCK.COM

Gentian family. Herbs with varying soil moisture preferences. Gentians, flowering in late summer and fall, have opposite leaves and erect, vaselike, blue flowers, usually in terminal clusters. Wetland species include fringed gentian *(Gentianopis crinita)*, smaller fringed gentian *(Gentianopsis virgata)*, soapwort gentian *(Gentiana saponaria)*, and bottle gentian *(Gentiana andrewsii)*. Other names: closed or blind gentian *(G. andrewsii)*.

Among our most beautiful wildflowers, the fringed gentian is blue as "the male bluebird's back," wrote Thoreau, but the deepest blue probably belongs to the bottle gentian (all of the gentians occasionally produce white flowers, too).

Wetland gentian species differ somewhat in their flower forms. Fringed gentian species show four flared-out petals with fringed edges; other gentians open only slightly or, as in closed gentian, hardly at all. They differ, too, in their growth scheme. Unlike the vast majority of wildflowers, gentians are annuals (smaller fringed) and biennials (fringed), relying solely on wind-scattered seed for survival. The other wetland gentians are perennials, tending to persist longer in a given locale. Even the fringed gentians seem to begrudge opening for very long. They open in direct sunlight, but a cloudy day shuts them tightly. Wetland gentians apparently tolerate a broad range of soil chemistry. Fringed gentians favor fens and wet meadows, but these and other gentians also appear in acid bogs. Seldom, however, do they grow in great abundance anywhere.

Though technically bisexual, all gentian flowers develop mature pollen-bearing anthers before the female parts mature. This mechanism, seen in many wildflowers, actually amounts to sequentially unisexual flowers, one sex succeeding the other. It thus prevents self-fertilization; by the time a pistil becomes ready to receive pollen, the pollen-bearing anthers of the same flower have usually withered, and pollen must come from younger flower heads. Sometimes the fall season advances so far before pollen-bearing ceases that the female parts never catch up before frost occurs (in which case the flower ends up, by default, as unisexual male).

Compared with many flowers, gentians are relatively inhospitable to insects. Tubular gentian flowers, however, are especially adapted for bumblebee pollination; many "bumblebee flowers" are likewise blue. This powerfully built insect can shoulder its way past the entrance obstacles that discourage smaller, less efficient pollinators. Even the closed gentian admits the forceful entry of a bumblebee; the bee pries head-first into the flower, then backs out, combing the pollen from head and thorax into the baskets on its hind legs. Bottle gentian is one of the richest of all flowers in nectar quantity and sweetness. As with many deep, tubular flowers, bees sometimes perforate holes in the flower base from outside, thus short-circuiting the conventional frontal route to the nectar—a route that, in gentians, always offers resistance.

The name is said to derive from King Gentius of ancient Illyria (500 B.C.E.), who used the roots of European yellow gentian medicinally. "It is too remarkable a flower not to be sought out and admired each year," wrote Thoreau. Poet William Cullen Bryant thought so, too, and penned his famous lines to "The Fringed Gentian," making this plant on of America's foremost literary flowers.

In the years since Thoreau and Bryant admired them, however, gentians have suffered grievously from the loss and shrinkage of wetland habitats. They are now uncommon to rare plants in many areas that formerly supported abundant gentian populations. The fringed gentians, being seed-grown annuals and biennials, are especially vulnerable to habitat changes; only one year's aborted growth can wipe out an entire population, since the seeds remain viable for only a short time. Although gentians are legally protected flowers in most places, the wetland habitats they must have to survive remain underprotected and undervalued.

Grass-of-Parnassus
(*Parnassia glauca*)

Saxifrage family. Herb in fens, wet meadows, along streams. Flowering in summer and fall, grass-of-Parnassus shows solitary flowers with green veins lining the five cream-white petals. A small leaf clasps the flowering stem.

Neither a grass nor resembling one despite its name, this intriguing wildflower usually grows in small colonies, a resident of calcium-rich wetlands. Its bisexual, insect-pollinated flower is actually unisexually sequenced, with male parts developing and declining before the female parts mature. This virtually guarantees cross-pollination. The fruits are four-valved capsules.

The green lines on the petals are nectar guides. They show up especially well to pollinating insects, who perceive a strong contrast between the lines and the whiteness of the petals, which weakly reflect ultraviolet light. These rays are invisible to our eyes but are like neon to bees and other insects.

Note the plant's stalked filaments, called staminoids, bearing swollen heads that glisten like nectar droplets. If you touch one, however, you'll find it absolutely dry.

T. TRAVIS BROWN

These are sham nectaries (the real nectaries lie near their bases). The deceptive droplets are analogous to advertising hooks, which get the consumers into the store to discover the genuine goods.

Fen associates of this plant may include sedges, shrubby cinquefoil, reed, and orchids such as showy lady-slipper, rose pogonia, and bog twayblade. Flies, especially attracted by the false nectaries, are the chief pollinators. Small bees and butterflies, mainly skippers, also visit the flowers.

The similar Old World species *P. palustris* gave the plant its common name by supposedly having been first discovered growing on the slopes of Mount Parnassus in Greece.

Great Lobelia
(*Lobelia siphilitica*)

Lobelia family. Herb in swamps, wet ground. Identify this lobelia by its height (up to three feet) and its blue flowers in showy spikes. The flowers are lobed, showing two erect "ears" above and a divided lip below, with a white-striped flower tube. Other blue-flowered wetland lobelias are smaller plants; they include water lobelia *(L. dortmanna)* and brook lobelia *(L. kalmii)*. Other names: great blue lobelia, blue cardinal-flower, high-belia.

This is the blue version (though not quite so spectacular) of red cardinal-flower; great lobelia flower structure is much the same but on a somewhat smaller scale. One difference is that insect-pollinated great lobelia has a solid "landing platform"—the lobed, lower lip of the flower; cardinal-flower, being hummingbird pollinated, has no such surface. The two species sometimes hybridize, producing deep reddish or crimson-purple flowers and varying petal sizes and shapes. Occasional white-flowered variants also appear.

KRIS LIGHT

The male parts mature first on this bisexual flower, thus encouraging cross-fertilization, but self-fertilization also occurs. A unique feature of the flower tube is a top slit, which extends to its base and through which the stamens protrude. Numerous seeds spill from the fruit capsules when ripe.

Lobelias are relatively short-lived perennials, often lasting only two or three years. This lobelia never entirely dies back during its lifetime—it overwinters beneath the snow as a small, green rosette of leaves. This is a fen or swamp species, preferring alkaline or acid-neutral soils.

Great lobelia often associates with its red-flowered counterpart, which usually begins flowering a bit later in summer than great lobelia, but the latter lasts longer, so the two have a period of overlap. I often see great lobelia associated with other blue-flowered plants, including blue vervain, skullcaps, and monkey-flower. Boneset is also a frequent associate. As with most blue-flowered plants, bumblebees are the chief pollinators. Andrenid and halictid bees also collect pollen from the flowers.

Great lobelia once numbered among those many plants that were alleged to cure syphilis, hence its specific Latin name. They never had such powers—as is now known, early stages of the disease often progress into a remission of outward symptoms. American natives also used root decoctions in poultices for wounds, inflammations, and skin cancers and drank a leaf tea for treating colds and other ailments. The acrid, milky juice of all lobelias is toxic, so home remedies using lobelia are ill-advised.

Some botanists see the slitted flower tube of lobelias as an evolutionary landmark, representing the tendency toward development of multiple flowers (specifically, the strap or ray flowers) found in the most advanced plant family, the composites. Taxonomists generally rank the lobelia family just below this grouping.

Jack-in-the-Pulpit
(*Arisaema triphyllum*)

DAVID CARILLET/SHUTTERSTOCK.COM

Arum family. Herb in wet and mesic woodlands and swamps. Recognize this plant by its three-parted leaf or leaves, a striped floral leaf forming a hooded canopy over the enclosed clublike spadix, and its cluster of scarlet berries in the fall. Jack-in-the-pulpit adapts its size, coloration, and sex to environmental circumstances. It also traps insects inside the lower chamber housing the club-shaped spadix. Other names: Indian turnip, wild turnip, marsh-pepper, bog-onion, brown dragon, starchwort, wake-robin, dragon-root, cuckoo-pint.

There are three distinct forms or varieties of this familiar species, one of them favoring more mesic woodland habitats. The flowers are usually unisexual, but it's impossible to tell male from female without prying open the "pulpit" base to examine the spadix. Female flowers are round and berrylike on the spadix; the male pollen-bearing flowers are threadlike.

The plants arise from an underground stem called a corm. In any given year, a corm may produce either a male or female plant. The plants have no sex chromosomes as such. Which sex "happens" apparently depends on the size of the plant, hence the amount of food accumulated in the corm. This sex "decision" occurs in the fall, when the corm sprouts the plant that will appear aboveground the following spring. Individual corms may also bud off new corms, thus forming new plants; some corms survive for twenty years or longer.

A large plant bearing two compound leaves is almost invariably female. Small plants bearing only one leaf are male or asexual. Once a corm becomes large enough to produce a female plant, it may continue producing females for years. So Jack-in-the-pulpit adapts itself to varying environmental conditions, changing its sex to meet the circumstances of the growing season.

The lowermost chamber housing the spadix often traps small insects, because the slippery internal walls may prevent them from climbing out. This situation is probably an incidental consequence of the floral structure and not a capture mechanism, as in pitcher-plants. Still, though not technically considered an insect-trapping plant, Jack sometimes accumulates a sizable corpse litter in its basal floral chamber.

The insect-pollinated flower produces no nectar. Spadix bases, however, produce a funguslike odor that certain insects find irresistible. Pollinating insects are mainly fungus gnats, attracted by the odor. A species of thrips feeds in the flowers. The plant's chemical defenses make its foliage and corms extremely unpalatable to most insects and mammals, however.

Calcium oxalate crystals, found also in other arums, produce an intensely caustic, corrosive taste in leaves, corms, and fruits of Jack-in-the-pulpit. Meskwaki tribesmen made a war weapon of the fresh, grated corm; they added it to meat and offered it to their Sioux enemies, who ate it—and died in agony.

Thorough drying, however, rids the starchy corm of this substance. It then becomes safely edible, either sliced thinly or powdered into flour. Native tribes collected and dried the corms for food. They also used it in internal medicines for colds and bronchial ailments and externally for poultices on aches and sores.

This plant's common name was originated by a clerical-minded New Englander, one Clara Smith of Medford, Massachusetts. She sent a "flowery" verse to poet John G. Whittier for his approval. He tinkered with it, finally publishing it under his own famous name about 1884. Thus "Jack" suddenly became a good (if somewhat plagiarized) New England Calvinist flower.

Joe-Pye-Weeds
(*Eutrochium species*)

RON ROWAN PHOTOGRAPHY/SHUTTERSTOCK.COM

Composite family. Tall herbs in swamps, marshes, wet thickets. Flowering in summer and fall, Joe-Pye-weeds show pinkish-purple, domed or flat-topped flower clusters; whorls of three to seven long, toothed leaves; and often purple-streaked or purple-spotted stems. The most common wetland species include spotted Joe-Pye-weed *(E. maculatum)*, trumpetweed *(E. fistulosum)*, and coastal Joe-Pye-weed *(E. dubium)*. Other names: gravel-root, Indian-gravel, kidney-root, king or queen of the meadows, skunk-weed, marsh milkweed, quillwort, purple boneset or thoroughwort.

Their floral characteristics place Joe-Pye-weeds in the same genus as boneset, but their flower colors and leaf arrangements are much different. Joe-Pye-weeds also resemble ironweeds in form, again with leaf and flower differences.

Many composites, such as asters and daisies, have both disk and ray flowers. Joe-Pye-weeds are among those members of this huge family that, like thistles and others, have only disk flowers; in other words, if you pull off all the ray flowers ("petals") of a daisy, what remains is the central hub of disk flowers, which constitutes the sole flower head of Joe-Pye-weeds. The bisexual, insect-pollinated flowers come into bloom a few at a time in clusters atop the stem. Placement of their sexual parts often permits these flowers to self-pollinate as well, eventually producing furry heads of feathery achenes that are dispersed by wind in the fall.

The dead stalks often remain standing through winter, bleak swamp skeletons that imagination finds difficult to clothe with color. New stems arise in spring from horizontal, perennial rhizomes. These, with their roots, form a tough, tangled subsurface matrix that helps bind loose marsh soil into land.

Look straight down the stem of a Joe-Pye-weed and note how each leaf whorl is slightly rotated from the whorl above and below. This arrangement enables maximal light to reach each leaf. Joe-Pye-weeds require open sunlight and are not very shade tolerant.

These plants favor mineral-rich sites, often occupying transitional zones of rank growth between cattails and swamp loosestrife on the water side and goldenrods or Queen Anne's lace on the landward side.

Pollinating insects include various bees, flies, and butterflies, all attracted by the fragrant nectar deep in the tubular florets. Tiger swallowtails and fritillaries, plus many smaller butterflies, land frequently in patches of Joe-Pye-weed.

Who was Joe Pye? His name has come down through oral tradition. Scholars have diligently tried to trace this legendary Indian herbalist and healer who supposedly befriended New England pioneers, but the name on the plant is really all that remains of him. He may have been a Mohegan who lived and practiced his homeopathic arts near Salem, Massachusetts, in colonial times. It is said that he brewed decoctions of the plant bearing his name to induce sweating in typhus fever.

The names gravel-root and kidney-root resulted from the astringent rhizome's wide usage among natives and pioneers for urinary ailments. Forest Potawatomi, among other tribes, regarded the flowers as good-luck charms, especially effective for winning at gambling.

Lady's Slippers
(*Cypripedium* species)

Orchid family. Herbs in a variety of habitats; identify these orchids by their ballooning, pouch-shaped lower petal (called the labellum) and a large top sepal reaching above the flower. The three most common lady's slippers are pink lady's slipper *(C. acaule)*, large yellow lady's slipper *(C. parviflorum)*, and showy lady's slipper *(C. reginae)*. Other names: American valerian, stemless lady's slipper, moccasin-flower, Indian-moccasin, squirrel-shoes, nerve-root *(C. acaule)*; whippoorwill's-shoe, Indian-shoe, yellows *(C. parviflorum)*; queen's lady's slipper *(C. reginae)*.

These spectacular orchids vary widely in their habitat requirements. Most adaptable in its moisture tolerances is pink lady's slipper, which flowers in both bogs and dry, sandy uplands. Its main requirement is sterile, acid soil—wet or dry. Large yellow lady's slipper grows in both wet and mesic sites, favoring more neutral soils, including swamps and fens; it especially thrives in limestone areas. Showy lady's slipper, with its two-tone flower—white with streaked rose-purple labellum—is

MARC PARSONS/SHUTTERSTOCK.COM

one of our largest, most beautiful native orchids. It dwells much more consistently in wetlands than the previous two orchids, usually growing in fens and swamp openings and tolerating only light shade.

These bisexual, insect-pollinated flowers are deceptive in the extreme. Luring pollinators by color and an odor from the sepals and lateral petals, they offer little or no nectar. The insect enters the pouch through a front slit (in pink lady's slipper) or a circular opening at the top (in the two others). Fine, slanting hairs on the pouch's smooth-walled inner surface nudge the insect toward the sticky, overhanging female stigma, a constricted passage from which it cannot backtrack. It continues to squeeze through the passage, finally brushing against the pollen-loaded anthers. The exit passage is narrow and complex; the pouches sometimes become traps for insects that miss their cues on where to go.

Unlike many of the lipped orchids, lady's slippers cannot (or only rarely) self-pollinate. The flower's interior arrangement of sex organs requires that pollen be brought from another flower for fertilization to occur. The fruit capsules split to release clouds of powdery, wind-dispersed seeds. Only a few of them ever find the right combination of habitat and symbiotic fungus to grow and thrive. A germinated seed must be joined by a mycorrhizal soil fungus before it can absorb nutrition. The initial growth process may require two years or more, and the plant may not produce a flower for several more years. The subsurface plant forms a radiating complex of spaghettilike roots and round tubers, from which the new shoots arise in spring. The fungus is an absolutely necessary orchid partner. It functions as and in place of root hairs; without it, orchid roots cannot absorb soil nutrients. Many botanists believe that the relationship actually consists of orchid parasitism on the fungus. In bogs, pink lady's slipper usually occupies hummocks of sphagnum moss and other drier areas.

Midsize, ground-nesting andrenid and halictid bees, honeybees, and smaller bumblebees are the chief pollinators. Large bumblebees that get trapped sometimes bite their way free, leaving a mutilated pouch. Large yellow lady's slippers are frequently pollinated by the solitary *Andrena* and small carpenter bees. Common pollinators of showy lady's slipper include leafcutting bees.

Their relative infrequency makes orchids insignificant food plants for birds and mammals. White-tailed deer, however, apparently aid the germination of showy lady-slippers in cedar swamps, where deer often yard up in winter. By trampling and aerating the soil and overbrowsing the trees, thus creating forest openings, the deer help plant the orchid seeds. Old winter deeryards may display colonies of this spectacular orchid.

Orchids (especially lady's slippers) are ancient sexual and erotic symbols; the word *orchis* means "testicle" in Greek. Not only the scrotum shape of the labellum but also the roots and testiclelike tubers suggested uses as aphrodisiacs. Does some residual belief in orchid charms and powers lie behind our particular selection of these flowers as bodily adornment for ceremonial occasions involving courtship and marriage? May some such urge also drive the seemingly irresistible impulse in many humans to pick every available wild orchid in sight? That many species of our native orchids are not now extinct probably owes more to the difficulty in accessing orchid habitat than to legal protection or the forebearance of "flower lovers."

For some at least, the picking of lady-slippers can be a physically unpleasant experience. *Cypripedium* (especially showy lady's slipper) may produce a skin rash similar to that caused by poison ivy, in this case caused by a volatile oil and the resinoid cypripedin. Sedative properties of *Cypripedium* roots were well known to native peoples and American pioneers alike. Root teas were taken to calm the nerves; ease insomnia, depression, and menstrual disorders; and treat epilepsy. The Chippewa applied the dried, powdered roots to aching teeth. Other tribes used root decoctions for kidney and stomach ailments. Root foragers heavily harvested yellow lady's slippers during the last century for medicinal uses. Their populations have probably never fully recovered.

Lipped Orchids
(*Platanthera, Pogonia, Arethusa, Calopogon,* and *Spiranthes* species)

LEIGHTON PHOTOGRAPHY & IMAGING/SHUTTERSTOCK.COM

Orchid family. Herbs in a variety of bog, fen, and dry sites. Recognize lipped orchids (in contrast to the pouched lady's slippers) by a protruding, tonguelike lower petal, which shows various colors, shapes, and sizes among species. Two smaller petals and three flaring, bractlike sepals, plus (in most genera) a protruding rear spur, complete the flower aspect. The flowers grow in spikelike terminal clusters. Leaves, usually sheathing the flower stalk, are parallel veined. Common names for these orchid genera and species include fringed orchids *(Platanthera)*; rose pogonia *(Pogonia ophioglossoides)*; dragon's-mouth *(Arethusa bulbosa)*; grass-pink *(Calopogon tuberosus)*; and ladies'-tresses *(Spiranthes)*. Other genera also exist, but these are the most commonly seen. Other names: rein-orchids *(Platanthera)*; sweet pogonia, adder's-mouth, snake-mouth, beard-flower, ettercap, sweet crest-orchid *(Pogonia ophioglossoides)*; arethusa, wild pink, Indian pink, bog-rose *(A. bulbosa)*.

All orchid flowers are bisexual and insect pollinated. The lipped orchids produce pollen in sticky masses or packages called pollinia, which adhere to insect bodies or heads. Both male and female parts are fused into a central column, beneath which the insect passes to seek the nectar. Pollination and deposition on the insect of new pollen occurs when the insect backs out of the flower. The complex interior arrangement of sticky surfaces is positioned so precisely that an insect can hardly fail to pick up and deposit pollinia in exactly the right places. Despite this mechanism, most of these orchids regularly self-pollinate.

The red, spurless orchids—rose pogonia and dragon's-mouth—bear only a single flower at the stem tip. Pogonia's lip is pink-fringed and -crested; dragon's-mouth's is conspicuously yellow-crested and clawed or slightly lobed. "No orchid in our flora is lovelier," wrote orchid botanist Fred Case of the latter. Case also likened the fragrance of rose pogonia to red raspberries—"a person familiar with the odor can sometimes detect the presence of the plants before seeing them." Thoreau, on the other hand, thought pogonias smelled like snakes.

Grass-pink, also red, reverses the usual orchid flower orientation; its lip protrudes from the top, making the flower appear upside down. In all other native orchids, the flower ovary turns 180 degrees so that the lip petal, which actually forms in an uppermost position, as in grass-pink, becomes the lowest in position. Grass-pink flowers grow in a loose cluster atop the plant.

Ladies'-tresses, by contrast, show relatively inconspicuous spikes of small, white, unspurred flowers and long, grasslike leaves. A pollinating bee usually works the flower spikes systematically, landing on the lowest flower of a spike and spiraling up the flower stalk. Indeed, the "spiral staircase" form of *Spiranthes* flowers may represent the coevolved outcome of a bee's typical path up a vertical stem.

Orchid seed, often produced asexually in some species, is extremely fine, dustlike. Notoriously difficult to germinate in the laboratory or greenhouse, seeds remain dormant until, by some yet-unknown process in nature, their dormancy is broken. Although researchers have managed to germinate a few species under controlled conditions, raising native orchids from seed to flowering remains nearly impossible. Orchids guard their secrets well; this is part of the ongoing mystery and fascination of these complex, often bizarre plants.

Once germinated, the young plant must nourish underground, usually for a period of years, before it can produce aboveground leaves and flower stalk. The rhizome produces a new bud each fall, from which a new aboveground plant will rise the next year—provided it remains uninjured by frost, trampling, or other circumstances.

The sudden appearance of orchids where nobody has seen them before and likewise their disappearance from sites where they have usually grown are fairly common occurrences. In the former case, long-dormant seeds may have germinated and finally produced aboveground plants. In the latter, physical injury to plants, natural succession, or subtle changes in soil chemistry may wipe them out. In some cases, the lack of slight but continuous habitat disturbances can eliminate them. So specialized are the microhabitat requirements of some native orchids that they have probably always been (and always will be) rare. Where habitat conditions remain stable, however, other species may form long-lived, if localized, thriving colonies.

Vital to almost all North American orchids is the root-fungus symbiosis known as mycorrhiza, whereby fungal threads invade orchid root cells and provide their means of nutrient uptake. The fungus receives food from the orchid. For orchids, this relationship is one of absolute dependence; without it, germination and growth cannot occur.

Native peoples found scant use for orchids. Dragon's-mouth is said to have once been used as a toothache remedy. The tropical orchid Vanilla, source of vanilla flavoring, is the only plant of the family that yields an edible food product in any quantity.

Marsh Marigold
(Caltha palustris)

DABJOLA/SHUTTERSTOCK.COM

Buttercup family. Herb in wet meadows, swamps, fens, along shorelines. Its glossy, bright yellow flowers, among the first of spring, and its roundish, glossy leaves identify this common wetland plant. Other names: cowslip, meadow-gowan, capers, soldier's-buttons, boots, meadow boots, drunkards, crazy bet, kingcup.

This brightest herald of spring lacks petals; the golden-yellow flower consists of five to ten sepals. Like the petals of many buttercups, marsh marigold's sepals look wet and shiny. This waxy-yellow color can be scraped off with a fingernail, leaving colorless, translucent tissue. The yellow surface is "bee purple," reflecting ultraviolet light from all but the very center of the flower (a black spot to a bee), thus providing a nectar guide.

Marsh marigolds grow in saturated soil, frequently in the shallow margins of ponds, brooks, and springs. You will usually need boots (or bare feet) to get a close look at them. Although partially shade tolerant, they thrive best in full sunlight; at night or on cloudy days, the flowers close.

The bisexual, insect-pollinated flowers mature their male and female parts at the same time, but their placement (the anthers numerous and opening outwardly, the pistils fewer and very short) aids cross-fertilization. The flower "has no scent but speaks wholly to the eye," observed Thoreau. (Actually the flower has two "scent marks" at the base, but not many humans can detect the odor.) The seed cluster radiates outward in papery pods. These split open along the upper side, like violets, and often hold their seed rows exposed before the seeds fall out.

Summer is the time when marsh marigold does most of its photosynthesizing and energy storage. After flowers and seeds are gone, the leaves enlarge. Broadly heart-shaped, they now resemble the leaves of skunk-cabbage, a frequent associate. (A quick way to tell them apart: marsh marigold leaves are usually slightly toothed, while skunk-cabbage leaves have smooth, untoothed edges.)

Marsh marigold is one of those spring flowers that occasionally bloom again in the fall, when October day lengths correspond to their spring flowering period.

The glistening yellow flowers are especially attractive to flies. Syrphid flies, those beelike, often brightly colored hoverers, are probably the main pollinators. Many other flies as well as bees also seek nectar and pollen here. A 1962 Ontario study listed thirty-nine insect species that fed in the flowers. One of the most common pollen and aphid feeders is *Coleomegilla maculata*, a spotted lady beetle. Flower thrips are also common.

Most botanists have given up trying to remind us that this is not a true marigold. Common names often bear their own blithe insistence, and the name marsh marigold seems to wear quite well on this flower. Marsh marigold grows all over the world; early English poets called it simply "gold"—and certainly its sudden splashes of color in early spring become a golden feast for the eyes. The plant's Latin name means "marsh cup," and its flowers were once used for dyeing yarn.

Is this plant humanly edible? Yes, but . . . At flowering time, the young leaves (boiled in several changes of water) are said by some to taste better than spinach; others vehemently disagree. Marsh marigold leaves are rich in iron, and American natives used them for treating anemia. The flower buds can be pickled. But never should any part of this plant be eaten raw. (It's unlikely one would do so because of its exceedingly acrid taste.) Thorough cooking dispels bad taste and toxicity from the alkaloid jervine and the glucoside helleborin. The plant is also poisonous to livestock, but these animals usually avoid it.

Northern Pitcher Plant
(*Sarracenia purpurea*)

Pitcher plant family. Low herb in bogs and fens. Its semi-prostrate, purple-streaked leaves, forming keeled, pitcher-shaped water containers make this one of the easiest wetland plants to identify. Other names: northern or purple pitcher-plant, Indian dipper, huntsman's cup, side-saddle flower, Adam's-pitcher, fever-cup, smallpox-plant, dumb-watch, whippoorwill-boots.

Northern pitcher plant, along with sundews and bladderworts, ranks among the most common insect-trapping plants of North America. Its passive method is unique. The modified leaf that forms the pitcher has several easily seen interior zones. The topmost zone is a flared-out lip—a sort of landing platform—with nectar glands and conspicuous reddish veins. On the inside rim, a coating of fine, downward-pointing hairs and a numbing secretion make an insect's escape from the container almost impossible. Just below this zone is a slippery, smoothwalled, sticky constriction, a further impediment to escape.

KRIS LIGHT

Then comes the actual water container, where the prey dies by drowning. The water held in the pitcher is rain (though one observant naturalist has suggested that the hollow leafstalks may indicate water pressure from beneath). The liquid hosts bacteria and possibly plant enzymes, a "digestive fluid" that helps decompose trapped insects and converts their tissues into nitrogen and other nutrients absorbed by the plant. This absorption occurs by means of special cells at the bottom of the pitcher.

The lowest zone is the long, narrow stalk, where indigestible remnants of insects accumulate. Split open a dried pitcher leaf of a previous season (they often remain intact on the plant for months) to see the plant's scrap pile of insect parts. Plants that don't produce flowers in a given year, research has shown, actually don't do much insect digestion; the liquid remains relatively enzyme dilute.

Botanists once believed that nutrient-poor bog environments accounted for pitcher plant's evolved reliance on trapping insects for nourishment. But northern pitcher plants also grow in nutrient-rich fens where minerals are not in short supply. Yet some minerals may be rendered insoluble by chemical actions of other minerals, making even fens practically deficient at times in certain nutrients that plant carnivory can quickly supply.

The single flower rising a foot or two above the leaves is spectacular in itself, a large, maroon, nodding globe that is bisexual and insect pollinated. The pistil is large and umbrellalike, enfolded by the petals.

A five-parted seed capsule replaces the flower and frequently persists into the winter. The seeds require a period of freezing before germination can occur. Most of the plant's reproduction, however, occurs by continuous budding from the perennial rhizome.

At least a few dwarfed, evergreen pitcher leaves usually remain on plants throughout the year. Flowers and new pitcher leaves, radiating from the rhizome, appear only in spring and summer. New leaves are constantly replacing old ones, which die and detach from the plant. Living leaves often turn quite red in the fall. Usually fewer than eight pitcher leaves are present on a single plant at any given time. You can number the chronological sequencing of leaves by observing their stalks; the base of the newest stalk almost surrounds the plant stem, encompassing and overlapping all older leafstalks, and each next-youngest leafstalk does likewise. A new leaf develops almost opposite the position of the previous leaf in the radiating cluster. The younger leaves (those less than fifty days old) attract most of the insect prey. Older leaves seem to lose their attractant nectar and (possibly) odor.

"I never found a pitcher-plant without an insect in it," claimed Thoreau— remarkable if true, for in most pitcher plant populations, most of the containers do not show recent captures at any given time. The true indicator, of course, lies in the bottom scrap pile, if any, of the pitcher. Much research has been done on the number and types of insects that fall prey into the pitchers. In one Michigan study of 214 pitcher leaves, 504 individual insects from 13 orders and 49 families were recovered, most of them fly species. Another study found that almost half of the pitcher victims consisted of large calyptrate flies. Ants too are frequent victims; they sometimes nest inside dried and dead pitcher leaves.

Even more interesting than its victims, however, are the pitchers' guests. These not only resist the digestive brew of the leaves but thrive in it, feeding upon smaller residents: bacteria, diatoms, protozoa, rotifers, and nematode worms, plus fragments of drowned insect victims. They also contribute their own waste products to the mineral needs of the plant. Most of these residents operate in separate microhabitats of the pitcher. Probably the most common "guests" are the larvae of three fly species. The large flesh fly maggot, usually only one in a pitcher, feeds on freshly drowned prey at the pitcher's liquid surface. The pitcher plant mosquito grazes on organic debris in the pitcher liquid. And the pitcher plant midge burrows into the scrap pile of insect fragments to feed there.

In native tribal practice, this plant became a kind of medical panacea for the prevention and cure of smallpox. Tribal elders and medicine men prescribed infusions of the root for this purpose. Modern pharmaceutical research, however, has failed to find any therapeutic substance in the plant. Indians also used the root for various other ailments and drank tea of dried leaves for fevers and chills.

Another claim is that water contained in the pitchers of this plant is safer to drink than bog water. After sampling both, my own judgment is that pitcher-plant water is generally less untasty than bog water, but that the likelihood of protozoan presence in the pitchers would give preference, for safety's sake (should the need arise), to relatively less plankton-populated bog waters. American natives used the pitchers for improvised cups, but there is no record that they drank their natural contents.

Pickerelweed
(*Pontederia cordata*)

LEENA ROBINSON/SHUTTERSTOCK.COM

Pickerelweed family. Emergent herb in marshes, shallow margins of ponds, lakes, streams. Identify pickerelweed by its three-inch, violet-blue flower spike and its large, glossy, usually single arrowhead-shaped leaf with rounded bases. Other name: tuckahoe.

Beds of blue-spired pickerelweed provide color to shallows and shorelines from June to October, when the plants are in continuous flower. Look closely at the bisexual, insect-pollinated flowers. They come in three distinct forms, each in separate colonies, based on the three varying lengths of the female reproductive parts. A pistil can only be fertilized by pollen from another flower's stamens of the corresponding length. This arrangement virtually guarantees cross-fertilization. The only other flowers in this book exhibiting a similar arrangement are loosestrifes.

The crowded flower spike is the work of an entire summer. Usually only a few flowers bloom at a time; blooming begins at the bottom of the spike and progresses upward as the season advances. Each nectar-rich flower lasts only about a day; after pollination, the upper petals close, and it develops a single seed called an utricle. When flowering is finished, the spike releases seeds into the water. Seeds require about two months of cold stratification in order to germinate. Most reproduction, however, occurs vegetatively by means of the creeping, mud-buried rhizome, from which arise numerous individual shoots producing the familiar colonial growth form. Thoreau noted the prevalence of pickerelweed borders on the inside curves of stream meanders, where most sediment is deposited—"the river has its active and its passive side."

Pickerelweed seldom grows in water over three feet deep. Like many aquatic leaf stalks, those of pickerelweed have aerated chambers that function as interior flotation devices, holding the leaf upright in water. Leaves of pickerelweeds stranded on summer mud banks lie prostrate, for they have no supporting tissue of their own. Other emergent aquatic plants with arrowhead-shaped leaves (arrowheads and arrow-arum) often occupy the same shoreline habitats as pickerelweed.

Pickerelweeds are frequent birth sites of adult dragonflies and damselflies. The aquatic nymphs climb this and other emergent plants when they are ready to shed their final nymphal exoskeletons and take to the air. The cast skins of these insects often remain attached to the plant for days. Some female adult *Odonata,* such as the green darner dragonfly and black-winged damselfly, return to the plants and deposit their eggs in stem tissues just below the water surface.

Seeds are eaten by surface-feeding waterfowl, most notably black ducks, gadwalls, mallards, pintails, teal, and wood ducks, but in its general value to wildlife, however, pickerelweed ranks lower than many of its emergent plant associates. Although it does provide shade and shelter to aquatic organisms, the plant has no special associations with pickerel or other fishes.

Leaves and seeds of this common plant are edible and nutritious. The young, unfurled leaves can be used in salads or cooked for greens. Starchy pickerelweed seeds can be eaten off the plant or dried, roasted, or ground into flour.

Purple Loosestrife
(*Lythrum salicaria*)

Loosestrife family. Tall herb in marshes, swamps, wet edges. Its spire of magenta flowers, with six petals, and its opposite or three-whorled, stalkless leaves mark this attractive, ubiquitous plant. Almost all loosestrife species in our region are wetland plants. This is the most common purple-flowered loosestrife. The yellow loosestrifes (*Lysimachia*) belong to a different family, the primroses. Other names: spiked loosestrife, spiked willow-herb, long purples, black blood.

Charles Darwin spent much time and effort analyzing the insect pollination scheme of purple loosestrife. The bisexual flowers display three separate forms, each on a separate plant or clone. Each form is based on the length of male and female floral parts. Darwin's experiments proved that pollen from a stamen of one length functions best on a pistil of the same length. The flowers can also self-fertilize. This happens in the medium-length form more often than in the others. A single plant may produce three thousand individual flowers. Thirteen hours of daylight are required for flowering to begin. Blooming

DABJOLA/SHUTTERSTOCK.COM

begins at the bottom of the spike and moves upward as the season progresses. The last flowers of the season bloom at the very top.

Purple loosestrife produces prolific seed. Each seed capsule contains about one hundred seeds, which are gradually dispersed by wind in the fall and winter. In water, the seeds immediately sink. Not until they germinate do they rise and float, dispersed as tiny seedlings.

Most perennial wetland herbs reproduce mainly by spreading rhizomes, but purple loosestrife colonies originate largely from seed. Each stem dies back to its base in the fall; new stems arise in spring from root buds, which form only slightly larger clones each year. In addition, new plants can sprout from broken green stems that have fallen.

Purple loosestrife thrives in fen areas but can also tolerate slightly acid soil. It does best not in water but on land that rises no more than inches, or a few feet at most, above the water table. Thus, in dense vegetation along watercourses, its zonal growth tells you quite accurately where land begins. The plant prefers full sunlight but can tolerate light shading.

Major flower pollinators include bumblebees, honeybees, leafcutting bees, and carpenter bees. Butterfly pollinators, such as the European cabbage butterfly, common sulphur, and wood nymph, are also frequently seen. Biological control agents, mainly various beetle species, have been used with unimpressive results to control this plant in Europe. Birds rarely consume the seeds, but they probably play some role in dispersing the plant by carrying seeds in mud clinging to their feet.

An alien species from Europe, purple loosestrife arrived on our shores sometime before 1850, probably via immigrant gardeners and ships' ballast. Until the turn of the century, however, it remained localized and nonaggressive. This plant thrives in disrupted wetland habitats, so subsequent dredging and development of inland waterways, canals, and ditches provided numerous highways for its travel. It soon began spreading across the continent, competing with and often eliminating much of our native wetland vegetation by its dense, colonial growth. Today thousands of wetland acres have been taken over by this colorful loosestrife, and its spread continues. It remains essentially unstoppable.

The situation is an easy one for environmentalists to deplore. This plant, like few others, stirs our alien prejudice. Our native cattails, for example, are almost as rudely aggressive and competitive in many wetland areas as purple loosestrife. Yet, because cattails obviously "belong here," they seldom evoke the same outraged feelings against their existence.

Plants, after all, go and grow only where habitats invite them. And once they begin to establish themselves, a series of complex adjustments involving the entire habitat community also begins. There are winners and losers. But the weight of evidence shows that after a vigorously aggressive phase, invasions usually run their course. What usually happens is that community self-regulating mechanisms—herbivory, parasitism, diseases—begin to limit and restrict the invasive dominance of a species. Eventually it becomes integrated into changed but relatively stable community structures that display their own survival strategies. This process operates on its own schedule, requiring time and seasons. With the spread of purple loosestrife, we have (at least) new opportunities to witness the phases of an ever-recurring ecological process.

Despite its aggressive habit and low wildlife value, purple loosestrife is not universally despised. Gardeners and landscapers use it for colorful plantings (deep rose and clear pink varieties are popular), and beekeepers rank its dark honey high in taste and sweetness.

The first-century Greek physician Dioscorides bestowed the name *lytron,* signifying blood or gore from a wound, on this plant. As "dead men's fingers" and "long purples," it appears in Shakespeare's plays.

American natives didn't know the plant, of course, but purple loosestrife teas were popular European folk remedies for stomach upset and sore throat. They were also used for cleansing wounds. Modern pharmacology has found that the plant contains antibiotic properties. As an astringent, it also stops bleeding.

Skunk-Cabbage
(*Symplocarpus foetidus*)

PAUL MOZELL/SHUTTERSTOCK.COM

Arum family. Low, colonial herb in mud of swamps, woods, stream borders. Its streaked, mottled purple, shell-like spathe that envelops the round, fleshy flower cluster; large, broad leaves; and unpleasant odor identify this common wetland plant. Other names: swamp cabbage, meadow cabbage, foetid hellebore, skunk-weed.

Skunk-cabbage is probably the earliest flowering plant to emerge from the ground. Its rolled-up, spirelike spathe often pokes up through February snow. The plant is actually well advanced by then; emerging cone-shaped buds of next year's growth often begin to show in early fall. It is usually in flower by March or April, its bulging spathe enclosing the knoblike flower cluster, called the spadix, like a monk's cowl. The spathe gaps open on one side, allowing entry to insects. Lavender, flesh-colored flowers on the surface of the spadix are bisexual and pollinated by some of the earliest flying insects of the year.

In late winter, as the flower buds enlarge, they increase in temperature, often melting snow around them. When the surrounding ground and air warm to above freezing, respiration of the spadix produces a quite constant warmth of about 72 degrees F, which the surrounding, air-pocketed spathe helps maintain. The tiny flowers on the spadix have no petals. Their female parts mature first; they begin to bloom at the spadix top and progress downward. By the time the lowermost flowers emerge, the upper ones have produced their male parts and are beginning to pollinate. Male flowering likewise descends on the spadix. After pollination, the spadix bends toward the ground on its stalk, the spathe disintegrates, and the bright green leaves push up in vertical, rolled-up spires. Soon after opening, the cabbagelike leaves increase in size on their thick stalks, often becoming two feet long or longer by early summer. The smaller leaves are easily confused with marsh marigold leaves, but the latter leaves are slightly toothed whereas skunk-cabbage leaves have smooth margins.

The spadix, turning black with age, now becomes a compound fruit. The heavy, marble-size seeds are released as the old spadix decomposes. Seeds usually germinate within a few feet of the parent plant. Five to seven years of growth are required before the rhizome becomes large enough to permit flowering. The thick, vertical rhizomes center a radiating mass of long, descending roots that resemble earthworms. These roots contract slightly each year, pulling the rhizome and the entire plant downward several millimeters, thus keeping the surface parts close to the ground. The rhizomes, which sometimes grow two feet long, may be quite long-lived, perhaps surviving indefinitely in stable habitats. Some skunk-cabbage rhizomes have apparently persisted for centuries.

Look for skunk-cabbage at just about any time of year—flowers in early spring, leaves and fruits in summer and fall, emerging shoots in fall and winter—in the muddiest areas of marshes, fens, and shorelines. The plant is probably the first pollen source in spring for honeybees, which do not fly well in air that's below 65 degrees F but are sometimes seen inside skunk-cabbage plants when air temperature drops as low as 42 degrees. The warmth in successive spathes, it is theorized, serves as a "heat stop" for the bee, allowing it to restore energy for flights between spathes and to and from the hive. Sometimes bees become trapped in narrow-gapped spathes.

Skunk-cabbage is doubly misnamed; it is unrelated to cabbage and other mustards, and its odor only slightly resembles mammal musk. Various descriptions usually include the words putrid or foul. Thoreau noted its resemblance to the odor of certain currants. Whatever odor one associates with the plant, its volatile, odoriferous chemicals mimic putrescence successfully enough to attract insects that specialize in scavenging dead and fecal matter.

Like most arums, skunk-cabbage is full of calcium oxalate crystals that produce an intensely acrid, burning sensation if eaten raw. Grazing mammals usually let it alone. Only thorough drying, not boiling, removes this toxic property. After treatment, the leaves can be added to soups or stews and the rhizomes ground into a cocoalike flour.

American natives found many internal and external medicinal uses for the plant. Menomini tribes also used the rhizome in combination with other herbs as an ingredient for tattooing the skin as a talisman against disease. Physicians once valued the dried rhizomes (under the drug name Dracontium) as an antispasmodic for treatment of epilepsy and asthma. They also used the leaves as poultices for skin irritations.

This same species occurs in Japan and other locales in eastern Asia, its probable origin. Paleobotanists believe that the plant migrated to North America via the Pleistocene land bridge that existed at several times between Siberia and Alaska. This makes skunk-cabbage—like humans—a relative newcomer to our continent.

Smartweeds
(*Polygonum* species)

T. TRAVIS BROWN

Smartweed family. Emergent and shoreline herbs in marshes, shallow water, lake and pond margins. Recognize smartweeds by their swollen stem joints encased by sheaths and pink or white flower spikes at the top. Some fifty species of *Polygonum* exist in the region, but only about ten of these favor wet habitats. The most common include water smartweed *(P. amphibium)*, with short, stubby flower clusters and floating leaves, or erect stems on muddy shorelines; swamp smartweed *(P. coccineum)*, equally variable in growth habit but with long flower spikes; and mild water-pepper *(P. hydropiperoides)*, with sparsely flowered spikes and fringed sheaths at joints. Other names: jointweeds; water persicaria, amphibious bistort, willowweed, ground-willow, heartsease, red-shanks *(P. amphibium)*. (The dry-land species of this large genus are called knotweeds, showing flowers in the leaf angles.)

Pink, emergent flower spikes of smartweeds, standing several inches above the water surface in large, colorful colonies, are familiar sights along shorelines in summer. Water and swamp smartweeds adapt well to changing water levels, appearing in aquatic forms with floating leaves or as erect, land-based plants in muddy habitats—true botanical amphibians.

Smartweeds display so many variants that botanists puzzle whether certain of them are true species or mere forms and varieties of other species. Almost every plant manual treats them differently—in itself a significant indicator of plants undergoing rapid evolutionary changes. Botanists are likewise uncertain as to what extent many smartweeds are natives or aliens introduced from Europe and Asia.

Smartweed flowers, usually pink but with white variants, are bisexual and insect pollinated. Lacking petals, the tiny flowers on the spike show colored sepals. Both annual and perennial species exist. Annuals, including arrow-leaved tear-thumb, common smartweed, and nodding smartweed, rely exclusively on seed production to reproduce. Perennials such as water smartweed, swamp smartweed, and mild water-pepper reproduce by means of extensive rhizome systems.

In water smartweed, each new shoot from the rhizome is able to sprout new shoots if broken off. Water and swamp smartweeds display two kinds of flowers, each on separate plants: long styles with short stamens or short styles and long stamens. Smartweed seeds are achenes.

Water smartweed is probably the most aquatic species, thriving in shallow water and rarely flowering on land. Mild water-pepper also grows in water but can tolerate situations where water levels are sporadic or seasonal. Other species favor shoreline habitats.

Insects gain little from smartweed flowers. Both pollen and nectar quantities are sparse. Yet, in one seasonal study of mild water-pepper, sixty-nine insect species were recorded as visitors. Pollination is chiefly effected by small bees and flies. Foliage feeders include several caterpillars. Yellowish-green, sluglike caterpillars are probably bronze copper butterflies.

"Any aquatic area bordered by extensive growth of smartweed is likely to be popular with ducks," reported one research team. Indeed, smartweeds are the wetland counterparts of ragweeds in their value and importance to many seed-eating birds, especially fall migrants and winter resident species. Only bulrushes rival them as a seed source for wildlife.

Smartweed leaves have a peppery taste ranging from mild and pleasing to acrid and inedible, depending on the species. For cooked greens or eating raw in salads, mild water-pepper is one of the best—and common smartweed one of the worst. Juice from stems and leaves can cause skin irritation in allergic individuals. These plants provided medicinal teas and tonics for generations of both Old and New World users, chiefly as astringents for external poultices and for internal bleeding. Rutin, a glycoside ingredient found also in tobacco and buckwheat leaves, strengthens blood capillaries, acting as a coagulant to prevent or stop bleeding.

Sundews
(*Drosera* species)

MARTIN FOWLER/SHUTTERSTOCK.COM

Sundew family. Tiny, ground-level herbs in bogs and fens. Recognize sundews by their radiating rosettes (about three or less inches across) of small leaves covered with reddish, glandular hairs that exude a sticky juice. Of some seven species in east-central North America, the most common are round-leaved sundew *(D. rotundifolia)* and spatulate-leaved sundew *(D. intermedia)*, differentiated by their leaf shapes. Other names: rosa solis, dew-plant, eyebright, youthwort, lustwort, red-rot, moor-grass; long-leaved or oblong-leaved sundew, love-nest sundew *(D. intermedia)*.

Together with the unrelated pitcher-plants and bladderworts, sundews make up the third common group of American insect-trapping plants. Their trapping method is different from those of the other two. Sundew's "flypaper trap" enmeshes insects in a sticky secretion, which glistens like morning dewdrops at the ends of the leaves' tentacles. An insect, visually attracted by the crystal droplets, alights on the leaf and becomes stuck. Its struggles trigger movement (actually an extremely rapid cell growth) in the tentacles, which begin folding over the insect body in about a minute, further securing it. Insect prey may be entirely enfolded in twenty minutes. The leaf itself also gradually rolls inward over the prey.

Sundew tentacles only move if they are touched several times in a few seconds; a falling leaf, dead insect, or inanimate particle will not trigger the mechanism or will trigger it only sluggishly. Charles Darwin, who thoroughly studied these plants, suggested that such a selective response was an energy-saving adaptation, preventing wasted movement of the tentacles.

Having captured the insect, the tentacles release an anesthetic that seems to stupefy the prey, along with digestive enzymes that dissolve the creature's internal organs. This dissolved nutrient is absorbed by the tentacles and transported into the plant's vascular system. The entire digestive process, leaving only the insect's exoskeleton, may take a week or more. A single leaf contains up to one hundred tentacles, though usually less.

In summer, the bisexual, insect-pollinated flowers, white or pink, arise in one-sided clusters on a stalk surmounting the leaf rosette. Flowers open one at a time along the linear cluster. The chafflike seeds occur in capsules. Although insect prey is not vital to a sundew's survival, sundews that succeed in trapping insects tend to thrive and flower to a greater extent. The plants also reproduce vegetatively from buds on horizontal or subsurface stems. Often on spatulate-leaved sundew, the living leaf rosette crowns a series of previous rosettes, now dead, that remain on the stem. Sundew leaves are highly vulnerable to frost; they die back in the fall—and sometimes too after several false starts in cold spring weather.

The chief flower pollinators are small insects: flies and gall wasps. Midges and other small flies also constitute the plants' main prey. But many other insects also fall victim to the sticky tentacles. Fairly common ones include marsh beetles and crane flies. Moths often escape capture because of the detachable scales on their wings, which also protect them from adhesion to spider webs. But even large butterflies frequently become trapped by their legs.

As might be expected, sundews remain remarkably free from insect attack. One moth caterpillar, however, feeds with impunity on the tentacles from beneath, consuming the end droplet, the glandular bulb, and then the tentacle itself. This plume moth larva, active only at night, may denude leaves of all their tentacles, then eat the leaf itself. It also scavenges partially digested insect remains on the leaf. Its long bristles apparently function as "feelers," enabling it to avoid bodily contact with the sticky droplets. This caterpillar often attaches its cocoon lengthwise on the flower stalk.

More than ninety sundew species exist worldwide, some of them much larger than our native sundews. In American wetlands, sundews are fragile species and do not tolerate much human encroachment. Most states legally protect them.

Folk remedies using these plants once abounded, though American natives apparently made little use of them. Sundew teas were especially recommended for respiratory and hypertensive ailments. They were also taken as an aphrodisiac. External applications are said to cure pimples, corns, and warts—a function of sundew's proteolytic enzymes. Plumbagin, another constituent, is an antibiotic. Many better medicines for these purposes now exist, however. Sundews should not be collected for any purpose.

Swamp Loosestrife
(*Decodon verticillatus*)

Loosestrife family. Arching shrub or herb in swamps. Recognize swamp loosestrife by its arching growth habit; lavender, bell-shaped summer flowers tufted in the upper leaf angles; and paired or three-whorled leaves. Other names: Water-willow, whorled loosestrife, swamp willow-herb, grass poly.

This is our most common native loosestrife, quite unlike the alien purple loosestrife in habit and appearance. Botanists can't decide whether it's shrub or herb; it has woody stems, but unlike those of true shrubs, they die back in the fall. Most elect to call it "shrubby" and let it go at that. Its distinctively ridged, arching stems, three to nine feet long, are thickened and spongy at the base; ridged stems in plants can support more weight than round ones of the same diameter. On land, stem tips root where they touch the mud, sending up another arching stem in a sort of looping, leapfrog growth that may extend one plant over many feet. More often, however, these are land-building plants of the shoreline edge. Typically arching over the

KRIS LIGHT

water, their tips float, expand, and send down roots. Dense tangles of their roots trap, anchor, and build up sediments, in which other emergent vegetation takes root. Led by vanguard loosestrife, the shoreline advances, in some places by a foot or more each summer.

The flower is bisexual, insect pollinated, and (like its close relative) trimorphous. It produces urn-shaped seed capsules. Like most wetland plants, however, swamp loosestrife reproduces most vigorously by the vegetative means mentioned. "Those in the water do not generally bloom," noted Thoreau.

Look for swamp loosestrife on shrubby shoreline edges. Buttonbush and shrub willows are frequent associates. On offshore edges, swamp loosestrife roots trap soil, providing rooting areas for arrowheads, pickerelweed, and rushes. Swamp loosestrife is generally a good indicator of soft, unstable ground—places to step carefully if you're exploring a swamp or water's edge.

Dodder is a parasitic seed plant that often twines around swamp loosestrife, tapping into its stems. Dodder vines draping and enmeshing swamp loosestrife in the fall resemble heavy, yellow cobwebs when seen from a distance. This parasitism seems to affect loosestrife abundance very little. Bumblebees, honeybees, and other bees are the usual pollinators. Tiger swallowtail butterflies often alight on the flowers and pollinate them. A large, green caterpillar with a rear "horn" found feeding on the leaves may be a hydrangea sphinx moth. Mallards, ducks, teal, and wood ducks eat the seeds. Muskrats relish the thickened submersed stems.

Swamp Milkweed
(*Asclepias incarnata*)

KRIS LIGHT

Milkweed family. Tall herb (two to four feet) in swamps, ditches, along pond margins. Its domed, pink or purplish-red flower cluster atop the plant and its narrow, mostly opposite leaves and slender, erect seed pods identify this milkweed. Most other milkweed species occupy dry upland fields or woods. Other names: rose milkweed, white Indian hemp, water nerveroot, water silkweed.

The small but complex flowers of milkweeds show distinctive bent-back petals with both male and female flower parts united in a single central structure. Surrounding this organ are five clasping hoods enclosing five incurved, nectar-secreting horns. The pollen occurs in waxy masses called pollinia, which adhere to the legs of insects. Struggling to gain footing on the flower, an insect steps into one or more of the small slots in the flower base, where the pollinia ensnare the leg with filaments. Carrying these pollinia "saddlebags" as it leaves the flower, the insect similarly struggles in another flower, often breaking the pollinia and thus effecting cross-fertilization. Milkweeds are called obligate outbreeders because self-pollinated flowers (including flowers pollinated from others in the same cluster) are rarely fertile.

If each flower were to develop into a seedpod, the plant would be loaded with them. As it is, only about five pods (containing some fifty seeds) develop from about seventy-five or so flowers per plant. The control mechanisms are unknown. Each seed has a tuft of hairs, which assists dispersal by wind and water.

Swamp milkweed favors "wet feet," often rising in shallow water marginal to shores or swamp pools. In contrast to common milkweed, its rhizomes are small and produce few cloning stems. Like most milkweeds, it requires full sunlight.

The major pollinators are bumblebees and honeybees, though other insects also pollinate the plant. Among these are thread-waisted wasps and butterflies, including the monarch, swallowtails, mulberry wing skipper, and black dash skipper. Watch for all of these insects carrying the aforementioned yellow pollinia on their legs. Insects may get their feet or tongues trapped in the pollinia slots; the sight of dead insects hanging from milkweed flowers is not uncommon.

Milkweeds, like goldenrods, center a sizable community of insects that occur quite exclusively on these plants. Several of them (especially the beetles and bugs) display bright warning colorations. These insects sequester the milkweed toxins in their bodies and thus are often unpalatable or poisonous morsels to bird predators, who learn to avoid them.

The alkaloid compounds containing cardiac glycosides found in the milky latex of milkweeds are toxic and distasteful to most vertebrates. This feature hardly prevented some notable masochistic attempts to find medicine in the plant. "The root tea is said to drive the worms from a person in one hour's time," reported an observer of the Meskwaki tribe. Indeed, such tea is strongly laxative and also induces vomiting. American colonists used it in various concoctions for a variety of ailments, but milkweeds remain dangerous plants to sample for experimental remedies.

With repeated boilings, young shoots, top leaves, and flowers are edible and, it is said, tasty, but the similarities of young plants to highly toxic dogbanes and butterfly-weed advise against collecting them for food. American natives also braided the stem fibers for strong cordage.

less difficult. Inside the flower now, a sterile fifth stamen obstructs nectary access to all but the larger, long-tongued insects, which can reach over the bar. The flower's sexual organs all project from the inner roof of the tube.

The oldest flowers are at the base of the cluster. They often become ragged and unkempt as new flowers above them open through late summer and early fall. The winged fruits, produced in capsules, are dispersed by wind. Turtlehead usually grows isolated or in small clumps from perennial rhizomes.

Turtlehead is the foremost larval food plant of the Baltimore butterfly. The spiny, orange, black-banded caterpillars emerge from hibernation in spring and feed singly on the leaves, where they also pupate in suspended, whitish cocoons. Then they transform into the black, orange-spotted adult butterflies, which seldom visit the flowers. They lay crimson masses of eggs on leaf undersides. Turtlehead's chief pollinators are bumblebees. Sometimes they partially destroy the flower tube by biting their way in from the side.

Leaf teas of turtlehead, exceedingly bitter, were staples of folk medicine introduced by similar native usage. Healers of various stripe often prescribed them for jaundice and liver ailments, as well as for worms and as an appetite stimulant and laxative. Decoctions of the plant were applied externally to tumors, herpes, and hemorrhoids.

Water-Hemlock
(*Cicuta maculata*)

KRIS LIGHT

Parsley family. Tall herb in wet meadows, fens, and swamps. Features of water-hemlock include its smooth, purple-streaked stem; compound, reddish-tinged leaves; and white, umbrella-shaped flower clusters. Other names: spotted cowbane, spotted water-hemlock, beaver-poison, musquash-root, poison parsnip.

Many plants of the parsley family look much alike. Water-hemlock grows up to six feet tall, its flowerhead much resembling that of the common Queen Anne's lace, except it is looser and the clusters are more widely spaced ("like so many constellations or separate systems in the firmament," wrote Thoreau). The plant even more closely resembles water-parsnip, which (unlike Queen Anne's lace) grows in the same habitats. Flowers can be unisexual or bisexual. Water-hemlock also reproduces vegetatively from its tuberous roots.

Some authorities believe this to be the most violently toxic green plant in North America; eating even small amounts is usually fatal to humans and other mammals. The deadly poison is the alkaloid cicutoxin, a yellowish, oily liquid contained in all parts of the plant (except, probably, the flowers).

Flowers and nectar attract bees, wasps, and butterflies—many more of these insects, according to some accounts, than visit most parsley family flowers. Almost all parsleys are favored food plants of black or parsnip swallowtail butterfly caterpillars. American natives, well acquainted with this plant, knew that it killed beavers that fed on it.

Indians generally avoided this plant except when seeking it deliberately for suicide (a not uncommon practice even among presettlement tribes), which the plant accomplished swiftly, if painfully. Use of the root for poultices and mixing the seeds with tobacco for smoking are also recorded.

This is not the same plant that Socrates took in a deadly potion—that was probably the closely related poison-hemlock, which has somewhat less violent toxic effects. Many parsley family plants are edible and tasty, but unless you are completely familiar with the wild-growing members of this group, it is wisest to sample none. Accidental deaths (many of them children) have resulted from only casual tasting of this plant, usually when it was mistaken for a similar-appearing parsnip or carrot. Without immediate, aggressive treatment, fatality is almost certain.

Water Lilies
(*Nymphaea odorata* and *Nuphar* species)

ALMONDD/SHUTTERSTOCK.COM

Water lily family. Floating-leaved and emergent herbs in ponds, slow streams. Three common species are fragrant water lily *(Nymphaea odorata)*, yellow pond lily *(Nuphar advena)*, and common spatterdock *(Nuphar advena)*. Recognize water lilies by their broad, platterlike, surface-floating or (in spatterdock) emergent leaves and their large, floating, bright white or yellow flower heads. Other names: white, American, or sweet-scented white water lily, water-nymph, water-cabbage, alligator-bonnet *(N. odorata)*; yellow water lily, beaver-root, cow lily *(N. advena)*.

A pond seems hardly a pond without water lilies in spring and summer bloom and covering the water surface with their broad leaves from spring to fall. Leaves of fragrant water lily are usually rounder and broader-notched where the leafstalk connects than the more oval, narrow-notched yellow pond lily leaves. Nonfloating, wide-notched common spatterdock leaves stand erect several inches above the water surface. Thus, even without flowers present, these water lilies are all fairly simple to differentiate.

Some aquatic ecologists believe that all floating leaves have tended to evolve toward circular, untoothed shapes. Such shapes (manifested most obviously in water lilies) provide maximum protection against tearing from wind and wave action. Water lily leaves, leathery in texture, also resist penetration by heavy rains and hail. The upper leaf surface bears a heavy, waxy, water-repellent surface cell layer. Also, in contrast to aerial plant leaves, the air pores are located on the upper, air-exposed surface rather than the underside. Leaf undersides and stems bear a thick, slippery, mucous coating, which probably protects against some aquatic herbivores and also abrasion when plants rub together in waves or currents. The red pigment on leaf undersides of white water lily is believed to raise leaf temperature slightly above the water temperature, thus speeding transpiration.

Water lily stems, rising from thick rhizomes in the bottom mud, are intriguing marvels of plant engineering. Several air-filled, tubular passages called lacunae run throughout the stems, giving them buoyancy. But the enclosed air is not static; studies of yellow water lily have shown that the stems conduct gases both to and from the leaves. These "internal winds" flow under considerable pressure. Down in the sediment, carbon dioxide and methane diffuse into the lacunae and travel upward to older leaves, "spraying" into the air from the leaf stomata. In younger leaves, the stomata draw air into the leaf lacunae, whence it travels down to the buried rhizome and roots. The process works like a pump; pressure generated in the young leaves is vented finally through the less-pressurized older leaves, which serve as the transport system's exhaust.

Fragrant water lily and yellow pond lily flowers vary somewhat in anatomy and form. Fragrant displays numerous white petals surrounding the central, golden-yellow sexual parts. The large flower, sometimes five inches across, opens in the morning, closes in afternoon. In yellow pond lily, six large, yellow, overlapping sepals surround the small, yellow, stamenlike petals, which themselves surround the central barrel-shaped, yellow-green "brandy bottle" of sexual parts. This flower is often odorless.

Spatterdock's six sepals are green outside, yellow or purplish inside, and form a barely open spherical cup when it first blooms; the triangular aperture over the disklike stigma is just wide enough to admit a pollen-bearing insect. Next day, after it has been fertilized, the flower widely expands, exposing the now-mature anthers with their pollen ready to shed on insect visitors.

After fertilization and pollen release, the flower closes and its stem begins to coil, pulling the flower head underwater. There the seeds (some six or seven hundred of them) mature in about a month inside the fleshy aril, which breaks off, floats to the surface, and, after a time, releases the seeds. The seeds sink, germinating the following spring. In fragrant water lily, the new plant requires three years to flower; it remains submersed the first year and produces only floating leaves the second year.

Few flowers attract as many insects as the fragrant water lily. Chief pollinators include honeybees and small halictid bees. During first-day blooming, you may find halictid bees drowned in the small bowl of liquid atop the concave pores. Insects land on the surrounding palisade wall of flexible stamens, which bend inward under the insects' weight, causing them to fall into the stigmatic fluid. Most of them escape, however.

For certain mammal herbivores, these plants are important. Muskrats consume the rhizomes and other plant parts. Beavers relish them, sometimes storing the rhizomes. (In summer, beavers in some areas feed almost exclusively on aquatic vegetation rather than woody growth). Their damming activities create water lily habitat, and they widely disperse the plants by dropping rhizome fragments hither and yon. Porcupines also relish the plants, as do white-tailed deer. For moose, water lilies are principal foods.

American natives made extensive use of the extremely astringent rhizomes. Medicinal teas treated bowel disorders, and skin poultices helped stop bleeding and heal cuts, sores, and swellings. For food, they cooked the young leaves and unopened flower buds and fried or parched the oil-rich seeds. The rhizomes of yellow water lilies can also be eaten after plenty of boiling. Water lily pollen grains bear sharp, microscopic spikes, sometimes causing irritation to human nasal passages.

Related Old World water lily and lotus species have carried much religious and symbolic significance throughout history. Water lily petals decorated the funeral wreaths of Egyptian pharaohs, and various white water lilies became emblems of purity, virtue, and innocence—the more so because they arise from the slime and mud.

Water-Plantain
(*Alisma plantago-aquatica*)

KRIS LIGHT

Water-plantain family. Emergent and shoreline herbs of ponds, marshes, ditches, and stream margins. Recognize water-plantain by its long-stalked, broadly oval, parallel-veined leaves and taller flower stalk with whorled branches bearing tiny, white, three-petaled flowers. Other names: mad-dog weed, devil's spoons.

Like the related arrowheads, water-plantain adapts its growth form to its aquatic circumstances. In shallow-water habitats, it may develop lax, narrow, ribbonlike leaves and broader floating leaves; in its muddy shoreline habitats, the leaves stand erect. The inconspicuous flowers, resembling miniature arrowhead flowers, are bisexual and insect pollinated. The male stamens ringing the central stigma point outward, thus minimizing chances of self fertilization. To obtain nectar droplets at the stamen bases, insects landing on the stigma must subsequently brush against the pollen-bearing anthers. Nutlets are produced in a ringlike head. The plant rises from perennial tuberlike corms.

Syrphid flies are probably the major pollinators. Foliage and stem invertebrate feeders are generally the same as for arrowheads. Water scorpions—brownish, elongated, predatory bugs that resemble walkingsticks—lay eggs in submersed water plantain stems.

Surface-feeding ducks such as mallards, pintails, teal, and the diving scaups feed on the seeds to some extent, as do ring-necked pheasants. This plant is not, however, a major food source for wildlife.

Modern medical research has verified the therapeutic properties and diuretic effects of water-plantain root in kidney and other ailments. American natives knew about these benefits and drank root teas of the plant for urinary disorders and lung ailments. They also used external poultices of the root for bruises and wounds. Animal experiments with this plant indicate that its medical usages may extend to lowering blood pressure and glucose levels and inhibiting fat storage in the liver. The leaves redden and irritate the skin when rubbed on, sometimes a useful treatment for certain sores or swellings.

Wild Calla
(*Calla palustris*)

T. TRAVIS BROWN

Arum family. Herb in shallow water and swamps and on pond and bog edges. Identify wild calla by its golden, club-shaped flowerhead clasped by a white bract and its broad, heart-shaped leaves. Other names: water-arum, bog-arum, arum lily, swamp robin, female dragon, water dragon, marsh calla.

All of the arums have tiny flowers crowded on a blunt, vertical "club" sheathed or hooded by a modified leaf. This leaf in wild calla is petal-like and white with somewhat rolled edges. Calla's yellow florets are mostly bisexual, but a cluster of exclusively male florets often crowns the flowerhead. The flowers are somewhat ill scented. In late summer, the plant becomes more conspicuous with its terminal cluster of bright red berries replacing the flowerhead.

Wild calla often grows in small or large colonies, reproducing vegetatively from flattish green rhizomes as well as by seed. A good place to look for wild calla is on margins of the mineral-rich moats, which often surround sphagnum bogs.

The plants are also quite common in alder swamps.

Pollination is mainly accomplished by midges and other small flies attracted to the plant by its white flag and fetid odor. Pond snails and other aquatic snails also pick up, carry, and deposit pollen as they glide over the floret surfaces.

Most arum fruits will severely burn your mouth if you taste them. Wild calla's attractive berries—the entire plant, in fact— contain calcium oxalate crystals, which are extremely acrid and irritating to mucous membranes. Crushed berries will also burn and irritate the skin. Thorough drying removes this acrid property, and the dried seeds and rhizomes can be ground to make a nutritious, if not very tasty, flour. The Lapps in northern Europe, however, made a palatable bread of it.

The forest Potawatomi used the pounded root of wild calla as an effective poultice for swellings. Other tribes made a medicinal tea-tonic from the dried rhizome. In England, the rhizomes of the closely related *A. maculatum* provided the source of white starch used to stiffen those huge ruffled collars seen in Elizabethan portraits.

Wild Irises
(*Iris* species)

MARTHA MARKS/SHUTTERSTOCK.COM

Iris family. Herbs in marshes, fens, wet meadows, and upland areas. Recognize the larger blue flag *(I. versicolor)* by its showy, purple-veined blue flower. Yellow iris *(I. pseudacorus)* has a large, all-yellow flower. Both raise erect, straplike, bluish-green leaves, which resemble cattail leaves, though shorter. Other names: blue iris, wild iris, fleur-de-lis, flower-de-luce, flag lily, snake-liver *(I. versicolor)*; water flag *(I. pseudacorus)*.

Some twelve irises (not all of them wetland) species grow wild in east-central North America, but these two are by far the most common. The spectacular flowers are, more literally than most flowers, exhibitionistic "flags" that capture the attention of pollinating insects. Each flower is bisexual. While a single flower stalk may produce several flowers, the flowers bloom sequentially, not all at once. Lines called nectar guides adorn the largest, tonguelike part, which consists of three fused sepals. The three upright parts are the petals, and the curved structures above the sepals hold the sexual parts. An insect pushing beneath this curved entrance (actually the female flower) is "combed" of pollen as it enters, and it also brushes against the pollen-bearing anthers. The female parts face away from the anthers, so the chances of self-pollination are reduced. The fruit, a three-lobed capsule, splits to release the stacked seeds. These can float on water, thus aiding in dispersal.

Irises rise from thick, creeping rhizomes that branch and spread. They typically appear in small, cloning patches, seldom in large, pure stands. New plants usually produce only leaves for the first year or two, so a flowering iris represents more than a season's effort. Irises thrive best in full sunlight, but they can also tolerate light shade.

Flower pollinators are usually large insects such as bumblebees, smaller halictid and other solitary bees, mason bees, digger bees, and syrphid flies. Common insect residents in iris flowers include thrips and the flower beetle *Trichiotinus piger*, a pollen feeder. Several nonpollinating nectar feeders are frequent flower visitors. These include two orange-brown, medium-sized butterflies: Harris' checkerspot and the bronze copper. Several yellowish skippers are also common visitors.

Irises and rainbows have ancient connections. In Greek mythology, Iris was the rainbow, a messenger goddess designated to transport women's souls to the Elysian fields after death. Colonial France's blue national flag during the years of early American exploration was nicknamed the fleur-de-lis because of its iris symbol. The significance of this flower for the French originated as far back as the first century C.E., when it adorned the banners of Gaul. Louis VII, the Crusader king, adopted the iris as his personal emblem, and the fleur-de-Louis became the "flower of chivalry" with "a sword for its leaf and a lily for its heart," wrote John Ruskin. Napoleon later discarded the symbol as a royal anathema (and replaced it with some iris pollinators, golden bees). Yellow iris, a European native, escaped from colonial cultivation into our wetlands. In early Christianity, yellow iris became associated with the Virgin Mary.

Like all irises, the native *I. versicolor* is toxic to humans and cattle. Rhizomes contain irisin, an acrid substance used to produce the drug iridin, and are exceedingly bitter. American natives brewed small fragments of the rhizome for drastically powerful cathartics and emetics. They also used them as poultices for external wounds and sores. Various tribes used the leaves as sources of green dye and for weaving mats and baskets. The Ojibwa carried pieces of the root as charms against snakebite, believing the scent protected them.

Woodlands

SHAIITH/SHUTTERSTOCK.COM

Bellworts
(*Uvularia* species)

MELINDA FAWVER/SHUTTERSTOCK.COM

Lily family. Herbs in moist woods and thickets. These spring ephemerals show nodding, bell-like, yellow flowers. Parallel-veined leaves occur in different arrangements for the three main species: perfoliate bellwort *(U. perfoliata)*, large-flowered bellwort *(U. grandiflora)*, and sessile bellwort *(U. sessilifolia)*. Other names: merrybells, straw bell.

Perfoliate and sessile bellworts prefer acid soils, but the large-flowered species thrives best in limy soils. Bellworts rarely gang together like spring beauty or violets. Instead, these solitary plants rise inconspicuously from slender perennial rhizomes amidst the mosaic of the showier crowds.

Probably because its flower dangles rather than presenting "wide-open sex" to the sun, bellworts give an impression of modesty. The bisexual flowers nevertheless attract pollinating insects with a slight fragrance emanating from the nectaries at the flower base. Rough, dustlike orange particles on the perfoliate's inner flower surface may aid an insect's foothold.

As a six-parted lily, the bellwort is older on the evolutionary scale than the attention grabbers around it. Yet its method is manifestly adequate for its reproduction. Bellwort will never carpet the earth after all, and in that subtlety and grace lies its interest.

Native Americans made an infusion from bellwort rhizomes as a backache treatment and massage lotion for sore muscles. The young shoots, minus the leaves, are edible when boiled like asparagus, as is the rhizome. The great Sweidsh naturalist Linneaus choose bellwort's generic name *Uvularia* because its drooping flowers reminded him of the uvula in the human mouth.

Bloodroot
(*Sanguinaria canadensis*)

KRIS LIGHT

Poppy family. Low herb in moist, humus-rich woodland. Its showy, white flower, only briefly appearing in early spring colonies, is always partially clasped by a single, pale green, lobed leaf, which lasts much longer. Other names: Red puccoon, Indian paint.

The bisexual flower of this spring ephemeral is usually gone by the time seasonal warmth convinces us that spring is not just another winter thaw. This flower produces prodigious amounts of pollen and is usually self-pollinated. This ensures maximum chances for seed production despite unreliable appearance of insect pollinators in early spring. A single flower usually lasts about two days.

Cloning stems rise from a thick perennial rhizome. During the flowering season of two to three weeks you may find stems of the same clone in virtually all phases of development. As the oblong seed case develops, the leaf grows taller to shelter it.

Despite bloodroot's reliance on self-pollination and cloning, its flower shows most of the typical structural invitations and devices for insect pollination. This, when it occurs, is accomplished most often by pollen-collecting bees, notably the solitary halictids and andrenids, plus bumblebees and honeybees. Pollen-eating syrphid flies are also frequent visitors. When mature seed cases are present, look for ant activity; bloodroot seeds are dispersed by ants, and the plant may owe its distribution largely to these seed collectors.

Bloodroot's staining juice (the source of its name), highly toxic if ingested, contains the alkaloid sanguinarine. Native Americans used it not only as a dye for baskets and clothing but also as an insect repellent and facial paint. The Iroquois used it to treat ringworm. Commercially sanguinarine is useful as an antiplaque agent for toothpastes and mouthwashes.

A tea made of the root was a favorite rheumatism treatment among tribal nations of the Mississippi region. American pioneer families used drops of the juice on lumps of sugar for coughs and colds—an uncertain, rather hazardous, remedy.

Canadian Mayflower
(*Maianthemum canadense*)

Lily family. Low herb in moist, shaded woods. One to three alternate, heart-shaped stem leaves, a short terminal cluster of white flowers, and pale red, speckled berries in autumn identify this delicate little plant. Other names: wild (or false) lily of the valley, two-leaved Solomon's seal, bead ruby.

Canadian mayflower is a cloning herb rising from perennial rhizomes and underground extensions. Shade and moderate moisture are the only consistent requirements for this species, which often forms a lush, matlike ground cover in rich woods. Leaves are not invariably two—some individual plants may have only one, others three—but one-leaved plants seldom produce flowers. In most colonies, the one-leaved, sterile plants outnumber the flowering ones, probably diverting energy to them through the subsurface connections. The four-pointed, bisexual flowers are extremely fragrant.

Though related and somewhat similar to the true lily of the valley and three-leaved false Solomon's seal, Canadian mayflower is the only member of its genus found in east-central North America.

KRIS LIGHT

Probably the foremost insect pollinators are bees. Slugs sometimes eat holes in the leaves, and snowshoe hares have also been known to consume the leaves to some extent. The translucent red berries are eaten by ruffed grouse, chipmunks, and white-footed mice. The bittersweet berries, although not poisonous to humans, are not very palatable.

Cleavers
(*Galium aparine*)

Bedstraw family. Herb in shady moist woods and thickets. Whorls of six or eight leaves surround the square, prickly stem at intervals, and the plant generally sprawls in tangles over other vegetation. Some thirty *Galium* species grow in the East, many in dry woods and edges. Most have smooth stems. *G. aparine,* however, is one of the most common. Other names: bedstraw, goosegrass, catchweed, scratchgrass, stickleback.

Its scratchy, recurved prickles are like Velcro, just strong enough to adhere to your shirt if pressed—hence the name cleavers. The fasteners seem not to be a plant defense but rather a means of dispersal. The plant, with its burry twin seed heads, lies ready to hitch a ride on any passing pelt or pants; the stem easily breaks off when pulled.

This *Galium* is an annual, reproducing entirely by seed; such an exclusive reliance on seed reproduction is unusual among woodland plants. The small, white, bisexual flowers rise on short stalks from the leaf whorls. Seeds germinate in the fall, gaining the plant a head start for

KRIS LIGHT

spring growth. This is mainly a plant of beech-maple and oak-hickory forests.

Upper leaves with inrolled edges signify the presence of *Eriophyes galii,* a mite. A gall gnat called the bedstraw midge may produce aborted flower buds. Moths to watch for include the drab brown wave, the common tan wave, and the large lace-border. These are all inchworm or geometer moths whose twiglike caterpillars move by "looping." Webs of the chokecherry tentmaker, a tortricid moth caterpillar, grow to encompass entire branches and tops of shrubs. Masses of these caterpillars may defoliate the plant.

Dutchman's Breeches
(*Dicentra cucullaria*)

TIM MAINIERO/SHUTTERSTOCK.COM

Poppy family. Herb in rich woods. The distinctive flowers of these spring ephemerals are white, yellow-tipped, and double-spurred like upside-down leggings. The feathery, gray-green leaves are finely cut and many-lobed. Other names: white hearts, soldier's caps, ear-drops.

Two of the four petals are united to form the two-spurred bisexual flower, with the other two petals inside and projecting liplike over the stamens. The two horns or "breeches" contain the nectaries. These are not quite so difficult for insect access as the similarly upended wild columbine, but they still require long, specialized mouth parts. Flower clusters, rising on separate stems directly from the root, last for about eleven days. Presence of this woodland perennial, which often grows gregariously from clustered, grainlike tubers just below the surface, indicates a neutral to slightly acid soil rich in humus.

Besides bees, not many insects can successfully manage the pendulous flower structure of Dutchman's breeches. Most insects are much better at working down than climbing up to nectaries. Early-ranging bumblebees are the main nectar feeders and pollinators. Their eight-millimeter-long tongues reach just far enough to secure a drop or two from each "legging," and in so doing, the insects brush against stamens and stigmas. The honeybee, with only a six-millimeter tongue, can't plunge this deeply, but it does collect pollen from the flower. Bumblebees occasionally nip holes through the spurs from outside, thus bypassing the conventional route. The long seedpods, which mature in late spring, open lengthwise. The seeds are widely dispersed by ants.

Leaves of Dutchman's breeches should not be nibbled or used in salads—they contain an alkaloid that can produce a narcotic effect and have been known to kill cattle.

Gaywings
(*Polygala paucifolia*)

KRIS LIGHT

Milkwort family. Low herb in moist, rich woods. Its broad, evergreen leaves that resemble wintergreen and its pink-magenta flower consisting of two flaring, lateral sepals and a bushy, fringed central tube identify this plant. About a score of *Polygala* species occupy various northeastern habitats; this is one of the most common.

Other names: fringed polygala, flowering wintergreen, fringed milkwort, bird-on-the-wing.

Flowers of gaywings superficially resemble pea blossoms. The fringed, central pouch is actually a landing platform for insects, whose weight depresses the pouch and forces the rigid sex organs through a slit at the top and into direct contact with a furry belly. Cross-fertilization is thus achieved.

Like such plants as touch-me-nots and violets, gaywings also develops another kind of flower that never opens and is entirely self-fertilized. This insurance provision produces viable if not genetically diverse seed. Such cleistogamous flowers are pouchlike in shape and located on tiny, subsurface branchlets that can't be seen unless one carefully hunts for them. The fruits of gaywings are small capsules. The plant rises from a slender, perennial rhizome, sometimes a foot long. The leaves turn bronze-red on the plant in winter.

Investigation of how both aerial and cleistogamous seeds are dispersed has revealed an interesting coaction with at least three ant species. Saclike appendages on the seeds contain an oily liquid appealing to the ants. These insects cut the seeds from the ripe capsules and carry them back to their nests. After consuming the oily appendages, the ants discard the seeds in heaps—where a new bed of gaywings may germinate. The plant's flower looks utterly unlike any other milkwort flower. Most others show cloverlike blooms.

Hepaticas
(*Hepatica* species)

KRIS LIGHT

Buttercup family. Low herbs of early spring in the woods. Hepaticas have three-lobed leaves, hairy flower stalks, and white to pink, lavender, or blue flowers. Identify the two most common species—round-lobed hepatica *(H. americana)* and sharp-lobed hepatica *(H. acutiloba)*—by the angularity of their lobe tips. Round-lobed prefers somewhat acidic soil; sharp-lobed is more common on limy soil. Both species often occur in the same woods, however, and the two may hybridize. Other names: liverwort, liver-leaf, squirrel cup, snow trillium, mayflower, blue anemone, kidneywort.

The flowers—some fragrant, some not—show generally the same structure as those of wood anemone; six to twelve lustrous sepals substitute for absent petals. Leaves are evergreen, lasting for a year, and new ones replace the old purplish ones soon after the flower wilts. Flowers close at night and may remain closed during cloudy days. Along with marsh marigold and spring beauty, hepaticas are among the earliest flowers of spring, sometimes appearing before all the snow has melted. Fruits are achenes. Sharp-lobed hepatica is chiefly a resident of beech-maple woodlands.

Hepaticas depend on insects not only for flower pollination but for seed dispersal as well. Early-flying bees and flies are the main pollinators. And the one-seeded achenes are collected and stored by ants. Earlier in the season, however, hepatica's new, densely hairy stems may keep small crawlers such as ants off the plant before the seed has set.

In a simpler age plant shapes and other features were believed to signal, by their resemblances to human body parts, their medicinal uses. It seemed unthinkable, therefore, that hepatica's liver-shaped leaf could have no use for liver ailments. At best, some remedies based on this idea may have been good placebos. At worst, they added toxic trauma to the original illness. Although hepatica leaves have probably never killed anyone, neither have they cured any livers.

Indian Pipe
(*Monotropa uniflora*)

DAN HANSCOM/SHUTTERSTOCK.COM

Heath family. Herb in rich, shady woods. No part of this plant is green; waxy-white, translucent stems, scale-like leaves, and a solitary, nodding white or pinkish flower identify it. Other names: corpse plant, ice plant, ghost flower, bird's nest.

Botanists of an earlier generation, convinced that nature had made a bad mistake, deplored this strange little perennial for its "degenerate morals." How dare a seed plant give up being green and become a parasite! Today, botanists call Indian pipe an epiparasite, for it feeds indirectly from the roots of green plants. Its source of nourishment is subsurface mycorrhizal fungi, which interconnect with the roots of nearby plants and derive nourishment from them. The fungi act as a middleman that processes food delivery to Indian pipe from its green neighbors.

Indian pipe has the basic bisexual flower parts, though its leaves are vestigial, since they carry on no photosynthesis. The terminal waxy flower nods until it is pollinated by an insect. Then it bends erect, forming a dry fruit capsule. The stalk turns black and may last, tough and dry, through winter. Germinating seeds form immediate mychorrhizal bonds, and several stems usually rise together in hooded "ghostly array" from a parent mycorrhizal mat. The plant always grows in shade, never in open sunlight.

Indian pipe's key associates, necessary to its survival, are the subsurface fungi by means of which it obtains nourishment. Look for Indian pipe in densely shaded pine and deciduous woodlands. Identity of the foremost pollinating insects remains largely unknown, though the flower's habitat, drooping position, and pale hue give us some clues about insect types to look for.

One would think that such a plant, given its appearance, must have a vivid folklore history. Instead it has often been mistaken for a strange mushroom. Its common name derives from the plant's supposed resemblance, when in flower, to a peace pipe. To some Native Americans, the clear sap was an eye medicine, believed to be capable of sharpening vision. Whether this use was medicinal or ceremonial (often a false distinction in tribal cultures) remains unclear.

Large-Flowered Trillium
(*Trillium grandiflorum*)

DOUG VINEZ/SHUTTERSTOCK.COM

Lily family. Herb in moist woods. Three broad leaves and three showy petals mark all the trilliums, of which some ten species exist in our area. This species, the largest, most common, and most variable, has a white flower that often turns deep pink as it ages. Other names: white trillium, common trillium, wake-robin, white wood lily.

The spectacular bisexual flowers rise from perennial rhizomes, making the spring woodland floor seem carpeted with lilies. The flowering of a large-flowered trillium, however, requires much longer than for most wildflowers. For at least six years, the plant produces only one-leaf and three-leaf forms before flowering for the first time. From then on, the plant blooms every spring if the habitat remains stable. A single flower lasts about two weeks before turning pink.

The fruit, technically a berry, is a swollen, ridged capsule that bends to one side as it matures. Seed pressure splits it, and the seeds fall out in clusters. Two winters in the soil are required, the first to release root dormancy, the second to release the shoot block. A germinating seed, following a winter in the soil, develops only a small root and won't even send a shoot above ground the first spring.

Often a giant flower or a flower showing an anomalous form will be seen. One April I found a flower consisting of nine petals set in three layers. Such anomalies are believed to result from an infection caused by mycoplasmalike bacteria.

The most abundant colonies of this trillium occur in beech-maple forests. Trout lily is a frequent associate. A commonly observed crab spider on the flowers is the goldenrod spider, a predator on visiting insects. Whitish with two red side stripes, it migrates to goldenrods in summer, where it turns yellowish. The main pollinators are bees and butterflies. Atortricid moth caterpillar feeds on the leaves. When the seeds spill, ants are attracted to an appendage on the seed where it was attached called the strophiole. Ants carry the seeds to their nests, where they eat the strophioles, thus helping to disperse the plant. On the whole, however, the seeds and foliage of trillium are generally unimportant foods for wildlife.

Native Americans used decoctions of the rhizome for various ailments, including ear infections and rheumatism, and as external dressings for inflammation. Trillium species were often used to control bleeding during childbirth. The effect of the solution is mainly astringent. Very young leaves are edible as salad greens but become bitter as they age. This plant is protected by law in some states, however, so should not be picked. Even clipping the leaves and flowers can quickly kill the rhizome, which has taken many seasons to become productive.

Smooth Solomon's Seal
(*Polygonatum biflorum*)

AZURE/SHUTTERSTOCK.COM

Lily family. Herbs in moist woods and thickets. Parallel-veined leaves on an arching stem, paired greenish-yellow flowers dangling beneath the leaves, and dangling blue-black berries in the fall identify smooth Solomon's seal. The false Solomon's seals show similar leaves, but their white flowers (and the fruits) occur in terminal clusters. Also closely similar in form are the twisted-stalks *(Streptopus)*.

The bell-like bisexual flowers of this spring ephemeral are six-parted and insect pollinated. Note that the tubular female style is much shorter than the six pollen-bearing anthers, an arrangement that probably helps prevent self-fertilization. Flower location beneath the leaves protects them from wind and weather. Stems rise from a perennial rhizome that produces a circular scar atop the rootstock after each season's growth so that one may age a plant by its number of scars.

Smooth Solomon's seal thrives in slightly acid soil. It usually grows as a solitary plant, not in colonial groups, though several may be found together. Often you may find both true and false Solomon's seals growing in proximity.

The flowers seem particularly adapted to pollination by bumblebees, though other insects also frequent them. The atortricid moth caterpillar often feeds on the leaves. Various birds consume the berries, thus aiding the plant's distribution, but Solomon's seal is not a major food plant for wildlife.

Though the berries are inedible, the young shoots can be eaten raw or cooked, and the fleshy rhizome can be boiled like a potato. This plant, however, is not usually so numerous that it can tolerate regular harvesting for food. Iroquois and other tribes dried and ground the rhizome to make a sort of bread. The Chippewas made a decoction of it, sprinkling it on hot stones and inhaling the vapors to relieve painful headaches.

The conventional explanation for this plant's ancient name refers to the round scars on the rhizome that, with some imagination, resemble the impressions created by signet rings for wax seals. But English herbalist John Gerard, writing in 1597, believed that the name involved the root's "singular vertue" to "seale up greene wounds." Naturalist Mary Durant has suggested that since Solomon's seal originally referred to the Star of David emblem with its six points, the flower may well have been named for this resemblance and then forgotten. Her theory sounds as plausible as any.

Spreading Dogbane
(*Apocynum androsaemifoium*)

KRIS LIGHT

Dogbane family. Shrubby herb in upland woods and thickets. Its red stems, paired blue-green leaves, nodding, pinkish flowers, and paired seedpods are distinctive. Other names: fly-trap dogbane, honey bloom, bitter root.

The bisexual flowers are traps—not for their proper pollinators, the long-tongued butterflies, but for smaller flies and moths that get caught by their tongues in the flower's V-shaped nectaries. These insects haven't the size and strength to pull out, so they dangle and die. Rose-striped lines inside the flower lead to those sometimes lethal nectaries, which are quite fragrant.

Though adaptable to sunny, open sites, spreading dogbane thrives best in light-shady edge locations, in which it spreads by perennial, horizontal rootstocks. Another clue to dogbane's identity is its acrid, milky sap, similar to that of milkweeds, which oozes from broken stems. It often hybridizes with the closely related Indian hemps, resulting in many mixed forms that are lumped under the name *A. medium.*

Almost anywhere spreading dogbane grows you will find its foremost insect associate, the shiny green and copper-colored dogbane leaf beetle. Resembling the notorious Japanese beetle, it feeds gregariously and almost exclusively on dogbane foliage. The beetles quickly roll off the leaves if disturbed. You may also find their yellowish egg masses on the plant's stems or leaves. Monarch butterfly caterpillars, though primarily milkweed feeders, also feed and pupate on dogbanes. Look for large, yellow-striped caterpillars and green, gold-dotted pupal cases on the plant. The snowberry clearwing, a sphinx moth with projecting rear horn and sphinxlike posture, feeds on dogbane, as does the dogbane tiger moth.

Few if any vertebrate animals consume dogbane. It induces vomiting when ingested. The milky sap contains cymarin, toxic not only to dogs and humans but to livestock and most other mammals. Insects that can synthesize this chemical are themselves toxic, at least in some cases, to creatures that cannot.

Dogbane stem fibers, long and stringy, can be twisted into strong, durable cordage to use for emergency laces and fasteners in the woods. Native Americans found a decoction of the roots useful as a diuretic. Potawatomies and Chippewas also used it as a medication for heart palpitations, and an extract has been employed as a substitute for digitalis.

Spring Beauty
(*Claytonia virginica*)

MARY TERRIBERRY/SHUTTERSTOCK.COM

Purslane family. Herb in moist woods. Its five white or pink petals lined with darker pink veins and its single pair of linear, grasslike leaves identify this spring ephemeral. The Carolina spring beauty *(C. caroliniana)*, occupying somewhat drier habitats, shows similar flowers but much wider leaves. Other names: Claytonia, Quaker ladies, patience.

The flowers range from white through shades of pink. Bisexual and insect pollinated, the male and female parts mature separately, thus reducing the likelihood of self-fertilization. Typically a mature female stigma receives pollen from a younger flower that is still producing it. The flowers, which close at night and during cloudy weather, last only about three days. The pink veins leading to the flower center guide insects to the nectaries; strongly reflected ultraviolet light from the male filaments does the same job. The fruit is a capsule that explosively ejects its seeds—often as far as two feet—by suddenly in-rolling valves.

Spring beauty rises from small, perennial, bulblike corms; the plants often densely carpet the ground. By late spring, the stems have died back, and the plant lives underground the rest of the year. The plant usually appears in flower a few days later than hepaticas, about the same time as bloodroot. Chief pollinators include bumblebees, the solitary bee, bee flies, and butterflies. Only the bulblike corms have much wildlife food value. These are often dug and consumed in spring by chipmunks and white-footed mice.

The corms are edible not only to rodents but to humans as well. Stripped of their skins and prepared in potato fashion, they are tasty. Many must be dug to make a meal, however, and they should be collected only where abundant.

Toothworts
(*Cardamine* species)

Mustard family. Herbs in rich, moist woods. Recognize these spring ephemerals by their opposite leaves, each divided into three leaflets, their terminal clusters of white (fading to pinkish) four-petaled flowers, and their slender, ascending seedpods. The most common species are the two-leaf toothwort *(C. diphylla)* and the cutleaf toothwort *(C. laciniata)*.

A four-petaled, cross-shaped flower often belongs to the large mustard family. Although most mustards favor wet or open, sunny ground, toothworts are among the few that thrive in woodlands. These perennials rise from fleshy rhizomes that show pointed, toothlike (hence the name) projections or constricted, necklacelike tubers.

Flowers are bisexual and insect pollinated, though self-fertilization does occur. A spot at the base of each petal reflects ultraviolet light, visible to bees. A flower lasts about four days. *C. laciniata* blooms earlier and lasts longer than *C. diphylla,* which flowers only briefly in May.

Cut-leaf toothwort appears at about the same time and places as yellow trout lily and the early violets.

KRIS LIGHT

Small pollen-collecting bees (andrenids, halictids) are the chief pollinators. On the foliage, look for solitary, velvety green and yellowish-striped caterpillars. These may be larvae of a butterfly group called whites, most of which feed on plants of the mustard family. The mustard white and Virginia white are two common feeders on toothworts. White-footed mice are the main seed-eaters.

The peppery rhizome can be chopped or ground and used as horseradish or a pungent addition to salads.

Violets
(*Viola* species)

CHARLES BRUTLAG/SHUTTERSTOCK.COM

Low herbs in dry or moist woods, meadows, wetlands. Some seventy-seven species range throughout North America. Most of them are blue-flowered, but there are also yellow, white, and a few purple, pink, and red species. Violets come in one of two groups: the stemmed species, in which leaves and flowers grow on the same stalk, and the stemless group, in which each grows on separate stalks. Most violets have heart-shaped leaves (a notable exception is bird-foot violet, *V. pedata*). The flowers are five-petaled, the lowest petal heavily veined and extending back into a spur. The most common blue, yellow, and white violets are, respectively, the common blue violet (*V. sororia*), the downy yellow violet (*V. pubescens*), and the Canada violet (*V. canadensis*). But the species continually hybridize—trying to identify a violet (especially a blue one) "by the book" often becomes an exercise in frustration.

It's the most visible beginning, this low, blue flame in the woods. I think of it as a pilot light that ignites the entire burst of resurrection we call spring. Violets have two kinds of flowers, one rarely seen. The colored petals of early spring attract pollinating insects, directing them inside the flower by lines called nectar guides. Yet this obvious flower is probably less important to the plant's reproduction than the later, hidden flower. It grows low and close to the root, never opens, and thus exposes no pollen for cross-fertilization. The seed produced from this self-contained flower carries genes only from its sole parent.

Violet plants seem extremely picky about where they will grow. Two plants from separate colonies that look exactly alike may not thrive or even grow in each other's microhabitat. This fastidiousness may be both a survival mechanism and a result of inbreeding. Because the violet that germinates from a self-pollinated seed is a genetic repeat of its sole parent plant, it is already precisely adapted to its own microhabitat. For a genetically distinct plant produced from two parent violets, the situation would be hit-or-miss. Thus violets show that it is sometimes advantageous for an organism not to evolve. The violet's dual means of reproduction guarantees its success in most circumstances.

Seedpods open explosively, sometimes shooting the seeds three or four feet—and sometimes not scattering them at all but holding them in the splayed pods.

Violets rely mainly upon the solitary bees as pollen vectors. Other insect visitors include syrphid flies, bee flies, butterflies, and moths. Bumblebees sometimes bite through the nectar spur of the flower, taking the payoff without performing the service. Irregular holes in the leaves generally indicate caterpillar feeders, most notably two genera of fritillary butterflies. The dark, spiny caterpillars feed only at night. During the day, look beneath the fed-upon plant, in the leaf litter, where they hide. A moth with translucent, pale-yellow wings is probably the beggar, whose caterpillar is an inchworm. Blistered leaves result from their egg laying. Large, ragged holes in leaves combined with trails of slime are signs of slugs. Ants collect seeds from the open pods and carry them to underground nests. It is the oil gland portion of the seed that attracts them. Investigations have shown that violet seeds manipulated by ants germinate faster, producing healthier plants, than seeds that simply fall to the ground.

Most wild violets have only subtle fragrance if any. Rich in vitamins A and C, the leaves may be nibbled raw, used as a salad or cooked green, and when dry, steeped for a tea. Flowers can be candied or made into jam, jelly, or syrup. Some of the yellow violets can be mildly cathartic and have been used as a gentle laxative. Native Americans used a rhizome decoction as an expectorant remedy for coughs and bronchitis. Used as a poultice, violet plants apparently have remedial effects on certain skin cancers, a subject of continuing research.

The sweet violet, blue and fragrant, is a common garden species native to Europe. It was the sacred flower of ancient Athens. Blue violets, the traditional nosegay flowers, symbolized faithfulness between lovers.

White Baneberry
(*Actaea pachypoda*)

KRIS LIGHT

Buttercup family. Herb in rich woods. This plant is most conspicuous in late summer, when its oblong terminal clusters of china-white berries on red stalks, each berry tipped with a dark spot, decorate the forest floor. Other names: doll's eyes, cohosh, necklaceweed, white beads, toadroot.

The white, bisexual flowers, blooming in May and June, contain no nectar but produce plenty of pollen, which attracts bees. All parts of this perennial, especially roots and berries, contain a poisonous cardiac glycoside.

Most of the bees seen on baneberry flowers are halictid species (which include the "sweat bees" that hover around our faces and arms on warm days). These semicolonial ground-nesters collect pollen for feeding their larvae. Baneberry is not a major food for wildlife. Only a few eaten berries may cause severe dizziness and nausea in humans, but a few species of birds, as well as mice and voles, feed on the berries with no ill effects. Observers note that toads seem attracted by the plant's odor.

This plant's name warns of a baneful experience for those who partake of its fruit. But those black-tipped white berries also gave the plant its other familiar name, doll's eyes. The berries yield a black dye when crushed and mixed with alum.

Wild Blue Phlox
(*Phlox divaricata*)

HOLLY KUCHERA/SHUTTERSTOCK.COM

Phlox family. Herb in rich, open woods. Its terminal flower clusters, five pale violet, wedge-shaped petals radiating from a central tube, opposite leaves, and sticky, hairy stem identify phlox. Some seventy species occupy various North American habitats, but the wild blue phlox is probably the most common. The garden phlox *(P. paniculata)*, widely escaped from cultivation, is also frequent. Other names: blue phlox, wild sweet-William.

Wild blue phlox's bisexual flower components are hidden inside the central corolla tube, so this plant obviously requires pollinating insects with specialized mouthparts. After phlox has flowered, the rootstock begins forming horizontal runners, which extend over the ground and remain there through the winter. New phlox stems will sprout from their tips next spring.

Tell phlox flowers from those of the unrelated wild pink by whether the petals are joined at their bases (phlox) or not (pinks). Flowers are pollinated mainly by bumblebees and butterflies feeding on the nectar of the slightly fragrant blooms. Examine the upper stem and flower stems for small trapped insects. The downy, sticky surface often proves a morass for crawling, would-be raiders on the nectaries. Foliage feeders include two-spotted spider mites, tiny sap-sucking arachnids that weave mealy webs beneath and between leaves, often causing them to yellow. The phlox plant bug, orange-red and striped, feeds on new leaves, producing whitish spots, and often deforms buds.

A common pest of many phlox plants is the stalk borer moth, whose brownish caterpillar bores into stems, causing them to wilt and fall over. A small, round hole in the stem may also indicate its presence. Phlox is also vulnerable to tiny nematode parasites called eelworms, which kill leaves and stunt plants.

The Roman scholar Pliny first used the word *phlox* (derived from a Greek word meaning "fire") for a red campion. Linnaeus then switched the designation to what is now phlox, some say because of the torchlike shape of the buds. The name sweet-William is a misnomer for blue phlox. Named for William the Conqueror, sweet William is a variably colored garden annual.

Native Americans made some use of blue phlox, brewing a tea of the plant and drinking it for stomach upsets. They also steeped the roots to make an eyewash solution.

Wild Columbine
(*Aquilegia canadensis*)

Buttercup family. Herb in dry or open woodland. Its drooping flower (red on the outside and yellow within) features five up-ended spurs. The three-lobed leaflets are also distinctive. Cultivated garden columbines are hybrids of this and several other species. Other names: red columbine, meeting house, rock bells.

Its form and color make wild columbine one of our best known and most popular wildflowers, virtually impossible to misidentify. Those long, upturned spurs are nectar repositories. The red tubes are the petals, culminating in the spurs at one end and the flowing, united red sepals at the mouth. The male stamens, maturing before the female pistils, protrude from a central column until all pollen has been discharged; then the pistils elongate. Since individual flowers mature at different rates, this sexual-timing arrangement helps guarantee cross-fertilization (self-fertilization is unlikely anyway, owing to the flower's pendant position).

Plainly these flowers are designed to attract a long tongue

HOLLY KUCHERA/SHUTTERSTOCK.COM

and an eye for red. Note how the tubes contract just below their tips, where the nectar is secreted; this is probably a defense against insects without sufficient equipment to tap so deeply. Following pollination, the flower tilts upright, and the dried ovaries become rattle-boxes in the wind, releasing seeds as they deteriorate.

This is a perennial plant, rising from a stout rhizome. A basal rosette of leaves that develops in late summer or fall stays green over winter, producing the flowering plant in spring. Columbine is an indicator of limy or near-neutral soils, preferring dry over moist sites.

Columbine leafminers feed beneath the leaf epidermis, leaving white trails behind. After their larval existence in the leaves, they emerge as adult flies. A dying plant often indicates the presence of the columbine borer, a moth caterpillar that bores into stems and roots. White, winding trails, very common on columbine leaves, are feeding tunnels of columbine leafminers, larval flies. As well, look for columbine dusky wing butterflies, purplish-winged skippers, hovering over the plant.

Columbine's nectaries are much too deep for most bees to reach, but honeybees and halictid bees often collect pollen from the flowers. Large bumblebees may sometimes penetrate far enough to reach the nectar, but even long-tongued moths and butterflies cannot easily position themselves on the inverted flower to bend their proboscises upward. Small nectar feeders often nip holes in the nectaries from the outside; such robbery is one hazard of being a long-spurred flower.

But this flower's most efficient pollinators and nectar-feeders are hummingbirds, with their needlelike bills and hovering flight. The flower's red color and long spurs indicate an evolved partnership; watch for ruby-throated hummingbirds wherever columbines are in flower.

Flowers are traditional tokens of love and esteem, but the gift of columbine was a token of war between the sexes, a symbol of cuckoldry and deserted lovers. To a woman, the gift was a stunning insult; to a man, it brought bad luck.

The great scientific namer Linnaeus made some strange analogies. He often affixed Latin names to plants based on their supposed resemblances to birds or mammals (has any vertebrate ever been named for its resemblance to a plant?). Thus *Aquilegia,* meaning eagle, refers to the flower spurs, bent like talons at their tips.The name *columbine* refers to another bird, the dove; those same bent spurs were said to resemble the heads of pigeons dunking around a water dish.

Nibble a flower spur for a sweet taste of nectar, but don't chew on the leaves—they contain enough prussic acid to induce an unpleasant narcotic effect on some.

Wild Geranium
(*Geranium maculatum*)

MALACHI JACOBS/SHUTTERSTOCK.COM

Geranium family. Herb in woodlands. Five-parted hairy leaves and five rose-purple petals on a long stylar beak distinguish this spring wildflower, the most common of some fifteen *Geranium* species in the northeast. Other names: spotted geranium, spotted cranesbill, alum-root, shame-face, rock weed.

The flower, like many bisexual flowers, actually goes through male and female unisexual phases in succession, thus preventing self-fertilization. By the time the long, beaklike pistil is ready to receive pollen, the male anthers have withered or dropped off. An individual flower generally lasts from one to three days. Depending on the weather, it may be a male flower for most of that time; on a warm, sunny day, it may convert to its female form within hours. Occasional flowers with blue anthers are known as blue-eyed geraniums. Nectar guides, those lines on the petals that direct insects to the white-woolly petal bases, show darker purple and translucent.

After insect pollination, the petals drop off and the long, beaklike pistil lengthens to an inch or more. This "crane's bill" is actually a sort of elongated tent, with its sidebands connected at the tip and held by tension at the bottom, where five seed containers are attached. As the seeds ripen, the sidebands dry and become taut. Suddenly they spring loose and curl up the central "tent-pole," flinging out the seeds. These symmetrical, curled-up catapults make identification of this plant easy in fall or winter.

A perennial, wild geranium grows from winter buds on thick underground rhizomes rich in tannin. As the leaves age in summer, some become white-spotted. This species prefers the light shade of open woods and thickets, thriving neither in dense shade nor full sunlight.

Feeding in masses on leaf and stem sap is the wild geranium aphid, yellowish green with black markings. Various butterfly species visit the flower for nectar—the common sulphur is a frequent one—but pollination is accomplished mainly by the larger bees. This plant, among many others, attracts Japanese beetles. The essence of its fragrance was once used as a bait in beetle traps for this destructive pest.

Geranium's thick, tannic rhizome provided an astringent medication for Native Americans. The Chippewas dried and powdered it, serving the bitter tea to their children for toothache, sore mouth, and intestinal upsets. It was also used as a coagulant to stop bleeding.

This plant's near relative, the European geranium is important in the history of science. Observing it in 1787, the German botanist Christian Sprengel figured out the mutualistic relationship between flowers and pollinating insects. The significance of cross-fertilization itself had to await the mind of Charles Darwin.

Wild Ginger
(*Asarum canadense*)

KRIS LIGHT

Birthwort family. Low herb in rich, moist woods. Two broad, heart-shaped leaves on hairy stalks surmount and shelter the solitary three-lobed flower, which is purplish-brown. Other names: Canada snakeroot, asarabacca.

An insect-pollinated flower must flaunt itself like the sexual creature that it is. To human eyes, however, ginger does not flaunt. Its single flower per plant seems rather to crouch beneath a broad roof of leaves. Its color is not a turn-on either. Clearly this flower, so low that it often lies partly buried in leaf humus, occupies a special niche of the forest ecosystem, resembling trailing arbutus in this respect.

The key to wild ginger's lifestyle lies in its early flowering, in April when the ground has barely warmed. Most active insects at this time consist of small flies and gnats. For these the cup-shaped flower provides abundant pollen for food and deep shelter from chill winds. In fact, this flower's structure shows a tendency toward the type of insect trap seen in its close relative, Dutchman's pipe.

In a reverse sequence of the unisexual flowering seen in wild geranium, the female pistil matures first, its lobes sticky; when it withers, a sex change occurs and twelve male stamens, loaded with pollen, arise. Cross-fertilization is also assured by the fact that only one plant grows from a perennial rhizome. As the seeds mature, the leathery capsule replacing the flower inverts, opens, and releases them.

Wild ginger grows in small or large colonies, sometimes covering many square feet in dense carpets. The leaves are evergreen with new ones replacing the old in spring. Ginger flower's color, resembling the liver hues of skunk-cabbage and red trillium, seems to attract flesh-eating flies such as blow flies and flesh flies. Watch too for other pollinating flies, which may include March flies, fungus gnats, and syrphid flies. Purplish-brown, tentacled caterpillars feeding side by side on a ginger leaf may be larvae of the pipe-vine swallowtail butterfly. The large adult butterflies, appearing in early spring, are brownish black with green iridescence on the hindwings. Seeds are collected and dispersed by ants.

Though the rhizome's odor and peppery taste closely resemble the spice used for flavorings, this is not the commercially marketed ginger (that spice comes from the root of the unrelated tropical ginger plant, grown in Indonesia and Jamaica). The dried rhizomes of wild ginger can, however, be substituted for commercial ginger, and an interesting candy can be made by boiling the rootstocks then simmering them in a sugar syrup. Native Americans used the powdered rhizomes as a seasoning. Ginger tea was also used to relieve gas and for indigestion, heart palpitations, and earache.

Wild Leek
(*Allium tricoccum*)

KRIS LIGHT

Lily family. Herb in rich woods. Its lilylike, onion-scented leaves and bulb and its spokelike umbel of white flowers identify this wild onion. Most other wild onions have grasslike leaves. Other names: ramp.

Colonies of wild leek indicate a damp, humus soil. Most green plants conduct their energy building and reproductive activities simultaneously. In this species, leaves and flowers operate on separate timetables. By the time flowers appear, the leaves have withered and died. The strong onion-flavored bulbs remain, either single or clustered on a rhizome. Bulbs are actually swollen stem bases composed of colorless leaves in multiple layers.

Probably the only significant insect feeder on leaves is the widely distributed onion thrips. Barely visible because of their tiny size, they leave signs on the leaves: whitish blotches, crinkled distortions, and browning tips.

In certain Appalachian and Amish communities, people collect wild leek bulbs for annual festivals and celebrate the coming of spring with steaming caldrons of wild leek soup. For less-intimidating soups or stews, a bulb or two in the pot will suffice for flavor; a leaf may add interest to a sandwich. Before the plant flowers, say leek gourmets, is the best time to collect leaves and bulbs.

Native Americans used the plant for food and flavoring but also used the crushed bulbs as a skin remedy for insect bites and stings. The Chippewas made a decoction from the bulb to use as an emetic ("quick in its effect," they said). Leeks are rich in phosphorus and sulphur plus vitamins A and C and are relatively high in protein.

This plant and its close relatives also have a place in history. Welsh defenders wore the plants on their headgear in 640 C.E when the Saxons invaded Wales. Leek thus became the Welsh national emblem. In our own country, the Menominee tribe identified a shoreline plain on southern Lake Michigan as *shika'ko* ("skunk place"), where leeks grew in abundance. "Skunk place" is now Chicago.

Wood Anemone
(*Anemone quinquefolia*)

KRIS LIGHT

Buttercup family. Herb in moist woods and dry or mesic prairie. Its white, solitary flower and deeply divided three-or five-part leaves identify this delicate spring perennial. Other names: windflower, mayflower, nimble weed, wood flower.

An examination of the bisexual flower shows that its apparent petals (usually five or six) are actually sepals—bracts that underlie the petals; real petals are absent. One of the earliest spring flowers, wood anemone thrives colonially in the sunlit woodland floor, which will later be shaded by the tree canopy. The light-sensitive flowers close at night or on cloudy days and are thus limited to insect pollinators that are active in the daytime. (Many other white flowers attract night-flying moths.) The flowers last about two weeks.

Flowerless anemone plants often have a single leaf of five leaflets; the flowering plants show three sets of three leaflets. This difference reveals the plant's means of energy conservation. It concentrates its dominant growth activity on either vegetative or reproductive forms.

Anemones are linked in mythology with the wind (the name derives from *anemos,* the Greek word for "wind"); just why remains obscure, unless this name refers to the flower's windlike, ephemeral existence. They are also linked with images of human sadness. In various accounts, these flowers sprang from Venus's tears over the dead Adonis or, in England, from the blood of Danes slain in battle. To the ancient Chinese, anemone was a "death flower," used in funeral rites. A meadow species of this little flower was probably the biblical "lily," with which Solomon's glory could not compare.

Yellow Trout Lily
(*Erythronium americanum*)

TIM MAINIERO/SHUTTERSTOCK.COM

Lily family. Herb in moist deciduous woods. Leaves mottled purplish or brown and a solitary yellow flower with reflexed petallike sepals identify this early-blooming spring ephemeral. Other names: Adder's tongue, dog-tooth violet, fawn lily.

Large colonies of this glossy-leaved little plant carpet the woodlands before the tree canopy shades the ground. Try to analyze from the leaf patterns which plants belong to separate colonies and how widely each colony spreads; the purple-brown "trout" patterns of separate colonies are never identical, but those within a single colony may be closely similar.

Yellow trout lily reproduces more by vegetative than by sexual means. Colonies result from the prolific budding of new perennial corms from previous ones. In a mature woodland, such colonies may be a century or more old, older than many of the surrounding trees. Many individual plants produce only one leaf and no flower; these far outnumber the occasional flower and two-leaved plants that rise among them. By the time May flowers bloom, erect green seed capsules have capped the stalks and the leaves have turned darker green, losing much of their mottled patterns. Then the plants are gone, retreating underground until next spring. Their long annual dormancy, however, belies their importance in the woodland nutrient cycle. The roots retrieve molecules of the trace mineral phosphorus from the runoff of spring rains, transferring them to the leaves, which ultimately enrich the forest soil. Trout lilies have been called living phosphorus sinks.

The bell-shaped, bisexual flower, slightly fragrant, attracts long-tongued insects, for its nectaries are deep. But this flower is not so pendant that it can't self-fertilize if a cool spring makes early insects scarce. A true sun-follower, it turns on its stalk.

The mottled color of the leaves attracts many flies. Chief pollinators are blowflies, the mining bee *Andrena erythronii,* and queen bumblebees. Other insect visitors include butterflies, often the small sulphurs and whites. Crickets and carabid beetles feed on the seed caruncles, helping disperse the plant. This lily is relatively free of pests; few insects feed on or deface the leaves. White-tailed deer nip off the seed capsules, and black bears dig up the corms to eat.

Young leaves and corms, though edible when boiled, may be slightly emetic to sensitive stomachs. A tea made of the leaves was said to be a sure cure for hiccups (but what isn't?).

This plant's various common names point to other characteristics: its appearance during trout-fishing season; its sharp, tongue-like shape as the shoot first emerges from the soil; and its two leaves standing erect like the ears of a fawn.

Glossary

Achene. Dry fruit, usually one-seeded, that does not split open slong suture lines.

Acropetal. Progressive ascending development of flowers toward an apex.

Alleopathy. One plant's inhibition of another by secreted chemicals, often from roots.

Annual. Plant that completes its entire life cycle within one year or growing season.

Anther. Pollen-bearing part of a stamen.

Apomixis. Development of fruit or seed without the fusion of sex cells.

Biennial. Plant that completes its entire life cycle within a two-year period, flowering and producing seed in its second year.

Bisexual. Having both male and female sex organs, as on a flower.

Cleistogamy. Process of self-pollination in flowers that remain closed in the bud.

Cyme. Stalk bearing flowers that develop and mature from stalk tip downward.

Epiphyte. Plant growing on another plant, using it as support but deriving no nourishment from it.

Floret. Small flower, especially on an aggregate flowerhead.

Inflorescence. Individual flowerhead or cluster of floral parts.

Mycorrhiza. Symbiotic relationship of a subsurface fungus with vascular plant roots.

Perennial. Plants that lives for three or more years, its aboveground parts often dying back to the roots in autumn.

Pistil. Female seed-bearing flower organ, consisting of overy, style, and stigma.

Protandry. Sex sequencing in a bisexual flower in which male parts mature and decline before female parts mature.

Protogyny. Sex sequencing in a bisexual flower in which female parts mature and decline before male parts mature.

Raceme. Flower stalk bearing flowers that develop and mature from the stalk base upward.

Rhizome. Horizontal underground rootlike stem that produces roots and cloning aerial stems.

Rosette. Cluster of leaves at the base of a stem.

Semelparous. Tendency of some biennial plants to delay flowering for one or more years.

Sepal. Modified leaf underlying the sexual parts of a flowerhead.

Stamen. Male pollen-bearing organ of a flower, consisting of anther and filament.

Stigma. Pollen-receiving part of flower pistil.

Stolon. Horizontal stem on the ground surface, giving rise to roots and shoots along its length.

Stratification. Period requirement of some seeds to undergo freezing in the soil before germination can occur.

Tepal. Sepal or petal when the two parts appear visually similar.

Umbel. Umbrellalike flower cluster with flower stalks radiating from a single point.

Unisexual. Having either male or female sex organs, but not both.

Utricle. One-seeded bladderlike fruit.

Index